Plain Language for Lawyers

Third Edition

Michèle M Asprey

BA, LLB

Solicitor of the Supreme Court of New South Wales
Plain Language Writing Consultant

THE FEDERATION PRESS

2003

Published in Sydney by

The Federation Press
71 John St, Leichhardt, NSW, 2040
PO Box 45, Annandale, NSW, 2038
Ph: (02) 9552 2200 Fax: (02) 9552 1681
E-mail: info@federationpress.com.au
Website: http://www.federationpress.com.au

First edition 1991
Second edition 1996
Third edition 2003

National Library Cataloguing-in-Publication
    Asprey, Michèle M
        Plain language for lawyers

    3rd ed.
    Includes index.
    ISBN 1 86287 464 6

    1. Law – Language. 2. Law – Australia – Language. I. Title.

808.06634

Typeset by The Federation Press, Leichhardt, NSW.
    Printed and bound by Southwood Press, Marrickville, NSW.

Contents

Chapter 1

What is this book about?

I know that you believe you understand what you think I said, but I'm not sure you realise that what you heard is not what I meant.

Richard M Nixon[1]

You might have noticed that this book doesn't have a foreword. It doesn't have a preface or a prologue or an introduction either. Or a conclusion. At least, the conclusion isn't at the end. It's at the beginning. That's so you'll read my conclusions when your interest is at its peak. Now.

You might have noticed these things were missing, but it is likely you didn't miss them, because you would have skipped the foreword and the preface and the prologue. There is a good chance that you would have skipped the introduction too, because if you looked at the table of contents and saw that there was a chapter entitled "What is this book about?", you would have started there. At the logical beginning. Where the first thing you want to know is explained.

If you get the answers you want about plain language in this chapter, you might not read any further. That puts an obligation on me, as a writer, to tell you right here what you want to know. That is why I've put my introduction and conclusions in Chapter 1. They are the most important parts of this book. They are what I want you to remember: anything else you can look up later. So even if you stop reading after Chapter 1, at least you'll know what plain language is about, why it is important for lawyers, and what you have to do now.

---

1 Quoted in *Australian Business*, 5 September 1990, p 89.

This book isn't a book on legal drafting in the usual sense of those words. It does deal with what we might call "drafting problems" and it does offer some drafting "solutions" or at least ideas to help you solve some drafting problems. The book does analyse text and deal briefly with some of the rules of interpretation. But it is not a book that will teach you everything there is to know about legal drafting, or give you step by step instructions in grammar and its role in clear drafting. What I want to do with this book is explain the basic principles of plain language drafting, and show how we as lawyers can make them work for us. For many of us, this means a significant change in the way we work, and it is this change that I am writing about.

So this book is about taking a different approach to drafting. About thinking of legal drafting as another aspect of all the communication we do every day. About doing more in our legal drafting than just recording a transaction or an event. About *really* communicating with our readers.

Drafting as communication

If what I have just said is true, then when we draft legal documents we should be able to use some of the same techniques that we use for other forms of communication: the techniques we use in everyday speech, for example, or ordinary letter writing. My task is first to convince you that that proposition is true.

I must show you that we should not treat legal drafting as if it has been elevated to some higher plane than other forms of communication, and that it *is* possible to write any legal document in the sort of language we use every day. That it will be just as "valid" and just as appropriate as a document written in what I might euphemistically call a "traditional legal style", but what the public calls "legalese".[2]

When I convince you of that, then I must get you started on the process of writing in plain language.

---

2   In Australia, the expressions "legal writing" and "legal drafting" tend to be used interchangeably, and I do the same in this book. Australians do not usually draw the same distinctions between them as US lawyers do, possibly because we do not have the same tradition of written advocacy as they do. But this could change as our courts move to limit the time allowed for oral addresses and require written submissions.

Can we change?

William Zinsser, in his excellent book *On Writing Well*,[3] ends his first chapter, on the need to achieve strength in writing without clutter, by saying: "Can such principles be taught? Maybe not. But most of them can be learned." I agree with Mr Zinsser.

The good news is that it is not at all difficult to learn the principles of plain language writing, even if we are talking about plain language drafting by lawyers. Those principles are simple, as I hope you'll see.

The hard part is "unlearning" all the bad habits we tend to pick up and cling to. And the really challenging part is putting what we have learned into practice when we are under pressure. That is the time when we cling most desperately to the magic formulas we've used for so long. Most of the time we've forgotten why we use the old formulas, if indeed we ever knew. Sometimes we just want the warm glow of security that they give us – and it is not easy to give that up.

Even if we know *why* we use a particular formula of words, we generally forget to ask ourselves why another, simpler form will not do as well. If we haven't asked that question, it is probably not because we don't care, but because we don't have time to think about it. And anyway, those words seemed to work last time (didn't they?) so why fix something that's not "broken"? Think of the professional indemnity position if we tamper with a tried-and-true formula …

Why should we change?

That's just my point. We can no longer be content to rely on the old words, the old clauses, the old precedents. Things have changed. The public perception of lawyers has changed. We are no longer seen as the learned custodians of unknowable secrets. We are no longer immune to challenge on our own ground. Our clients are asking questions. They are demanding the right to understand the advice we give and they want to be able to read the documents we draft for them. If they don't like the service we offer, they will go

---

3   2001, 6th revised (25th anniversary) edition, HarperResource Quill, New York, p 6.

elsewhere. If they ask questions, they expect intelligible answers. If they don't get them, and in a reasonable time, they can complain to various officials and *demand* the answers.

Governments, too, have taken notice of the language of the law.

In 1993, the Australian Parliament issued *two* reports that looked critically at lawyers' language and its effect on public access to justice. The first was the report by the Senate Standing Committee on Legal and Constitutional Affairs into the cost of Justice. It was called *The Costs of Justice: Foundations for Reform*, and was published in February 1993. On the issue of "lucidity", the Committee wrote:

> The law which people must obey should be readily understood by them ... Law, whether made by legislators or developed by judges, should be as comprehensible to members of the public as possible.[4]

The second report was a report by the House of Representatives Standing Committee on Legal and Constitutional Affairs. The Committee was specifically inquiring into legislative drafting by the Commonwealth of Australia. The report was published in September 1993, and was called *Clearer Commonwealth Law*. The conclusions and recommendations of the report begin like this:

> This report is about making laws, particularly Commonwealth laws, easier to understand.
>
> At present too many of our laws are difficult to understand.[5]

The Committee recommended 46 ways to make legislation easier to understand and use. The government issued its response to these recommendations late in 1995. It accepted the vast majority of the recommendations.

Now our laws are starting to look different. Jurisdictions in Australia and elsewhere have begun to draft in plainer language, to experiment with new drafting techniques and to produce legislation in new, easier-to-read formats.

Our courts, too are looking critically at lawyers' language. They have for a long time been willing to set aside contracts on the basis that people did not understand what it was they were signing. The doctrine of "non est factum" (literally, "it is not my

---

4   1993, Commonwealth of Australia, Canberra, p 27.
5   1993, Commonwealth of Australia, p xiii.

deed") is an old common law defence that enables a person who has executed a document in ignorance of its character to say that even though they executed it, it was not their act. In other words, the document they signed was different from what they thought they were signing.[6]

However, in recent times the courts are looking closer into whether the parties understand more than just the "character" of the document or what sort of a document it is. There are more claims by borrowers of unconscionable conduct by banks. In these cases, the courts are asking whether the parties *really* and *independently* understood the effect of the document. They are looking at the circumstances of each case to see if the parties are under any special disadvantages and whether or not they received any advice or assistance with the document. They are more willing to hold that documents are unenforceable because the parties cannot understand them. They are no longer prepared to assume that a party who can read, has signed a document, and knows what kind of a document it is, must be held to it.[7]

Our laws are beginning to specify that particular documents must be written so that they can be understood. For example, in Australia, there are now quite a few laws that require documents to be written (and in some cases, explained) in language that is "easy to understand", "easily [be] understood", "readily understood", "readily understandable", "intelligible", "comprehensible" or "expressed plainly". And some specifically require "plain language" or "plain English". Under the Consumer Credit Code that now applies in all Australian jurisdictions, certain documents issued by "credit providers" must be "clearly expressed".[8]

Whatever we think of the particular views of the various government committees and reports, we can't delay any longer. We can't wait until we are forced by law to write to be understood. We must take the initiative.

---

6   See, for example, *Saunders (Executrix in the Estate of Rose Maude Gallie) v Anglia Building Society* [1971] AC 1039; *Petelin v Cullen* (1975) 132 CLR 355; or, more recently, *Lloyd's Bank plc v Waterhouse* [1991] Fam Law 23; *The Independent*, 27 February 1990, CA.

7   See p 50 and following.

8   See, for example, section 162(1) of the Consumer Credit (New South Wales) Code. There is a list of some of these laws in Chapter 3, pp 44-46.

Showing our skill

To change our ways does not involve going back to kindergarten and writing only in words of one syllable. We will still be able to show our skill. In fact, we show our skill more keenly, more sharply, when we write in plain words. The frills, the frippery, the bells and the whistles are stripped away and what remains is pure and clear. No misunderstandings. Just the facts. A professional document that is accessible by its users. One that shows our skills and focuses its readers on the issues, rather than the periphery of unnecessary detail and unfamiliar style.

Plain speaking in Laramie

Let me illustrate what I mean with an example that shows how refreshing plain language can be. It is an extract from a letter written by a lawyer in Laramie, Wyoming, in the United States of America to another lawyer in California.

Ms Becky Klemt is a partner in the law firm Pence and McMillan, which in 1988 was a four-lawyer firm. She had won a child support judgment of $4240 for one of her clients and she needed to find another lawyer to collect the money from her client's husband in California.

Ms Klemt wrote to lawyer after lawyer in California, trying to find one who would be willing to collect such a relatively small amount for her client. She said that it was entirely possible that a single letter would be all that was needed. But she could not find anyone that was interested. Finally, she received a letter from a lawyer in California who had a most extraordinary practice.

"Without sounding pretentious", the California lawyer wrote, "my current retainer for cases is a flat $100,000". On top of that, he said, he charged $1000 per hour. He specialised in international trade and geopolitical relations between the Middle East and Europe. His client base, he said, was "very unique and limited". He declined the offer to collect the judgment.

Ms Klemt's letter in reply is worth quoting in full.

> Steve, I've got news – you can't say you charge a $100,000.00 retainer fee and an additional $1000.00 an hour without sounding pretentious. It just can't be done. Especially when you're writing to someone in Laramie, Wyoming where you're considered pretentious

if you wear socks to court or drive anything fancier than a Ford Bronco. Hell, Steve, all the lawyers in Laramie, put together, don't charge $1000.00 an hour.

Anyway, we were sitting around the office discussing your letter and decided that you had a good thing going. We doubt we could get away with charging $1000.00 an hour in Laramie (where people are more inclined to barter with livestock than pay in cash), but we *do* believe we could join you in California, where evidently people can get away with just about anything. Therefore the four lawyers in our firm intend to join you in the practice of international trade and geopolitical relations between the Middle East and Europe.

Now Steve, you're probably thinking that we don't know anything about the Middle East and Europe, but I think you'll be pleasantly surprised that this is not the case. Paul Schierer is actually from the Middle East – he was raised outside of Chicago, Illinois, and although those national newsmen insist on calling Illinois the Midwest, to us if it's between New York and the Missouri River, it's the Middle East.

Additionally, although I have never personally been to Europe myself, my sister just returned from a vacation there and told me lots about it, so I believe I would be of some help to you on that end of the negotiations. Hoke MacMillan has actually been there, although it was 15 years ago, so you might have to update him on recent geopolitical developments. Also, Hoke has applied to the Rotary Foreign Exchange Student Program for a 16 year old Swedish girl and believes she will be helpful in preparing him for trips abroad.

Another thing you should know, Steve, is that the firm has an extensive foreign language background, which I believe would be useful to you. Hoke took Latin in high school, although he hasn't used it inasmuch as he did not become a pharmacist or a priest. Vonnie Nagel took high school German, while Paul has mastered Spanish, by ordering food at numerous local Mexican restaurants. I, myself, majored in French in college, until I realized that probably wasn't the smartest career move in the world. I've forgotten words such as "international" and "geopolitical" (which I'm not *too* familiar with in English), but I can still hail a taxi or find a restroom, which might come in handy.

Steve, let us know when we should join you in California so that we can begin doing whatever it is you do. In anticipation of our move, we've all begun practising trying to say we charge $1000.00 an hour with a straight face, but so far, we haven't been able to do it. I suspect it'll be easier once we get to California where I understand they charge $500,000 for one-bedroom condos and everybody (even poor people) drive Mercedes. Anyway, because I'll be new to the area of international trade and geopolitical relations, I'm thinking of only charging $500-$600 an hour to begin with. Will that be enough to meet our overhead?

Becky added this postscript:

> Incidentally, we have advised our client of your hourly rate. She is willing to pay you $1000 per hour to collect this judgment provided it doesn't take you more than four seconds.

Becky Klemt's letter[9] created quite a storm. It appeared in the *Wall Street Journal* and she became something of a folk-hero. Her letter was described as a "masterpiece" by judges in the USA. The public perception seems to be that lawyers need to be brought back to reality and that Ms Klemt did just that *in plain words*. That made her not only news, but also a nationwide celebrity and a hero. A lawyer who writes plainly becomes a hero. It is worth investing a little time and thought, don't you agree?

So that's my introduction and conclusion. Lawyers need to take a different approach to legal writing. We have an obligation to communicate clearly and efficiently: with our clients, with our colleagues, with our opponents and with the general public. We cannot continue to pretend that legal writing is meant to be read and used only by lawyers. And we can no longer ignore the fact that legalese is not the only way: that legal writing *can* be simplified. If we do not take the time and effort to make a change in our bad writing habits, we will sooner or later pay the penalty. Society is demanding this change, the courts and the legislators require it, and our own professional integrity depends on it.

In the next chapter I explain what plain language is. In doing so I try to allay some of the fears and correct some of the misapprehensions lawyers often have about plain language. I look at some of the strange ideas we have about what legal language does and look at some "magic" words to illustrate why I believe we lawyers have little to fear if we give up some of our "time-honoured" language. Then in Chapters 3 and 4, I look in more detail at the forces that are urging us to adopt plain language.

By the end of Chapter 4 I hope you are convinced that lawyers need to use plain language and are not in danger if they do. The

---

9   Dated 17 August 1988.

following chapters go through the basic principles of plain language writing, with the aim of giving you guidelines you can follow in your daily work, so that you can recognise the areas in your writing that might need attention. I use examples that should be familiar to you and suggest a few new ways of looking at and attacking both familiar and unfamiliar language. Chapter 14 focuses on a relatively new area of lawyers' writing: email and the internet. Then we'll consider the *look* of the documents we produce, both on paper (in Chapter 15) and on a computer screen (Chapter 16). And in Chapter 17 we look at ways of testing whether what we've written works for our readers.

If you are already convinced of the need for plain language in law, you could probably skip to Chapter 5 now. But you might find the material in the next three chapters useful. It could give you confidence in using plain language as a lawyer, and help you justify yourself in the face of scepticism.

If throughout this book I am critical of legal writing, I hope you will realise that I write as a lawyer who understands the difficulties that lawyers have to cope with when they write. There are so many critics of legal writing, but so few who take seriously the problems that lawyers have to cope with in their writing, and so few with anything practical and constructive to offer.

I am critical of convoluted legal writing, but I also know that many lawyers do not write in "legalese" and never have.

I do not believe that lawyers are intentionally obscure, and I think that the vast majority of lawyers would embrace plain language in a moment if they knew what it involved and could be sure it was safe to do so. I have worked with many lawyers who have done just that. They have taken to plain language drafting with great enthusiasm, energy and creativity.

And we must not forget that "legalese" causes problems for lawyers as well as lay people. It weighs us down as a profession. It deadens our writing and drains us of creativity. Some of us have been tied up in the complexities of legal language for so long that we find it difficult even to contemplate change. Legalese is often as difficult for lawyers to read as it is for lay people. How many times do we find ourselves reading and re-reading a document, a law, a judgment, without understanding a word that is written? Sometimes we blame ourselves, when it is really the writer who is at fault. Young or inexperienced lawyers reading traditional legal writing can find themselves seriously doubting their powers of comprehension. They despair that they will ever be able to read legal writing without experiencing pain.

Why put up with the pain? The sense of liberation that using plain language can bring to us is tremendous. I hope that this book helps to liberate you.

There are other benefits as well. In the past 20 years or so, as the plain language message has begun to reach more and more of the legal world, lawyers are realising that their writing was a real barrier to communication with their clients. Now they are finding that plain language can actually help them strengthen their relationships with clients. They are finding that the documents they write and the advice they give both become more *usable* by clients, and more effective. But it takes a fundamental change in attitude for those lawyers to reach that point.

By the end of this book I hope to have you looking at your writing from a new angle. You might not feel you need to change a thing about your writing. You might realise that you are already writing in plain language. But whether you need to make a radical change in your writing, just a few adjustments, or no change at all, I hope that two things happen to you:

1. you see how important it is for lawyers to write so that they can be easily understood; and

2. you drop the defensive guard that most writers (and not just lawyers) have about their writing – "there's nothing wrong with the way I write; anyone could understand it" – and learn to see your writing as others see it.

If those things happen, you will be well on the way to writing in plain language.

Chapter 2

What is plain language?

What it is and what it isn't

The first thing to say about the term "plain language" is that it is the same thing as "plain English", except that because "plain language" includes languages other than English, it is a more useful expression. I prefer the term "plain language" for that reason, so that is the term I use throughout this book.

The second thing to say about plain language is that it has a problem. It has a bad name among some lawyers. This is usually because they don't understand enough about it to judge it properly.

There is also a problem with the word "plain". It sounds drab. Plain language isn't drab.

Next, people think that plain language is some new kind of language, with a separate vocabulary from normal language. That's not right either. Plain language writing is just the practice of writing English (or French or German or whatever else) in a clear and simple style. That's all.

Some people think that because plain language is simple, it must be simplistic – a kind of baby-talk. That is also wrong. Simple in this sense doesn't mean simplistic. It means straightforward, clear, precise. It can be elegant and dramatic. It can even be beautiful. It does not mean that we may only write in words of one syllable – although we may choose words of one syllable if they are better than the alternative. And they may well be. As William Zinsser points out,[1] of the 701 words in Abraham Lincoln's Second Inaugural Address, 505 are words of one syllable and 122 are words of two syllables.

Another criticism of plain language is that it is not "dignified enough" for lawyers to use in legal documents. They would prefer

---

1   2001, *On Writing Well*, 6th revised (25th anniversary) edition, HarperResource Quill, New York, p 69.

to use language that is more remote and less personal than ordinary everyday language. But if this is so then the judgments of Lord Denning, the opinions of Oliver Wendell Holmes and the will drafting advice of Justice Hutley of the Supreme Court of New South Wales are also not dignified enough.

Obviously, our tone must be appropriate for a formal document or letter, and we should not use the same tone as we would use for a note to a friend about our plans for the next weekend. But adopting an appropriate tone is different from adopting a remote, pompous or inflated drafting style in an effort to give more import to what we are saying.

As Mellinkoff puts it in his book *The Language of the Law*:

> There are those who believe that ordinary English is beneath a professional's dignity; as it should be when ordinary English is bad English or when law language is better. But ordinary English is not always bad English, and law language does not always say it better, or more precisely.[2]

Some people think that if you write in plain language you must use particular mannerisms – for example, always using "you" and "your" instead of giving the parties particular names like "Borrower" and "Lender". That is not a requirement of plain language writing. It might be helpful, but it is not essential. It is not compulsory. Plain language is not as rigid as that. In fact, one of its advantages is its flexibility.

There are many forms of plain language: not just one. What is appropriate in one context may be inappropriate in another. And it takes time to develop the necessary sensitivity to the problems of your readers. Those who try to write in plain language find that their skills develop with practice, and a natural style gradually emerges. If they look back over documents they have drafted in the past they can see the changes as they emerge. It is not possible to become a proficient plain language writer overnight, and there is no benchmark that tells you when you have become proficient. Improvement can continue for as long as you continue to write.

Writing in plain language is just writing in clear, straightforward language, with the needs of the reader foremost in mind. There are no hard-and-fast rules. There are no international

---

2   1963, Little Brown, Boston, p 345.

standards or infallible tests. The main thing to remember is that if what you have written could be unclear or confusing for your reader, or difficult to read, you should rewrite it so that it becomes clear, unambiguous and easy to read. The trick is to recognise those qualities in your own writing.

Unfortunately, because so many people have had these misconceptions about plain language, and have even grown to mistrust it, others who are keen to promote simple writing have shied away from using the labels "plain language" or "plain English". Some people have adopted other terms, such as "clear English" or even "user-friendly English". These terms make it look as though we now have a multitude of different dialects to choose from. That is a pity. The plain language movement, whatever label is used to describe it, is not about learning a new language, or even a new dialect. It is about simplifying our writing, and making it easier to read and understand.

One of the more recent criticisms of plain language is that it looks only at the words on the page, and ignores the other things that make documents difficult to read, use and understand. Again, this misunderstands the aims of the plain language movement.

When we draft in plain language we look at more than just the meaning of the words we are using and how they will be perceived by our readers. We also look at how the information is organised and presented. We look at the *organisation* of the words in a sentence, the sentences in a document and the *design and layout* of the document itself. All these things can have an effect on whether the document can be read and understood by its intended readers, at the level of understanding they need to have. We look at the issue of organisation in more detail in Chapter 6, and we look at the question of document design in Chapters 15 and 16. Then in Chapter 17 we consider how we can test whether our readers can actually understand what we write. All these things are integral parts of plain language writing. The more we explore these areas, the more we learn about what we can do to make our writing easier to read, understand and use. And we have much to learn from the experts in these areas, because the concepts of document design and testing are new to many lawyers. Most of us have not concerned ourselves with them until recently.

One thing lawyers pride themselves on is precision, and plain language lawyers agree. A plain language document needs not only to be clear and straightforward but also precise and complete. We never sacrifice completeness or precision for simplicity. We aim to achieve all of these things together. Sometimes there are trade-offs, because drafting can rarely be perfect in every respect – but we always aim high. Sometimes a plain language document can be longer than a document written in "legalese". This often happens when we have some extra explaining to do, perhaps to deal with a complex or technical concept. But whenever we can leave something unnecessary out, we do.

Paradoxically, plain language can be used to express highly technical or otherwise complex concepts far more effectively than convoluted drafting. And plain language does not ban all technical terms. But when plain language writers decide to use an uncommon or technical word in their writing, they usually do it for one of three reasons:

1. they know the readers will be specialists, who are familiar with the word; or
2. there is no accurate substitute for the word; or
3. the word will be a useful shorthand for a complicated subject matter that crops up more than just once or twice.

If the reader is not a specialist, the plain language writer will often give an explanation of the technical word – in plain language of course – and then continue to use the technical word as a convenient and accurate shorthand for a complex idea, perhaps even reminding the reader where to find the explanation each time the technical term is used.

Plain language writers also avoid using words that are no longer used in everyday speech – even if they are not "difficult". Of course, how far they take this idea depends on who their readers are and what the purpose of the document is. But as a general rule, plain language writers try to choose words that are most easily understood.

In summary, lawyers who write in plain language try to put themselves in the reader's shoes. They think about what they are writing and what it will mean to the reader – how the reader will react and how they can help the reader to understand what they have written.

In order to anticipate the problems a reader might have with a piece of writing, it helps to have some idea of the process that is taking place when the words we write are taken in by someone else.

Ways to communicate

I said in Chapter 1 that legal drafting is another facet of all the communication we do every day. We communicate with each other using various means: there are the obvious methods of speaking and writing. There are other means, such as traffic signals and other common signs. There are less obvious ones, such as gestures and facial expressions. And then there are more subtle means of communication involving time and space: for example, how long you are kept waiting at a reception desk, or for a telephone call or letter, or where you are placed at a table in relation to the guest of honour. All these things can send messages, whether they are intended or not.

Being precise communicators: are lawyers different?

We who work in law must be precise in most of the messages we send in our work. We cannot be ambiguous or vague. We must express ideas in such a way as they cannot be misunderstood. We have a great responsibility. Terrible things can happen if we get it wrong, leave something out or leave open a loophole. We are always worried about whether or not we've "covered all the bases" – not to mention our backs.

We do so much writing in such a precise and detailed way that we tend to think our difficulties with language are unique, and that therefore it is necessary, or even desirable, to use a special way of writing that is appropriate only for lawyers. We claim that legal drafting is special, important, different from all other forms of language. We deal with rights and obligations: the contracts between people that govern their activities, the laws that govern society. When we describe an obligation, we describe it in appropriate, precise, "legal" language. We believe we can't be casual or informal, because that would not be precise or appropriate. So when some lawyers write about obligations and rights, they write things like:

15

No person shall enter the Premises without prior written authorisation from the Lessee.

It is clear, isn't it? Crystal clear. And precise. And short, too. There are no "hard" words, really. Anyone signing a lease should be able to understand it. And if they don't, it's time they learnt.

Let's look at it more closely.

- *No person shall.* Well, *No person* means nobody – that's clear, isn't it? And *shall* – *shall* is a time-honoured word of obligation. We need to use *shall*. And anyway, people still use it for the future tense, so they should be able to understand it.

- *The Premises.* That's always used in leases. We didn't put *Demised Premises* because we knew you'd catch us out with that one! But surely *Premises* is OK. I mean, it's in the dictionary. It isn't really an uncommon word anyway. *And* we've defined it – see, there's a capital letter that shows it is defined – so they can look it up in the definition section and we even give the address of the premises there. That makes it really clear.

- *Prior written authorisation.* Well that's a common legal formula. And all those words are pretty ordinary – even plain, wouldn't you say? No need to change that.

- *Lessee.* Well, yes, some people might confuse *lessee* and *lessor* occasionally. Matter of fact, sometimes I do myself. But, look, it *is* defined, and it is a lease we're talking about here. Anyone with half a brain – who is about to sign a lease – will be able to work it out.

As a whole it really is quite a simple sentence. The words aren't too technical, it is short, straightforward and simple. No unnecessary legalese there. No need to change it at all, really. And it is a standard legal formula. Time-honoured. We all know what it means. No arguments over that sentence. It's the best way to put it. Right?

Wrong.

We're looking at it only from *our* point of view. A lawyer looks at that sentence and sees it in the context of someone protecting property. The lawyer doesn't ask why that person wants to impose the obligation. We lawyers just write the obligation into the contract. We either specify the consequences of disobeying it (or "breaching the contract", as lawyers prefer to describe it), or we leave the consequences unspecified and rely on the common law to punish those who disobey.

But let's take a different perspective. Imagine that the reason for the prohibition is that the property is in quarantine because the people who live there have been contaminated by radiation. Imagine that the "written authorisation" is a card that says you are protected from the radiation and can enter without endangering yourself and others. How effective would our drafting be in stopping people from entering? Sure, it is accurate, precise, complete and *relatively* comprehensible. But is it an effective warning? Would it stop anyone?

How would you rephrase that sentence if you knew it was for a sign on the door of a quarantined property? How would you tell someone about it if you saw them about to open the door? Would you use different words? Why? If you used different words, does that mean that you have changed the message? Is it less accurate? Is it more effective? Which way is better? Is one way right and the other way wrong?

Right and wrong

What I am getting at here is that there is no magic in the words themselves. Any idea can be expressed in many different ways. Each of them may be as valid as the next. Each may mean the same thing, but we are free to select the one we prefer. There may be many reasons for our selection. We may consider one form more appropriate, perhaps because it has a different emphasis, or sounds more or less formal. We may like the sound of one more than the other. We may want to sound serious, learned, stern or polite. We may want to show off our facility with language. There may be different shades of meaning in the words we choose, or no difference at all (if the words are true synonyms). One form of words might achieve a particular result and the other may not. But none of the words we use is of itself "right" or "wrong".

For example, if we are talking about handing over important documents and we are looking for a verb to describe that action, we may choose between the words *furnish* and *give*. We may decide on *furnish* because we like the way it sounds, but we should not delude ourselves that the word *furnish* is "right" and the word *give* is "wrong".

If we make that mistake then we fall into the trap of thinking that words are inseparable from what they refer to. That real distinctions exist when the distinctions are only in the symbols chosen to represent the ideas. In the example I just gave, both the words *furnish* and *give* would do the job. There might be a slightly different emphasis, and one word might be easier for some people to understand, but (leaving aside the issue of accessibility for the moment) both words do the job. Neither is the "right" word.

Magic words

The phenomenon of the "rightness" of particular words is described at some length by Glanville L Williams in his essay titled "Language and the Law".[3] He shows how the English law gradually moved away from what he calls "word fetichism",[4] when the need to use a particular formula of words was paramount, but says that we still tend to confuse the form of words with their function. We still think that by choosing different words – even if they mean the same thing – we will alter the result. We still think that something in the words themselves is what achieves the different result. That, in short, the words are magic.

We all know that judges have often said that "there is no magic in words", but Glanville Williams shows that the courts have often considered two different sets of words which describe the same thing, drawn fine distinctions between them, and stipulated quite different legal consequences.

Williams uses the example of the "penalty" to explain this point. Here's how it works.

If A lends money to B on mortgage and states that the interest payable is 5%, but that if the repayments of the loan are not made promptly, interest is 6%, then the last part of the provision is void because it is a "penalty". The law does not allow you to impose a penalty for late payment. Yet if A had said that interest was 6%, but if repayments are made promptly it is reduced to 5%, the whole provision is valid, because there is no penalty – merely a reduction in interest for prompt payment.

---

3   (1945) 61 *LQR* 71 at 74-81.
4   His spelling.

Glanville Williams says that although this has been described often enough as a "fine distinction" being drawn between two sets of words, in fact it is not a distinction at all.[5] The reality is that the interest rates paid in either case, whichever form of words used, would be *exactly the same.* It is pure fiction to describe one provision as a "penalty" and the other as "fair". If there is a different legal result, it is for policy reasons – not because the language requires it.

There are plenty of other examples in the same vein. Williams gives us the example of a covenant to pay an amount of £1000 "free of income tax", which was void under the United Kingdom Income Tax Act 1918. But a covenant to pay an amount which, after deducting income tax, would leave £1000, was considered valid because it did not offend against the section of the Tax Act that said that annuities made without allowing for a deduction for tax are void.

Or what about an agreement by A to give the whole of A's time to serve B? It clearly means that A will not be able to serve anyone but B, and Glanville Williams tells us it was held to be unenforceable. Yet an agreement by A not to serve anyone but B *would* have been enforceable, because it did not create a contract to provide "exclusive service", which was void.

The meaning of the alternatives in each set of words in these three examples is *the same*, but the legal result is different.

In each of these examples, there were two ways of saying the same thing. It was *exactly* the same thing, but expressed differently. And because it was expressed differently, the courts seized upon it and created a legal "fiction" which leads us to believe that there is a real distinction between the two sets of words. We all know that paying £1000 free of tax is the same thing as paying an amount which, after deducting tax, would leave £1000. But the court told us that it was quite different. There were reasons that the court chose to make that distinction and I'm certainly not saying that we should ignore the distinction, or draft as if it did not exist. What I *am* saying is that we should see that the distinction is a matter of *law*, and not of language.

There is nothing in the *words themselves* that makes that distinction. It is the policy that our courts or legislators impose on the words which produces a different legal analysis and a different result. Those words are only "magic" because the court has

---

5   "Language and the Law" (1945) 61 *LQR* 71 at 79.

decided to see them in a different way. And as long as we under-stand the reasoning of the court, we could no doubt select other words which would achieve the same result.

So what has all this word "magic" got to do with plain language drafting and the question that I asked earlier in this chapter – are lawyers different?

The point is this: we lawyers worry about the need to follow formulas of words that produce certain results. We think that because of the peculiar requirements of the laws of "penalties" or laws prohibiting contracts of exclusive service or making payments made free of taxes void, we are stuck with the old formulas of words and the strange and complex sentence structures that are not found in any other kind of writing.

But it is not so.

It is not the words or the complex sentence structures that the judges have prescribed – it is the concepts. It is the way the law reads what we write. And so, as long as we have a good under-standing of the result we have to achieve, we can adopt whatever style we wish.

We might select plain words for our interest provisions, and a simple structure to express clearly the way that interest is paid so that it is not a penalty. Plain words and simple structures work just as well, even when they are only there to avoid some unwanted legal consequence. As long as we draft to achieve the desired result, we can choose simple or familiar words. We are not required to use archaic language or complex sentence structures.

In fact, using plain words to deal with unusual or technical legal points often helps. It can draw attention to peculiar provisions in a contract, which might need explaining to a client. It might prompt the client to ask why such a strange provision is necessary.

The true meaning of words

Words might not be "wrong" or "right" in themselves, but choosing the right words does present a real problem for lawyers. We have to write words which will mean what we want them to mean not only now, when our clients are signing the contract we've just drafted for their new business enterprise, but also tomorrow when they open for business, next week when the first orders come in, next year when they have their first major disagreement and perhaps even in the next decade when the business collapses and they sue each other.

But words aren't static. Their meanings can change. Mr Justice Holmes, of the United States Supreme Court, understood this. 85 years ago, he said:

> A word is not a crystal, transparent and unchanged; it is the skin of a living thought and may vary greatly in colour and content according to the circumstances and the time in which it is used.[6]

The meanings of words can change because our courts or legislators impose a meaning on them or interpret them in an unusual way, which imposes a different legal result. They can change in the way language as a whole changes: with usage, as the years go by. Or the meaning of the words can seem to change because circumstances put a different light on them.

For example, two people might regulate their mutual business under a contract that deals with all the usual things that might happen in business. What if something happens that no-one thought of when the contract was written? And what if the words in the contract can be read as if the parties actually foresaw these unforeseen circumstances? What if the words coincidentally seem to be quite clear on the subject, but produce an unintended result? Of course this only causes a problem if one party intends to take advantage of the windfall in its favour. But either way the words of the contract have not changed: the circumstances have, and the contract can be read in a way that the parties did not intend.

Lawyers have to write today to cover tomorrow and they can't be sure what will happen tomorrow. So they try to do the best they can. They look for the "right" word. The word that "truly" means what they're trying to say. But unfortunately there are no "true", "proper", "actual" or "natural" meanings of words. There is more to communication than the words themselves. The communication takes place not only in the writing but also in the reading, not only in the telling but also in the hearing. What we think we're writing or saying might not be what the reader or listener is understanding.

I can best explain this as a linguistic principle, by using some examples used by Randolph Quirk in *The Use of English*.[7]

---

6 *Towne v Eisner* 245 US 418 at 425 (1918).
7 1968, Quirk, R, *The Use of English*, 2nd edition, Longman, London, p 47.

If I say something that sounds like *meel*, you may hear it as *meal* and think I am asking for food. If I said the same thing in France, the listener will hear it as *mille* and think I was counting. Similarly, the sounds that make up the English word *cry* mean *edge* in Russian and would mean something like *circle* to a German.

As Quirk says, "We must not expect the signs of language to be direct symbols of what they mean, in the way that an 'x' symbolises a crossroads or blue on a map symbolises the sea". It is only because we all agree on a convention – that the sound *meal* refers to food – that it actually does so. But if the listener does not operate under the same convention, the meaning I intend will not be conveyed to that listener. So which of us has the "true" or "natural" meaning then?

Of course, you might think my example is a bit extreme. Surely words have "true" or "natural" meanings when we all speak the same language. But even when we all speak and understand the same language, it does not make sense to say that words have a meaning within themselves. The effect of those words depends on how the reader or listener understands them.

Another example might explain what I mean. In recent years, the word *decimate* has come into vogue. But the meaning of the word is changing. This is reflected in the different dictionary definitions one can find. According to the Australian Concise Oxford Dictionary,[8] *decimate* has two meanings. The first, "destroy a large proportion of", is described as "disputed". A usage note explains that this is now the usual sense of the word, although it is often "deplored as an inappropriate use". The second meaning given is described as the meaning "originally": "kill or remove one in every ten of". This is a shift from 12 years ago,[9] when the same dictionary gave the words three meanings. The first two were "put to death one in ten of" and "destroy tenth or large proportion". The third, "disputed" meaning was "destroy ... *nine*-tenths of". That meaning has now disappeared, the "original" meaning has taken second place, and the second part of the second meaning is now the first meaning the Dictionary gives.

---

8   3rd edition, 1997.
9   When the 1st edition of this book was published.

So when a television newsreader described[10] an attack by armed forces as "decimating" their opponents, which meaning of the word *decimate* did the newsreader mean to convey? And which was understood? If we take the view that the "correct" meaning of *decimate* is the one in "the dictionary", then first we must choose the dictionary we prefer. If we prefer the Australian Concise Oxford Dictionary, then we must select from several listed meanings. If we have an out-of-date dictionary, or we select the "original" meaning of the word, we would say that the newsreader must have meant "one-tenth" and that is what the viewers should have understood. But if we did that in this case we'd be wrong.

The news that night was written on the basis that *decimate* meant destroying a large proportion of the enemy forces, not one-tenth. The news had adopted the newer meaning of decimate. The other, earlier meaning was neither intended by the newsreader nor understood, I suspect, by the majority of viewers. Only those who clung to the older meaning of *decimate* would have misunderstood the news item. So which meaning of *decimate* was the "true" or "correct" meaning?

Glanville Williams[11] goes into this issue in great depth. In summary, he says there are no "true" or "proper" meanings of words. There is only:

1. their "ordinary" or "commonly acceptable" meaning – which might be their meaning to the world at large or perhaps another meaning that operates within a small group of people, such as scientists or even lawyers, depending on the context the word is used in; and

2. a special meaning that is "assigned" by a particular person using it – like a definition given to a word by a lawyer (which I'll deal with in Chapter 7).

So if there is no "assigned" meaning – no definition – for a particular word, we are left with the "ordinary" or "commonly acceptable" meaning. Where do we find it?

---

10   ABC Sydney television 7pm news, 31 January 1991.
11   "Language and the Law" (1945) 61 *LQR* 71.

Looking at the past

As lawyers, when we are unsure of the meaning of a word we want to use, we go straight to the specialist legal dictionaries and "words and phrases" books to see if we can find any cases which will tell us "what it means" at law. But what do those books actually tell us? They tell us what the word was held to mean *in the past*, last time someone else argued over it. Unless we are lucky enough to be considering the meaning of the same word very shortly after it was last considered, the legal dictionaries and phrase books cannot help us with its *present* meaning. Those books give us more of a historical record of past meanings than a guide to likely present (or future) meanings. The past is an unreliable guide to the present meaning of a word, because meanings can change.

And then there is the different *context*. The words in the legal dictionaries are there either because others have argued about them, or because they were given a special meaning in a statute or a document. When we look up a word in the legal dictionaries, we are very lucky indeed if we find that it has been judicially considered in exactly the same context as ours. The odds are even worse against it having been considered recently.

As Dr Robinson points out,[12] this difficulty of context was recognised by the English courts in the 1960s. In *Sefton v Tophams Ltd*, the court had to consider the meaning of the word *permit*, Lord Wilberforce said:

> the use of precedents to attribute to plain English words a meaning derived from the use of those words in other documents is always of doubtful value and the inutility of this procedure is exemplified here. The cases in fact give no more than illustrations of the use of the word "permit" in certain isolated fact situations, and illustration is something less than we need.[13]

So how comfortable should we feel when we say that a word has years of case law behind it, which tells us what it means? Surely what we are actually saying is that people have been arguing over its meaning in various contexts for years. How can that represent an "ordinary" or "commonly acceptable" meaning?

---

12   1973, *Drafting*, Butterworths, Sydney, p 84.
13   [1967] 1 AC 50 at 84.

It seems to me that what we should aim for in our writing is that it can be understood by all those likely to be affected by it. So we should do our best to make sure that the words we use are used in the way that the reader would use and understand them. As I've said, we can't be sure that anything we write will stand the test of time, but it seems sensible to start with our likely readers understanding what we write today, rather than relying on what the words might have meant to others in the past, or in another context.

Much has been said over many years about the need for lawyers to simplify and clarify their writing. In the next chapter I look at who has been saying these things and what incentives there are to spur us into action. But in focusing on the difficulties that "traditional" legal language presents, both for the reader and the writer, we should not lose sight of all the difficulties that lawyers face when they try to write documents that are not only clear and precise but also will stand the tests of time and close scrutiny.

I have not said all I want to say on that subject. For example, we need to consider the effect of the rules of interpretation on our writing. In Chapter 12 I look at some of the rules that we are most likely to encounter, and consider whether they are an impediment to plain language writing. But for the time being, let's focus on the past, in the hope that it will convince us we need to change.

Chapter 3

Why plain language?

Who says there's a problem?

The idea of trying to simplify our writing is not new. Nor is criticism of verbosity and confused, foggy writing. Over the years there have been plenty of people ready with advice about writing. Here is a brief rundown of some of it. Some of it, but thankfully not all, is criticism of law, lawyers and legalese.

About writing and language in general

People have been advocating plain words since long before they began to focus on lawyers as the worst offenders. Even in the 4th century BC it seems plain words were admired. Roger Ascham (1515-1568) records that Aristotle had some advice for those who want to write well:

> He that will write well in any tongue must follow this counsel of Aristotle, to speak as the common people do, to think as wise men do; so should every man understand him, and the judgment of wise men allow him.[1]

Sir Ernest Gowers, himself a barrister, had this advice for all writers:

> Be short, be simple, be human.[2]

Even Albert Einstein had some useful advice for us about simplicity. He said:

> Everything should be made as simple as possible but not simpler.[3]

---

1   *Toxophilus* (1545) "To all gentlemen and yeomen of England".
2   Gowers (Greenbaum and Whitcut eds), 1987, *The Complete Plain Words*, 3rd edition, Penguin Books, London, p 19.
3   Attributed to Albert Einstein by *The Bloomsbury Treasury of Quotations*, 1994, Bloomsbury Publishing plc, London, p 629.

About politicians, scientists, journalists, officials and others

Arthur Wellesley, first Duke of Wellington (1769-1852) had some good advice for a new Member of Parliament:

> Don't quote Latin; say what you have to say, and then sit down.[4]

George Orwell, in his 1946 essay "Politics and the English Language", singled out political writing for criticism. He said:

> In our time it is broadly true that all political writing is bad writing.[5]

Chemists and other scientists have recognised they have a problem writing clearly. Robert Schoenfeld, who was a chemist, identified a separate subspecies of English, which he called "Chemist's English".[6] One of its chief characteristics is a high proportion of passive verbs, and another is its lack of first person pronouns.

Randolph Quirk, in *The Use of English*,[7] reviewed the styles of English used by those in industry and commerce, officials, scientists, journalists – and lawyers. He was very generous in his acknowledgment of the problems lawyers face in their writing – which, incidentally (and perhaps naively), he considers "obligatory, and not optional". But his final assessment was:

> In the last resort, the determiners of any linguistic form are mainly habit and fashion, however much we may like to believe there is some useful purpose justifying it.[8]

William Zinsser has a theory that weakness in writing style actually *increases* in proportion to education and rank. He gives us a lovely example of officialese. This is a government memo describing a blackout order in 1942:

> Such preparations shall be made as will completely obscure all Federal buildings and non-Federal buildings occupied by the Federal government during an air raid for any period of time from visibility by reason of internal or external illumination.[9]

---

4   Quoted in Muir, F, 1976, *The Frank Muir Book*, Corgi Books, London, p 90.

5   In *The Penguin Essays of George Orwell*, 1985, Penguin Books, London, p 361.

6   Schoenfeld, R, 1989, *The Chemist's English*, 3rd revised edition, VCH Verlagsgesellschaft mbH, Weinheim, Germany.

7   Quirk, R, 1968, *The Use of English*, 2nd edition, Longman, London, pp 169-182.

8   Same work, p 173.

9   2001, *On Writing Well*, 6th revised (25th anniversary) edition, HarperResource Quill, New York, p 8.

Zinsser tells us that when Franklin D Roosevelt saw this he took executive action. "Tell them", he said, "that in buildings where they have to keep the work going to put something across the windows".

About laws, lawyers and legal writing

Even as long ago as the 16th century, people were complaining about the proliferation of laws and the difficulties of legal language. King Edward VI (who reigned from 1547-1553) is said to have complained:

> I would wish that the superfluous and tedious statutes were brought into one sum together and made more plain and short so that men might better understand them.[10]

Jonathan Swift was a savage critic of legal language. In 1726 he wrote:

> there is a Society of Men among us, bred up from their youth in the Art of proving by Words multiplied for the purpose, that White is Black and Black is White, according as they are paid. To this society all the rest of the people are slaves.[11]

He was, of course, referring to lawyers.

Across the Atlantic and a little later, Thomas Jefferson was complaining about wordy statutes. He was head of a committee whose task was to revise the laws of Virginia after the Declaration of Independence in 1770. His committee pledged itself "not to insert an unnecessary word, nor to omit a useful one".[12] He criticised statutes which:

> from verbosity, their endless tautologies, their involutions of case within case, and parenthesis within parenthesis, and their multiplied efforts at certainty, by saids and aforesaids, by ors and by ands, to make them more plain, are really rendered more perplexed and

---

10 Quoted by Kennan, the Hon J, QC MLA, in "The Importance of Plain English in Drafting" in Kelly, D StL (ed), 1988, *Essays in Legislative Drafting*, Adelaide Law Review Association, Federation Press, Sydney.

11 Swift, J, *Gulliver's Travels* (Crown ed, 1947), pp 295-296.

12 1950, 2 Jefferson, *Papers* (Boyd ed) 325, quoted in Mellinkoff, D, 1963, *The Language of the Law*, Little Brown, Boston, pp 252-53.

incomprehensible, not only to common readers, but to the lawyers themselves.[13]

At around the same time, back on the other side of the Atlantic, Jeremy Bentham was railing against lawyers and their wordy jargon. He said the law was "spun out of cobwebs"[14] and "wrought up to the highest possible pitch of voluminousness, indistinctness and unintelligibility".[15]

As might be expected, Will Rogers (1879-1935) was even more blunt. He said:

> The minute you read something and you can't understand it, you can be sure it was written by a lawyer.[16]

In 1853, Charles Dickens had his say about the prolixity and fogginess of lawyers. In *Bleak House* (Chapter 1), he described Chancery practice, where the barristers were:

> mistily engaged in one of the ten thousand stages of an endless cause, tripping one another up on slippery precedents, groping knee deep in technicalities, running their goat hair and horse hair warded heads against walls of words, and making a pretence of equity with serious faces, as players might.

In 1878, Jessel MR had the task of construing a series of objects clauses in a memorandum of association and he said this:

> Now speaking for myself only, and knowing as I do the habits of conveyancers and the mode in which legal instruments are drawn in this country, I am never very much embarrassed by the suggestion that when a man uses ten words where two would do, I am bound to affix a separate meaning to every word of the ten. I do not consider myself so bound, and the same principle applies to the use of three words instead of two.[17]

---

13 1905, *The Writings of Thomas Jefferson* (Lipscom ed), p 65, quoted in Mellinkoff, *The Language of the Law*, pp 252-53 (cited at note 12).

14 1843 5 Bentham, *Works* (Bowring ed), p 485, quoted in Mellinkoff, D, 1963, *The Language of the Law*, p 261 (cited at note 12).

15 1843 6 Bentham, *Works* (Bowring ed), p 332, quoted in Mellinkoff, D, 1963, *The Language of the Law*, p 261 (cited at note 12).

16 Quoted in the information kit issued by the Canadian Law Information Council's Plain Language Centre, 1989.

17 *In re Florence Land & Public Works Company; Ex parte Moor* (1878) 10 Ch D 530 at 538.

More recently, we have Professor Carl Felsenfeld of Fordham Law School, New York City, who was one of the masterminds behind one of the first consumer documents to be "translated" into plain language – the First National City Bank (now Citibank) consumer loan note. He tells us:

> Lawyers have two common failings. One is that they do not write well and the other is that they think they do.[18]

In 1987 the members of the Victorian Law Reform Commission told us:

> The measure of success for legal writing is not how well drafters manage to sound like lawyers but how well they achieve accuracy of content combined with plainness of expression.[19]

And in 1993, in his opening address to a conference of judges of the Supreme Court of New South Wales, the former Chief Justice of the High Court of Australia, Sir Anthony Mason criticised his fellow judges. He said:

> Unfortunately, judgements do not speak in a language or style that people readily understand. That is why academic lawyers tell me that students are much more interested in reading speeches and papers presented by particular judges than the judgements they write, even though they may cover the same ground. The judgement is so encrusted with discussion of precedent that it tends to be forbidding.[20]

Finally, here's MM Corbett, a former Chief Justice of South Africa, on the reasons why society doesn't trust lawyers:

> There is no reason why the law should be, and remain, an occult science understood only by lawyers. In fact society's distrust of lawyers and the law is mainly due to the tendency of lawyers in the past to keep the law to themselves.[21]

I hope after that list that we can agree that there has been sufficient criticism for us to recognise that there is a serious problem

---

18 "The Plain English Movement in the United States" (1981-82) 6 *Canadian Business Law Journal* 408 at 413.

19 30 June 1987, Law Reform Commission of Victoria Report No 9, *Plain English and the Law*, Appendix 1, p 1 – Drafting Manual.

20 Text of speech given by the former Chief Justice on 30 April 1993, as reported in *Rapport* No 8, June 1993, p 7.

21 "Writing a Judgment" (1998) 115 *South African Law Journal* 116 at 122.

with much of our writing – and it is not just non-lawyers who are doing the criticising. But lawyers are not alone. As Zinsser says,[22] "every profession has its growing arsenal of jargon to fire at the layman and hurl him back from its walls".

So just how did we lawyers get this way?

How did it get so bad?

Mellinkoff examines the origins of the problem in great detail in his book *The Language of the Law*.[23] During the early 15th century in England, law and legal procedures had gradually moved from the oral to the written. This meant that written pleadings had to be prepared outside the courtroom and could no longer be altered by the lawyer in court, depending on which way the evidence was shaping up and the way the court seemed to be leaning. It became more attractive to work from what had worked before.

Then in the mid-15th century, the printing press hit Europe. The market was ready, and the technique of printing spread rapidly. It reached London in 1480. Nearly every aspect of Western society felt its effects, and, according to James Burke, it almost completely destroyed the oral traditions of Western society.[24]

Printing is an invention that many commentators on legal history have pinpointed as a major contributing factor to the deluge of words. Mellinkoff tells us[25] that by the 17th century it was already being viewed with alarm by commentators such as John Locke (1669), and, in 1671, the Lord Chief Justice Sir Matthew Hale, who referred to it as "the rolling of a snow-ball".[26]

It seemed nothing could stop the printing presses from spewing out the growing mass of law. Almost two centuries later Benjamin Disraeli (1804-1881) echoed that view when he said:

> The greatest misfortune that ever befell man was the invention of printing.[27]

---

22   Zinsser, W, 2001, *On Writing Well*, p 16 (cited at note 9).
23   Cited at note 12.
24   See Burke, J, 1985, *The Day the Universe Changed*, British Broadcasting Corporation, London, p 112.
25   Mellinkoff, D, 1963, *The Language of the Law*, p 140 (cited at note 12).
26   1 Hargrave (ed), 1787, *A Collection of Tracts*, 271 (quoted in Mellinkoff, D, cited at note 12).
27   Quoted in *The Frank Muir Book*, p 125 (cited at note 4).

The problems in the legal world were exacerbated by the discovery in the 16th century of the concept of the filing fee. The courts of those days were not completely supported by public funds. To generate income, they devised a system of fees for preparing and filing documents that was based on the number of pages; the longer the document, the higher the fees.

To compound matters, lawyers and clerks were also paid by the length of the documents they prepared. They filled out documents with unnecessary words. This was the heyday of the recital and the preamble. Drafters found they could lengthen their documents and repeat material by "reciting" it. But there were some attempts made to curtail this practice, and we have evidence that the judges were not afraid to act – and act creatively – to discourage overlong documents.

A dramatic attempt occurred, it seems, in 1596 (although Tothill gives the date as 1565) when Chancellor Egerton sentenced an offender – whose pleading was 120 pages long – to have his head put through a hole cut in his document, and to be led "bare headed and bare faced round about Westminster Hall".[28] Strangely enough, the offending document in that case was not drafted by a lawyer, but by the son of the person bringing the case to court, and happily the Chancellor was wise enough to punish the son rather than the father! We are left to wonder whether the offender would have received the same punishment had he been a lawyer.

In fact, although Chancellor Egerton was quick to punish non-lawyers whose pleadings were inflated or full of irrelevant or defamatory material, there is some evidence that lawyers did not completely escape punishment. During the reign of Elizabeth I, Lord Bacon ordered that if any pleadings were found to be of "immoderate length", *both* the litigant *and* the counsel who signed them should be fined.[29]

---

28 *Milward v Welden* (1565) Toth 102; 21 ER 136 – described in more detail (as *Mylward v Weldon* (8 & 10 Feb 1596)) by Spence, G, 1846, in *The Equitable Jurisdiction of the Court of Chancery*, Vol 1, V and R Stevens and GS Norton, London, p 376, note (e). Spence quotes as his reference Reg Lib A 1596, fol 667 and fol 672. He states that the reference in Tothill's reports (Toth) is "as usual, erroneous". The incident is also described, without noting a year, in Holdsworth, Sir W, 1945, *A History of English Law*, Sweet & Maxwell, London, 3rd edition, Vol 5, p 233, quoting Monro, *Acta Cancellaria* 692-693.

29 Spence, G, 1846, *The Equitable Jurisdiction of the Court of Chancery*, p 377 (cited at note 28).

In the centuries that followed, the amount of law and legal text increased dramatically. Court reports became available in print, and we begin to see the inexorable rise of the precedent: both in the sense of the book of forms and in the sense of prior decisions of the courts. Laws multiplied prodigiously as society and commerce became more complex. "Forms and precedents" books (of varying standards) became more readily available to lawyers, who took to them with enthusiasm. Some made wildly extravagant claims about their accuracy and efficacy, and sought legitimacy by invoking the mystical blessing of "precedent".

And so here we are today, weighed down by centuries of legal precedents, hog-tied by the precedent and form books, chained to our own drawers and folders full of "tried and true" precedents, trying to communicate with our clients clearly and efficiently in the 21st century. It is not easy to change the habits of a career, much less of a whole profession. Why bother? What's in it for me?

What's in it for me?

Does it save on costs? As we'll see in Chapter 4, the United States introduced various "plain language" laws beginning in 1975. But companies like Citibank moved to a plain language policy *before* the laws were introduced. In 1973 Citibank began the process of rewriting a consumer promissory note in plain language. That note became an icon of the plain language movement.

The moving force behind the decision to change was the feeling among the senior managers that rewriting an important consumer document in plain language was an important service they could provide to consumers. Citibank is on record as saying that it has achieved better communication with its consumers, improved its image and saved costs on consumer litigation by simplifying documents.[30] After it finished rewriting the first document, Citibank went on to revise all its consumer forms. Teams of lawyers work with Citibank managers to simplify the documents.

Imagine the position in 1973 when the decision was made to do the rewrite. A massive loan portfolio was to be "put at risk" by adopting what was thought to be "new" and "untested" language.

---

30 US Department of Commerce Office of Consumer Affairs, *How Plain English Works for Business*, US Government Printing Office, Washington, p 3.

Now, 30 years later, Citibank is still committed to the policy of simplifying its documents. And they say they can show that the new documents actually result in *fewer* suits against consumers.

Many US corporations, such as Sentry Insurance, St Paul Fire and Marine Insurance Company, Aetna Life & Casualty, Home Owners Warranty Corporation, JC Penney Company Inc, Shell Oil Company, Pfizer Inc, Hoffman La Roche Inc and Target Stores, have publicly stated that adopting plain language increased their efficiency and improved their profiles in the market. None has complained of increased litigation about the meaning of the words in their documents and some say there has actually been a decrease in litigation since they adopted plain language.[31]

The question "Does Quality in Document Design Pay?" was asked by a US commentator in an article published in the US journal *Technical Communication*.[32] She presented 16 examples of organisations which had saved time and money or won customers by rewriting and redesigning documents and forms. Some of the examples the author gives are:

- The Motorola Corporate Finance Department estimates that rewriting the directions on its forms and computer screens has helped it save US$20,000,000 per year.
- The Southern California Gas Company estimates a saving of US$252,000 a year because it simplified *one* billing statement form.
- The Federal Communications Commission rewrote its regulations for citizens band radios and was able to reassign five employees who had done nothing but answer questions.[33]

In Australia, NRMA Insurance Limited was so happy with its decision to move to "Plain English" car and home insurance

---

31　Same work.

32　Schriver, KA, "Quality in Document Design: Issues and Controversies", (1994) 40 *Technical Comm* 239 at 250-251.

33　Professor Joseph Kimble has collected more evidence about the money (and time) saved by using plain language, in his article "Writing for Dollars, Writing to Please" *Scribes Journal of Legal Writing*, Vol 6 (1996-1997), p1. He lists 11 case studies of time and money saving from the US, Canada, UK and Australia. The article also deals with the ability of plain language to please and persuade readers.

policies that it undertook further reviews of its policies: reviewing language, format and layout to make the policies even more "user-friendly". NRMA Insurance takes the view that insurance is a difficult enough concept for the average person to understand: it says there is no need to make things more difficult by using complicated traditional language.

Far from experiencing difficulties with the language of the plain English policies, NRMA Insurance said that the new language has caused no significant problems at all. In 1991 I interviewed one of NRMA Insurance's legal advisors, Peter Mann,[34] who handled NRMA Insurance's insurance contract litigation from 1984. He said that in that time there had been "precious few" disputes over the meaning of words in the plain English policies. He could only recall "one or two" cases when judges had criticised any aspect of the policies' drafting style. Given the huge volume of insurance that is underwritten by NRMA Insurance, that is quite remarkable. "You could say", he said, "that the relative absence of any litigation involving an interpretation of the NRMA Insurance policies would tend to support the assertion that the move from traditional insurance language to plain language is beneficial".

In fact, a case decided in 1994 in Canada shows that using plain language in legal documents may even result in more wins for insurers. In *Munro v Shackleton*, a decision of the Saskatchewan Queen's Bench, a judge was construing an insurance contract. The plaintiffs claimed that the insurance agent had arranged the wrong policy for them – they needed a policy that would cover commercial business premises. But the judge was not prepared to let the plaintiffs win on the basis of the agent's negligence. The judge found that the policy the agent arranged was written in plain English and the plaintiffs should have read it. They were literate adults capable of reading such a contract. Justice Larry A Kyle said:

> I am not prepared to hold that insured persons are under no obligation to read the contracts which they make. There was a time when insurance policies were so poorly drawn that no-one could reasonably be expected to understand them without special training. Efforts made by insurance companies to relieve this problem have resulted in documents such as those filed in evidence in this case. It

---

34 Partner, Abbott Tout Russell Kennedy (as it then was), interviewed on 5 March 1991.

is not appropriate to place the entire burden upon the insurance agent to meet the needs of the applicant unless the facts demonstrate a complete reliance ...[35]

Can we measure the benefits? Several Australian companies, including NRMA Insurance Limited, have tried to measure their savings from documents that were redesigned and rewritten in plain language. NRMA Insurance Limited estimated its savings at $500,000 a year and Capita Finance Group estimated $530,000 of savings a year, on the basis of reduced staff time and fewer customer errors.[36] Another insurance group, the Norwich Group, has estimated that 30% of its staff's time is wasted on tasks that have to be performed because a written communication is inadequate. They believe that rewriting documents in plain English cuts that waste dramatically.[37]

The public sector has also experienced the efficiencies of plain language drafting. The Victorian Attorney-General's Department said it had saved over $400,000 a year in staff time after rewriting and redesigning just one court form.[38]

After the United Kingdom government adopted a plain English policy for government forms in 1982, various government departments rewrote, redesigned and eliminated many thousands of forms. They estimate that they have saved millions of pounds as a direct result, and that in 1984-85 alone they saved £4 million. The sorts of costs that were saved were related to reduced errors in completing forms – leading to less staff time, telephone calls and visits being devoted to correcting those errors and answering questions, and reduced delay in clients receiving service and benefits to which they were entitled.[39]

---

35   *Munro v Shackleton* (1993) 115 Sask R 104 at [9].

36   Duckworth, M and Mills, G, 1994, *The Costs of Obscurity: a discussion paper on the costs and benefits of plain legal language*, Centre for Plain Legal Language, Centre for Microeconomic Analysis, Law Foundation of New South Wales, Sydney, p 3.

37   Balmford, C, "Plain English Policy Making" (1993) 8(10) *Australian Insurance Law Bulletin* 79.

38   *Reader Friendly Campaign Materials*, 1990, published by the International Literacy Year Secretariat, Department of Employment, Education and Training, Canberra.

39   1987, Law Reform Commission of Victoria Report, No 9, *Plain English and the Law*, p 60.

But so many of these figures are just estimates. Is there any hard evidence? One of the most systematic attempts so far to collect hard evidence was made by the Centre for Plain Legal Language and the Centre for Microeconomic Policy Analysis (both then operating within the University of Sydney). First, they established the analytical framework needed to evaluate the costs and benefits of using documents written in plain language, and tried to work out a way to identify and measure them. In 1994 they published a discussion paper outlining the existing anecdotal evidence, and previous attempts to quantify the benefits of plain language. They also looked at some of the problems and the methodology involved in such a study.[40]

The results of their research study were published early in 1996. Unfortunately, for reasons beyond the control of the researchers, there was not enough data for a complete cost-benefit analysis. But they report that they found important statistical information and useful qualitative information.

Based on three case studies, together with their knowledge of other plain language projects, the researchers found statistical evidence of the following benefits of plain language writing projects:

- time saved in completing forms
- reduced need to amend forms later
- less effort to understand forms
- fewer questions from form processors
- fewer applications rejected because of form problems.

In the case studies, the researchers also found that a plain language project often revealed legal and policy problems with old documents.[41]

In Canada, the project co-ordinator for the Alberta Agriculture, Food and Rural Development took the trouble to take measurements before and after their plain language forms review project. By April 1996, 92 of their 646 forms had been revised. Using

---

40 Duckworth, M and Mills, G, 1994, *The Costs of Obscurity: a discussion paper on the costs and benefits of plain legal language* (cited at note 36).

41 Mills, G, & Duckworth, M, (1996), *The Gains from Clarity: A research report on the effects of plain-language documents*, Centre for Microeconomic Analysis, Centre for Plain Legal Language, Law Foundation of New South Wales, Sydney.

surveys, focus groups and participant descriptions, the co-ordinator was able to prove to Alberta Agriculture that improving the forms had saved them a minimum of C\$3,472,014 in salaries. And the amount of staff time saved on just six of the forms was 62.1 workdays or C\$9077.[42]

Another project in which the organisers took the trouble to measure the results of their efforts was the Veterans Benefits Administration (VBA), a section of the US Department of Veteran's Affairs. Because they were concerned at the potential cost of training staff in a wide variety of geographic locations in their "Reader-Focused Writing Tools" course, they undertook a careful cost-benefit analysis.

The formal results found by the independent evaluators were:

- Significant increase in performance. The participants' writing improved markedly when measured by two separate scales of evaluation.
- Sustained and retained learning and application. Evaluation which took place over a year after the course showed that participants remembered what they'd learned and continued to apply it: they took lasting benefits from the course.[43]

Does it save time? Most of the available figures on the savings and benefits of plain language relate to commerce or government. It is more difficult to estimate in concrete terms the savings that lawyers in private practice might expect to make by adopting a policy of writing in plain language. The Victorian Law Reform Commission has attempted to do so. It ordered a study aimed at comparing the time it took to read, understand and apply law written in the traditional manner with law written in plain English. They used traditional and plain English versions of the Companies (Acquisition of Shares) Act 1980 and the Futures Industry Act 1986.[44] The psychologist who conducted the study asked groups of lawyers to read extracts from those laws and apply the law to

---

42 For more information, see Mowat, C, "Alberta Agriculture saves money with plain language", *Clarity* No 38, Jan 1997, p 6.

43 Summarised from Kleimann, Dr S and Mercer, M, "Changing Bureaucracy – One paragraph at a time", *Clarity* No 43, May 1999, p 26.

44 Both now repealed.

hypothetical facts. They found that the standard of accuracy of the answers did not vary significantly between the groups of lawyers, but that the lawyers who were working from the plain language versions took *one-half* to *one-third the time* to get the answer that the lawyers working from the traditional version took.[45]

A study done in 1980 by the Document Design Center (later the Information Design Center) of the American Institutes for Research in Washington DC showed that a plain language version of an administrative rule was quicker to work with than the original rule. Those who had used the plain language version of the rule to answer a set of questions did 102% better on the test than those using the original rule, and they finished the test in *just over half the time* that the others took.[46]

In a 1983 study of medical consent forms presented to readers in the original form and in a revised form, readers of the revised form were able to respond to questions in less than two-thirds of the time of those using the original form.[47] And in Chapter 17 I mention the testing involved in the project to rewrite New Zealand tax laws. Researchers showed that even tax professionals found the plain language versions of tax laws quicker to comprehend than the original versions.[48]

Faced with the results of this objective kind of test and all the other efficiency-related benefits that flow from plain language, it seems pointless to argue about whether or not it takes more or less time to write in plain language. Blaise Pascal (1623-1662), the theologian, mathematician and incidentally the inventor (at the age of 18) of the calculator, seems to have thought that it takes longer to write less. He said in 1656:

> I have made this letter longer than usual, only because I did not have the time to make it shorter.[49]

George Orwell also thought it takes longer to write less. He said:

---

45   1987, Law Reform Commission of Victoria Report, No 9, *Plain English and the Law*, p 61.

46   Redish, JC, 1991, *How to Write Regulations and Other Legal Documents in Clear English*, Document Design Centre, Washington, p 43.

47   Kaufer, DS et al, "Revising Medical Consent Forms: An Empirical Model and Test" (1983) 11 *Law Medicine & Health Care* 155 at 161.

48   See p 291.

49   Lettres Provincales, XVI.

> It is easier – even quicker, once you have the habit – to say "In my opinion it is a not unjustifiable assumption that" than to say "I think".[50]

But it is not just a matter of measuring how long it takes us to write. If we want to work out whether writing in plain language makes us more efficient, we must count not only the time it takes us to produce the first draft, but also the extra time involved in improving the first draft so that it meets a proper professional standard. And this does take time if you are at all interested in the quality of your writing, because you are involved in a "write", and then one or more "rewrites". Remember what Orwell said: "It is easier – even quicker – *once you have the habit*" – to write badly. It is the *habit* – the habit of picking up the dictaphone and speaking off the top of our heads with no thought for the reader and no attempt to plan how we will arrange our information – that makes it *seem* quicker to write in legalese and with no planning. But the result is often poor writing, which needs rewriting. It is much more efficient to put in extra time at the planning stage, so that the time is invested, not wasted, and the quality of the end product is high.

Whether we can say that speed is one of the advantages of plain language drafting depends on whether we measure it with a stopwatch which starts when the writer takes up a pen or a dictaphone and stops when the document goes off to be typed, or whether we look at the process as a whole, right through any edits by the writer, to the moment when the client or colleague reads the letter and says "I understand. Now I know what to do." On the latter scale of measurement, plain language wins every time.

Is it more effective? This question of whether a reader understands what you have written and can act on it is an important but difficult one. But there is hard evidence that plain language improves comprehension. Much of this evidence has been cited by Professor Joseph Kimble in his article "Answering the Critics of Plain Language".[51] He lists about 20 studies (including a few of his own). For example, there have been several studies involving oral instructions given to juries. Each showed that plain language

---

50 "Politics and the English Language", in 1985, *The Penguin Essays of George Orwell*, Penguin Books, London, p 360.

51 *The Scribes Journal of Legal Writing*, Vol 5 (1994-95), p 51.

instructions improved jurors' comprehension by significant margins – in one study there was 100% improvement.[52]

I have already mentioned the study of medical consent forms that showed that readers could respond faster to questions about the forms if the forms were in plain language.[53] Readers of the plain language forms also answered more questions correctly – they did 91% better, in fact.[54] And I have also mentioned the Victorian Law Reform Commission study using traditional and plain English versions of the Companies (Acquisition of Shares) Act 1980 and the Futures Industry Act 1986.[55] I mention more studies in the context of document testing in Chapter 17. There have been many other studies using legal documents, forms and legislation written in plain language, in which readers are asked questions about the documents.

In each study, readers are more accurate in their answers if they are using the plain language version. In some cases the improvement is only slight. In others it is massive. The evidence is there, even if it is difficult to pin down exactly what it was that improved the readers' comprehension.

The fact is that we don't yet know exactly what it is that best helps readers to understand a document. There are so many variables involved in the studies done so far, and so many different factors like individual reader capacities and requirements. That is one reason why "testing" documents has become such an important aspect of plain language writing. There is more about "testing" in Chapter 17.

Will it give me a competitive edge? This is another benefit that is difficult to measure. I've already mentioned that various United States corporations have gone on record as saying that adopting plain language increased their efficiency and improved their profiles in the market. There are many Australian corporations and firms who have experienced similar benefits from writing in plain

---

52   Steele, WW Jnr and Thornburg, EG, "Jury Instructions: A Persistent Failure to Communicate" (1991) 74 *Judicature* 249 at 250.

53   See p 39.

54   Kaufer, DS et al, 1983, "Revising Medical Consent Forms: An Empirical Model and Test", pp 155, 161 (cited at note 47).

55   See pp 38-39.

language. I've already mentioned corporations such as NRMA Insurance Limited, Capita Finance Group and Norwich Group.[56] And I've already referred to the possibility of cost and time savings. These can all contribute to the competitive edge. But there is another, less tangible factor for lawyers: the expectations of their clients.

It used to be thought that clients expect their lawyers to write in legalese and would be disappointed if they didn't. Those days are receding fast; public attitudes are changing. In fact, my experience is that clients respond very well to plain language documents. I've actually had the experience of delighted clients writing and calling to say things like "Your documents were a joy to read" and "I could understand every word."

Law firms that have adopted a plain language policy can testify that they have actually picked up new clients because of the policy. New clients can *become* new clients because they are impressed by the plain language documents they see when they participate in other transactions. Next time, they may well instruct lawyers who have experience in drafting in plain language.

Australian firms with an eye on Asian markets are also seeing the advantages of plain language drafting in legal documents. They understand that these markets have special needs, and one of those needs is for clear and straightforward communication to minimise the problems caused by language and cultural differences. The benefits of plain language writing are clear in that context. Why export legalese to Asia?

Not only is it possible to pick up new clients who like their documents in plain language, it is also possible to pick up an entirely new type of work: the business of drafting special purpose plain language documents. In Australia, this is still a relatively new market, which is being driven by the recent atmosphere of law reform, the attitude of the courts to poorly written documents, and the increasing number of laws that require documents to be written so that they can be understood.

For example, in 1992, the Australian Trade Practices Commission issued a comprehensive discussion paper on the home building industry, and recommended that home building contracts

---

56   See p 36.

should be written in plain language. Soon afterwards, the first plain English building contracts emerged.

Also in 1992, the Trade Practices Commission issued a comprehensive report on the insurance industry. One of the criticisms made in the report was that superannuation and life insurance proposals and policies are difficult for people to understand. At about the same time, the Life Insurance Federation of Australia was briefing lawyers to prepare model plain language documents that are intended as industry standards. Several insurance companies had pioneered plain language in home and car insurance policies in the 1970s. Now some are moving to tackle life insurance as well.

When the Australian government announced plain language reviews of both the Corporations Law and the tax laws,[57] the government looked to private lawyers and language experts for help. In the case of the Corporations Law Taskforce, two of the Australian law firms that have established plain language policies won the right to help with the redrafts.

Then there are the banks. They have been running into more and more trouble in Australian courts because their documents can be hard for customers to understand. A 1988 government inquiry into banking, the Martin Inquiry, called on the banks to adopt plain language, especially in security documents. The Australian Bankers' Association responded by issuing a Code of Banking Practice in November 1993, most recently revised in August 2002.[58] The Code states (under the heading "Our key commitments to you") that banks will "provide information to you in plain language".

Some banks have realised the advantages of plain language documents. Several Australian banks have produced security documents, such as residential property mortgages, in plain language. And banks across Australia rewrote their credit contracts, guarantees and notices so that they comply with the Consumer Credit Code requirement that those documents be "clearly expressed".

It is well over 10 years since the idea of law firms marketing legal services in plain language was a novel one in Australia. Now it is seen as mainstream by the larger firms. Smaller firms, too, have

---

57 See pp 69-70.

58 The new Code does not commence until August 2003 and there may be changes in the meantime.

also seen its advantages.[59] Some of these firms are advertising their special plain language services and issuing brochures describing what they can do. They are setting up plain language units. They've realised that plain language drafting is here to stay, and they're making it work for them.[60]

Are there laws that are relevant to legal language or drafting? I mentioned in Chapter 1 that there are already quite a few laws that require us to write certain documents, or otherwise communicate, in simpler language: language that is "easy to understand", "easily [be] understood", "readily understood", "readily understandable", "intelligible", "comprehensible" or "expressed plainly", or requiring us to use "plain language" or "plain English". They include the following Commonwealth laws:

- Workplace Relations Act 1996[61]
- Crimes Act 1914[62]
- Family Law Act 1975[63]
- Therapeutic Goods Regulations 1990[64]
- National Health Act 1953[65]
- Telecommunications (Interception) Act 1979[66]
- Sales Tax Assessment Act 1992,[67]

the following New South Wales laws:

- Fair Trading Act 1987[68]

---

59 See Kabos, J, 1995, "The Small Firm Perspective: Kabos Elder", *Clarity* No 33, July 1995, pp 44-45 and Miles, T (Precedents Manager of Australian Law Firm Spark Helmore), "How Dolly Cruickshank Changed the Writing Culture of a Law Firm", *Plain Language Association International (PLAIN) Fourth Biennial Conference Proceedings Toronto, Canada, 26-29 Sept 2002*, <http://www.nald.ca/PROVINCE/ont/PLAIN/movement/1.htm>.

60 Accountants, too, have seen the benefits of plain language drafting and find that their clients notice and appreciate it: see McKerihan, S "Plain English in a Big 5 Accounting Firm", *Clarity* No 43, May 1999, p 34.

61 Section 143(1c) and (2A) and section 49(8) in Table A of the Notes to the Act.

62 Sections 16F, 19B and 20.

63 Sections 63DA(1), 112AF and 112AG.

64 Schedule 12, reg 9A(1), Schedule 13, reg 9A(1A).

65 Section 78(7).

66 Section 103A(2).

67 Section 130B.

68 Section 60F.

- Credit Act 1984[69]
- Legal Profession Act 1987[70]
- Subordinate Legislation Act 1989[71]
- Children (Community Service Orders) Act 1987[72]
- Workplace Injury Management and Workers Compensation Act 1998[73]
- Gas Supply (Natural Gas Retail Competition) Regulation 2001[74]
- Electricity Supply (General) Regulation 2001,[75]

in Victoria:

- Legal Practice Act 1996[76]
- Local Government Act 1989[77]
- Fair Trading Act 1999[78]
- Sentencing Act 1991[79]
- Adoption Regulations 1998,[80]

in Queensland:

- Industrial Relations Act 1999[81]
- Queensland Law Society Act 1952[82]
- Fair Trading Act 1989,[83]

in South Australia:

- Retirement Villages Regulations 2002[84]

---

69   Sections 147, 152 and 153 (and their equivalents in the other Australian jurisdictions which adopted the "uniform" consumer credit legislation).
70   Sections 179 and 208D(2).
71   Section 4 Schedule 1 clause 4.
72   Section 6.
73   Section 74(2B) refers to "plain language" but sections 62 and 255 refer to "ordinary language".
74   Schedule 1 Part 1 clause 1(1).
75   Schedule 1 clause 1(1).
76   Section 88(1).
77   Schedule 8 clause 1(f).
78   Sections 83 and 163.
79   Section 95.
80   Regulation 17.
81   Sections 126 and 333.
82   Section 48(2).
83   Section 58(2).
84   Regulation 6(2).

- Local Government Act 1999[85]
- Industrial and Employee Relations Act 1994[86]
- Industrial and Employee Relations (General) Regulations 1994,[87]

in Western Australia:

- Fair Trading (Retirement Villages Interim Code) Regulations 2003[88]
- Young Offenders Act 1994[89]
- Poisons Regulations 1965[90]
- Industrial Relations (Superannuation) Regulations 1997,[91]

in Tasmania:

- Subordinate Legislation Act 1992,[92]

in the Australian Capital Territory:

- Crimes Act 1900,[93]

and in the Northern Territory:

- Retirement Villages Act[94]
- Retirement Villages Regulations[95]
- Local Court Rules[96]
- Work Health Court Rules.[97]

There are too many similar provisions to list them all.

Then there is the Consumer Credit Code, which applies in all Australian jurisdictions. Section 162(1) requires that all credit contracts, guarantees and notices given under the Code by credit providers:

---

85   Section 247(g).
86   Section 93.
87   Regulations 6(3)(a) and 7(3)(a).
88   Schedule 1 Division 4 para 4.1(1).
89   Sections 44, 52 and 137.
90   Regulation 52(3)(g).
91   Regulation 4(1)(b).
92   Section 19 Schedule 1 clause 4.
93   Section 359(1) and (2).
94   Section 48(2)(b).
95   Schedule 2 – Retirement Villages Code of Practice Section 12(1)(a).
96   Rule 5.09(1)(a).
97   Rule 8.01(a) and Forms 9A and 9B in the Schedule.

(a)   must be easily legible; and
(b)   to the extent that it is printed or typed must conform with the provisions of the regulations as to print or type; and
(c)   must be clearly expressed.[98]

Section 70 also allows the court to reopen transactions that gave rise to contracts, mortgages or guarantees that are "unjust".[99] When doing so, the court is to have regard to (among other things) "the form of the contract, mortgage or guarantee and the intelligibility of the language in which it is expressed".[100]

The Queensland Residential Tenancies Act 1994 requires residential tenancy agreements to be "written in a clear and precise way".[101]

The old Rules of the Supreme Court of Queensland used to have an admirable penalty for long-winded lawyers. Order 22 rule 1(5) said that a court or judge could:

> inquire into any unnecessary prolixity, and may order the costs occasioned by such prolixity to be borne by the party responsible for the same.

Sadly, it is no longer on the books. But the good news is that all the rules have been superseded by a new, streamlined, simplified and uniform set of rules for the Supreme, District and Magistrates Courts of Queensland. The Uniform Civil Procedure Rules 1999 have been drafted in a plain language style. And, to replace Order 22 rule 1(5), there are rules requiring pleadings to be "as brief as the nature of the case permits"[102] and allowing the court to strike out pleadings and order indemnity costs against a party whose pleadings are considered to be "an abuse of the process of the court", for being "unnecessary" or "frivolous", among other things.[103]

In addition to these specific laws, there are other laws that deal in wider terms with the fairness of a contact, or whether a party was fully informed before entering the contract, or misled or deceived in some way.

---

98   Section 162(1).
99   Section 70(1).
100   Section 70(2)(g).
101   Section 39(5).
102   Rule 149(1)(a).
103   Rule 171.

With that in mind, we need to consider seriously whether it might be foolish – even negligent – to ignore plain language techniques in our drafting.

The Contracts Review Act 1980 is a New South Wales law that describes itself in its long title as "an Act with respect to the judicial review of certain contracts and the grant of relief in respect of harsh, oppressive, unconscionable or unjust contracts". Section 9 allows the court to look at all the circumstances of a case when it considers whether a contract or a provision of a contract is "unjust". One of the things the court can look at is:

> where the contract is wholly or partly in writing, the physical form of the contract, and the intelligibility of the language in which it is expressed.[104]

We also have, in Australia, laws that protect people in a more general way from misunderstandings about contracts and their terms. The Trade Practices Act 1974 is another federal law, which prohibits corporations from being involved in certain "unfair practices".

Three sections are particularly relevant for our purposes. First, section 52 prohibits a corporation in trade or commerce, from engaging in conduct that is "misleading or deceptive or likely to mislead or deceive".[105] Next, section 51AA prohibits a corporation, in trade or commerce, from engaging in "conduct that is unconscionable within the meaning of the unwritten law, from time to time, of the States and Territories".[106] We know from the Explanatory Memorandum to the Bill which contained the new section 51AA, that these words were not intended to cover conduct that is merely unfair or unreasonable. Rather, the section is aimed at the concept of "unconscionable conduct" as recognised by the High Court of Australia in cases like *Blomley v Ryan*[107] and *Commercial Bank of Australia v Amadio*.[108] In *Blomley v Ryan*, Justice Kitto explained the concept this way:

---

104   Section 9(2)(g).
105   Section 52.
106   Section 51AA(1).
107   (1956) 99 CLR 362.
108   (1983) 151 CLR 447 (discussed on p 50).

This is a well-known head of equity. It applies whenever one party to a transaction is at a special disadvantage in dealing with the other party because illness, ignorance, inexperience, impaired faculties, financial need or other circumstances affect his ability to conserve his own interests, and the other party unconscientiously takes advantage of the opportunity thus placed in his hands.[109]

Even with the twin requirements of "special disadvantage" and "taking advantage", it is still easy to see how that equitable principle could apply to a person who has had difficulty reading a document written in complex legalese. And that was exactly what happened in *Amadio's* case.[110]

Similarly, section 51AB prohibits a corporation in trade or commerce, in connection with the supply or possible supply of goods or services to a person, from engaging in conduct that is "unconscionable" in all the circumstances. In deciding whether conduct is "unconscionable", the court may look at, among other things:

whether the consumer was able to understand any documents relating to the supply or possible supply of the goods or services.[111]

Sections 51AB and 52 of the Trade Practices Act 1974 are mirrored in the Fair Trading Acts of New South Wales, Victoria, Queensland, South Australia, West Australia, Tasmania and the Australian Capital Territory.

Other laws take different approaches to matters of fairness and intelligibility in more specific circumstances. At this stage there is no indication that any one standard of readability, objective or subjective, will be applied to Australian legislation.

But regardless of what might or might not be on the horizon, lawyers who take the plain language initiative will be seen by their clients and potential clients as modern, progressive, efficient and responsive to their clients' needs and the needs of the public in general. And what better way to counter all the criticism of the language lawyers use?

What are the courts doing? As we saw earlier in this chapter, throughout history judges have criticised legal writing for being wordy, pompous and so on. I quoted a few examples, and I could

---

109   (1956) 99 CLR 362 at 415.
110   (1983) 151 CLR 447 (discussed on p 50).
111   Section 51AB(2)(c).

have used dozens more. But what are the courts doing about the problem?

As I said in Chapter 1, the courts are beginning to focus more closely on whether people understand the effect of their contractual obligations.

Look, for example, at what the High Court of Australia did in *Commercial Bank of Australia v Amadio*.[112] It set aside a mortgage and guarantee given by Mr and Mrs Amadio to a bank as security for their son's debt to the bank. It did so on the basis that the transaction was unconscionable, and that it would be unfair to allow the bank to rely on the guarantee. In coming to that conclusion, the court looked at all the circumstances, including the fact the Mr and Mrs Amadio were elderly and did not have a good command of English, especially written English, and that the bank manager knew this. There were other factors that added up to a finding of unconscionable conduct, including the fact that Mr and Mrs Amadio were accustomed to rely on their son's judgment in business matters. But the court paid particular attention to the capacity of Mr and Mrs Amadio to *understand* the document they were signing and the obligations they were undertaking. Justice Deane said:

> there was no proper basis at all for any assumption that Mr and Mrs Amadio had received adequate advice from Vincenzo [their son] as to the effect of the document which Mr Virgo [the bank manager] presented to them for their signature. Even if that were not the case, it would be difficult to accept as reasonable a belief that Vincenzo had successfully explained to his parents the content and effect of a document which embodied eighteen separate covenants of meticulous and complicated legal wording ...

In several cases since then, including *National Australia Bank Ltd v Nobile*[113] (a decision of the Full Court of the Federal Court of Australia), Australian courts have looked at the capacity of the parties to read and understand the documents they sign. Sometimes, as in *Amadio's* case and the *Nobile* case just mentioned, someone was at a disadvantage because English was not their first language. Other times, such as in *Goldsbrough v Ford Credit Aust Ltd* (a decision of the Supreme Court of New South Wales, Equity

---

112 (1983) 151 CLR 447.
113 (1988) 100 ALR 227.

division[114]) the parties have not had difficulties with English, but there have been difficulties with the document itself. In that case, Justice Young singled out a lease agreement for special criticism. He mentioned during his judgment the "rather disorderly fashion" in which the lease appeared to have been prepared. He mentioned the "relatively small print". He mentioned the difficulty that he had trying to work out what two of the clauses meant. Of one clause, he said:

> The default interest rate which they were also guaranteeing is, as I have said, hidden away in cl 5(m) among matters as venial as reporting a deficient odometer. The lease transaction was written in such legalese that not even the New South Wales office manager of the defendant realised what it meant.

Justice Young was critical of the structure of the document, which, he said, "made it impossible to work out the commencement value of the goods in the document itself" and he said that the complicated rebate formula "made it impossible to work out with any accuracy the rebate". He said these were "matters which cry out for relief". He held that the lease was unenforceable.

In 1992 another difficult-to-read document caused problems for the parties to it. In the Supreme Court of the Australian Capital Territory, in *Houlahan v Australian & New Zealand Banking Group Ltd*,[115] Justice Higgins held that a bank could not rely on a guarantee to cover advances it made above the overdraft limit that it had originally agreed with the Houlahans. The reason was that there had been a mutual mistake about what each side thought was in the agreement. In fact, no one involved in the transaction, including senior bank staff, really knew what was in the document. Even the barrister for the bank was unable to explain the first clause of the guarantee when the judge asked him. Justice Higgins pointed out that the first clause was:

> a single sentence of 57 lines in length couched in the most incomprehensible legal gobbledy-gook. That is, it must be conceded, the most extreme example. However, many of the other clauses would be understood only by a commercial lawyer with the time and patience to read them carefully.[116]

---

114   (1989) ASC ¶55-946.
115   (1992) 110 FLR 259.
116   (1992) 110 FLR 259 at 263.

Another interesting aspect of *Houlahan's* case is that at the end of the guarantee, the Houlahans had signed a statement, which read in part:

> I HEREBY ACKNOWLEDGE that I have carefully read and understand the purport of the within Guarantee ...

That statement did not save the bank. As Justice Higgins dryly observed, it was obvious that the statement was false.

The same bank's security documents came under scrutiny again in the Supreme Court of NSW. In *Karam v Australia & New Zealand Banking Group Ltd*, Justice Santow compared the case to *Houlahan's case* and observed that the bank's counsel appeared to have similar difficulties with this mortgage:

> That obscurity in terms of the mortgage relied upon by the Bank was evidenced by the difficulties experienced by Counsel for the Bank in dialogue with the bench in the present case. Experienced Counsel initially had difficulty even identifying the relevant clauses, let alone their exegesis or proper explanation ... How could lay people, the more so if only educated to the degree that the Karams were, be expected to understand its complex obscurities without proper legal advice?[117]

In 1998 the High Court of Australia handed down a landmark decision on the need for banks to ensure that their guarantee documents are properly understood. In *Garcia v National Australia Bank Limited*,[118] a married woman signed a guarantee for the debts of her husband's business. She did not fully understand the obligations she was assuming under the document. The Bank had left it to the husband to explain the guarantee. The court ruled that in the circumstances the onus was on the bank to ensure that she properly understood the effect of the guarantee. The court set aside the guarantee.

In a recent decision of the Supreme Court of the Australian Capital Territory,[119] the court had yet another bank guarantee to consider. In that case parents had mortgaged the family home to help out their son-in-law and daughter's business. The court found that the parents did in fact understand at least the general nature of

---

117 [2001] NSWSC 709 at [215].
118 (1998) 194 CLR 395.
119 *Watt v State Bank of New South Wales Ltd* [2003] ACTCA 7.

the obligations under the guarantee. But Justice Madgwick, noting how common this sort of case was becoming, suggested a legislative solution:

> Given the frequency of litigation involving people who have put themselves in ruinous situations by entering into guarantees to assist others to whom they are in a very close relationship, a better and swifter course might well be for the national parliament to intervene, at least in relation to guarantees in favour of institutional lending corporations. It is difficult to see why, as a matter of modern policy, such a lender should not be obliged, as a condition of enforcing a guarantee, to have taken every reasonable step to advise personal guarantors in plain language of the ways and the extent to which they might become liable and to ensure that they have been independently advised as to the wisdom of entering the guarantee transaction.[120]

So the courts, relying on various doctrines and laws, are quite willing to hold that documents are unenforceable because they cannot be understood. This directly implicates the lawyers who drafted them. How far away is the time when the courts expressly state that it is a lawyer's duty to write documents that can be understood? In other words, that a lawyer who drafts an unintelligible document is negligent. And even if unintelligible drafting does not actually amount to negligence, what does it say about the professional standards of lawyers if they draft documents that few can understand?

In the 1983 in the United Kingdom, that finding of negligence for unintelligible drafting came close to happening. On 7 October that year *The Times* reported that a firm of London solicitors had been ordered to pay £95,000 damages for giving "disastrous" advice to a client.[121] The judge was reported as saying that part of the letter was in "very obscure" English, and that it wasn't surprising that the client couldn't understand it. *The Times* described the letter as being "badly worded", and said it led the client to think that a lease could not be terminated, and that the client had to let the tenant stay on at the same rent for several years. The solicitors who wrote the letter had to pay damages to make up the difference in rent.

---

120 [2003] ACTCA 7 at [38].
121 *Socpen Trustees v Wood Nash & Winters*, The Times, 7 October 1983.

In fact, the problem was not so much the *way* the letter was written, but the fact that the advice, if you could decipher it, was just plain wrong. Nevertheless, the judge chose to blame the obscure language for at least part of the problem, and so the result, for cautious lawyers is the same. Badly written advice, right or wrong, may constitute negligence.

What about our image? People's opinion of lawyers seems to have hit a new low. The law and lawyers are subject to criticism as never before. A survey carried out by the American Bar Association in 1993 showed that only 8% of those surveyed had "great confidence" in lawyers. Compare that with 1974, when 24% had "great confidence". And those who despised lawyers most were male, upper class, salaried white-collar workers earning more than $50,000 per annum. That sounds suspiciously like many of our clients!

Things have not improved much in recent years. An American Bar Association survey in April 2002 found that only 19% of Americans are "very" or "extremely" confident in lawyers and the legal profession (and that's two categories combined). In the same month, Columbia Law School reported the results of a survey of one thousand people. According to that survey, many Americans think lawyers are dishonest and overpaid. 39% of respondents thought lawyers were either "especially" or "somewhat" dishonest. Only politicians scored worse. 60% thought lawyers were overpaid, compared to the other professions.[122]

The position in Australia is comparable. The Morgan Gallup Poll regularly rates the professions most admired by Australians for ethics and honesty. In the 12-year period from 1984-96, lawyers were consistently ranked fifth from the bottom. They were rated ahead of business executives, parliamentarians, journalists and car salesmen, but behind bank managers, accountants, police, dentists, teachers and the medical professions.[123] The November 2001

---

122 Reported in "CBA Professional Reform Initiative Task Force Interim Report to the Board of Governors" (2002)_ 31(7) *The Colorado Lawyer*, <http://www.cobar.org/tcl/tcl_articles.cfm?ArticleID=1754> and in Dorf, MC, 17 April 2002, "Can the Legal Profession Improve its Image?" *Findlaw's Writ*, <http://writ.news.findlaw.com/dorf/20020417.html>.

123 Eltis, K, 1997, *Fighting for the Teaching Profession*, paper prepared for the Australian College of Education, <http://wwwaustcolled.com.au/statebranches/nsw/nswresources/eltis.html>.

Bulletin-Morgan Poll, which rates a wider range of occupations, rated lawyers 13th out of 28 occupations for ethics and honesty. But the basis of that ranking was that only 32% of Australians thought lawyers had "high" or "very high" standards of ethics and honesty.[124]

Professor Deborah L Rhode, a legal ethics specialist at Stanford Law School, has pointed out that the legal profession seems to have been in a permanent state of decline throughout history. For 2000 years, she says, commentators have observed the lowering standard of behaviour of lawyers. If there had been a fall from grace, she concludes, it must have happened at an early stage of history.[125]

And how about our writing skills? How are they perceived? In a Canadian survey done in 1991 by the Plain Language Institute of British Columbia, respondents rated lawyers and politicians as the most difficult to understand out of eight vocations. Out of 10 kinds of publications, respondents rated legal documents as the most difficult by far: 57% said legal documents were hard to understand. This was almost 40% higher than instruction manuals rated, and they were rated second-hardest to understand. 64% said they always or sometimes feel frustrated or angry when they read legal documents.[126]

What do clients want? Strangely, when I first began preaching the plain language word, some lawyers were astounded to think their clients might have a negative opinion of them because of the peculiar way they used language. These lawyers used to say that their clients *wanted* them to write in legalese. Ninety-nine times out of 100 they were wrong.

A survey done in Australia in April 1994 by a large advertising agency then called George Patterson, supports what I've been telling lawyers for years – that clients really do want their legal advice in plain language.

---

124 Interestingly, this was up 3% from the same poll in October 2000. See <http://oldwww.roymorgan.com/pressreleases/20012/article-222.html>.

125 "The Professionalism Problem" (1998) 39 *William and Mary Law Review* 283 (quoted in Gleeson, M, CJ, *Are the Professions Worth Keeping?*, a speech to the Greek-Australian International Legal & Medical Conference 31 May 1999, <http://www.hcourt.gov.au/speeches/cj/cj_areprofe.htm>).

126 Plain Language Institute Report, 1993, *Critical Opinions: the Public's View of Lawyers' Documents*, Vol 11, pp 5-6.

The agency assembled "focus groups" of corporate executives – executives who were responsible for making legal decisions for their companies. Only major corporations were included in the groups. The psychologist conducting the study asked these corporate decision-makers to talk about law firms, and monitored their responses.

When the discussion came around to the image of law firms, the overall impression was that they were arrogant. And one of the key areas of arrogance was seen to be in "Legal speak". One of the most common requests made in the focus groups was: "Give me plain English advice".

These people said they wanted their lawyers to give them practical, commercial advice that they could actually use to solve their problems – and they wanted it in plain language. They wanted to feel confident and empowered in their dealings with lawyers. They wanted to have a true business partnership with a law firm that understood their business. Is that so very surprising?

A 1994 analysis of complaints made against solicitors in New South Wales revealed that by far the largest proportion of complaints related to problems caused by poor communication.[127] The Law Society of New South Wales has recognised that this is a major problem for the profession, and sees communication as one of the most important duties of lawyers. The Society's Statement of Ethics for solicitors in New South Wales, proclaimed in 1994, lists the duty to "communicate clearly with their clients" second in a list of 12 duties.

Nearly 10 years later, it seems not much has changed. Issues of negligence, poor communication and overcharging dominate clients' concerns about their lawyers: those categories make up 45.2% of complaints to the Office of the Legal Services Commissioner in New South Wales in the years 2001-02.[128] The Office has co-regulated the disciplinary system for lawyers in New South Wales since 1994. For all that time, according to their 2001-02 Annual Report, poor communication has been "one of the major catalysts in the evolution of a complaint".[129]

---

127 Source: Ian S Bowden, Lawcover, 1994.

128 Office of the Legal Services Commissioner, *Annual Report 2001-2002*, p 5.

129 *Annual Report 2001-2002*, p 14.

In 2000, Australian law firm Phillips Fox conducted a survey to find out what clients and potential clients thought of the firm. They found that the survey participants recognised – and valued highly – the clarity of the firm's advice and documents, and its plain language rewriting services. Even survey participants who were not Phillips Fox clients knew of the firm's expertise in plain language writing.[130] That's more clear evidence that plain language is what today's clients want from their lawyers, and they are prepared to pay for it.

Between the devil and the deep blue sea?

So are we now confident enough to make the jump and embrace plain language? Or would we prefer to stay with traditional legalese? At least we know and understand legalese, don't we? We feel comfortable with it, perhaps, but do we *really* know and understand it?

When was the last time we looked at all those familiar clauses in our forms and precedents and remembered why each clause was there? Has there ever been a time when a client asked us what a particular provision meant and we couldn't answer?

Let's be specific: in a security document, what does the provision that payments are to treated as *payments in gross* do? In indemnities why do we often see the words *and keep indemnified*? Do they do anything more than the word *indemnify* on its own? What about the words *and save harmless*? What do they add?

If we can't answer straight away, how can it be that we think using traditional language is safer than using plain language? Imagine yourself in a witness box explaining on oath *why* you chose those words. Surely it is a minimum requirement of a being a lawyer that we understand what we ourselves have written.

But what of the alternative? How is plain language different from legalese? Is it dangerous? What are we likely to lose by updating our language?

---

130 See Balmford, C, "Plain Language: beyond a 'movement'", *Plain Language Association International (PLAIN) Fourth Biennial Conference Proceedings Toronto, Canada, 26-29 Sept 2002*, p 6, <http://www.nald.ca/PROVINCE/ont/PLAIN/movement/1.htm>.

It is easy for lawyers to say that using plain language in legal documents is dangerous, but where is the evidence? Certainly not in cases like the controversy over the prospectus issued by the NRMA, which has been quoted by some as a warning against the "dangers" of plain language.

In that case,[131] an Australian motorists' association (the NRMA) and its related insurance company decided to change their structures. They wanted to change from being mutual organisations, without share capital, and instead operate through a company with shares listed on the stock exchange. The proposal had to be approved by the members, but in return they would get shares in the new company.

The NRMA issued a prospectus booklet to its members. In keeping with the NRMA's reputation as a supporter of plain language, the prospectus was well designed and tried to explain the proposal in simple language. But it frequently mentioned that members would get "free shares" if they approved the plan.

NRMA officials who were not in favour of the proposal tried to get court orders to stop it. One of their grounds was that the booklet breached section 52 of the Trade Practices Act 1974, which prohibits misleading or deceptive conduct in trade or commerce. They said that the shares were not "free" at all: members had to give up their mutual ownership of the organisations and the benefits of membership.

The Federal Court of Australia agreed. It held that the prospectus booklet was misleading.

The decision in the *NRMA* case was claimed by some to vindicate using technical language. They said it justified the need for long and complex documents for important and complex legal procedures. That is not so. And the court said as much. It said:

> The need to make a full and fair disclosure must be tempered by the need to present a document that is intelligible to reasonable members of the class to whom it is directed, and is likely to assist rather than confuse ... In complex cases it may be necessary to be selective in the information provided, confining it to that which is really useful. Clearly the present case was one of this kind.[132]

---

131   *Fraser v NRMA Holdings Ltd* (1995) 15 ACSR 590.
132   (1995) 15 ACSR 590 at 603.

Others claimed that the case showed that people should be particularly cautious about documents written in plain language. But this is misguided. The main problem with the prospectus was not that it was written in plain or simple language, or that it left out complex explanations. It just left out something that the court decided had to be said: that when the members received their "free" shares, they would be giving up something in return.

Summary

So that's the case in favour of plain language:

- Traditional legal language has been complained about and even ridiculed for centuries.
- Plain language is efficient – it saves time, effort and money, and we can measure those efficiencies.
- Plain language is effective – readers generally comprehend plain language documents better and quicker than documents written in traditional legal language, and we can measure those benefits.
- Plain language can give you a competitive edge.
- Many laws already require plain language, or similar standards of readability or comprehensibility.
- Our courts are quite willing to hold that documents are unenforceable because they cannot be understood.
- Plain language can improve the image of lawyers – surveys confirm this.
- Clients want good communication with their lawyers. They know plain language when they see it, and value it highly.
- Traditional legal language may not be as "safe" as we think it is.

There's still more persuasive evidence in favour of plain language. There's a history of almost 30 years of the plain language movement around the world. Plain language is truly international now, with a refreshing degree of cross-pollination and shared learning. To find out more, we can review the major developments in plain language around the world, which we'll do in Chapter 4. But if you're already convinced, or you are keen to get down to the practicalities of plain language writing, then skip to Chapter 5, which is where the writing process begins.

Chapter 4

Plain language around the world

A consumer-driven movement spreads worldwide

We saw in Chapter 3 that plain language has always been a valued commodity, even from ancient times. But in the past 30 years there has been a significant move to plain language in business, government and the law – all around the world.

In the first edition of this book I included information about developments in the United States, Canada, the United Kingdom, New Zealand and Australia. I explained how, beginning in the 1970s, the consumer movement prompted various corporations to explore the benefits of plain language documents. First in the United States and then soon after in Australia, banks and insurance companies developed plain language contracts and policies, which they believed would help decrease contractual problems and increase their market shares. Next, in the United Kingdom the National Consumer Council urged lawyers to write in plain language. The movement spread to Canada towards the end of the 1970s, and to New Zealand in the 1980s.

By 1996 and the second edition of this book, the plain language movement had spread further and gained in stature and maturity. I added information about plain language developments in the European Community, Sweden, Denmark, South Africa and India.

By 2003 and this third edition, the list of countries working towards plain language is even longer. In fact, there is so much information that it is not feasible to include it all here. Instead, you can go to <www.federationpress.com.au> and click on Book Supplements and then *Plain Language for Lawyers* to find an expanded version of this chapter listing the achievements of the plain language movement country by country

Here I will highlight major developments in plain language worldwide. My aim is to show that plain language can hardly be seen as a passing fad, or as something radical, foolhardy, or even dangerous. We have nearly 30 years of experience to draw on. The plain language movement may have begun as a part of the consumer movement. Its growth coincided with an era of demystification of (and disenchantment with) the professions, and a time of increasing interest by linguists and others in the *process* of communication. But it soon entered the mainstream of business and the law, quickly gaining legitimacy.

Beginnings – banking, insurance and the 1970s

United States The document that marks the coming-of-age of the plain language movement in the United States is the plain language consumer loan note launched on 1 January 1975 by First National City Bank (now Citibank). In 1973 Citibank made the decision to move to plain language because it had become worried by the large number of suits against consumers it had to run to collect its debts.[1]

Citibank found that not only was the bank praised by clients, consumer advocates, politicians and judges, but also there was a substantial reduction in the number of suits the bank brought against consumers.[2] Citibank acted voluntarily to rewrite its loan note, but legislation to require certain documents to be written in plain language was not far off.

In 1975, the Magnuson-Moss Consumer Product Warranty Act was passed by Congress. It stated that warranties must be written in "simple and readily understood language". Soon, US insurance companies[3] started thinking about simplifying a wide range of insurance policies, even though the Magnuson-Moss Act did not specifically apply to insurance policies. Other plain language laws would soon follow.[4]

---

1   See p 33.
2   US Department of Commerce Office of Consumer Affairs, 1984, *How Plain English Works for Business*, US Government Printing Office, Washington, pp 3-7.
3   Such as Sentry Insurance, St Paul Fire and Marine Insurance Company and Aetna Life & Casualty.
4   See p 63.

Australia Here, too, insurance companies were among the first corporations to join the plain language movement. NRMA Insurance introduced its "Plain English" car insurance policy in September 1976, and "Plain English" versions of all the other NRMA insurance policies were introduced over the next five years. Other insurance companies, such as NZI and AMP followed NRMA Insurance.

Canada The insurance and banking industries were at the forefront of the move to plain language in Canada as well. In 1979 the Bank of Nova Scotia worked with lawyer Robert Dick to redesign and rewrite its loan forms. At the same time Royal Insurance of Canada had produced a plain language insurance policy.

But even before this, in 1976, the Canadian Legislative Drafting Conventions had been produced and sanctioned by the Uniform Law Conference of Canada. These conventions adopt many of the principles of plain language drafting.

United Kingdom In 1979, Chrissie Maher and Martin Cutts founded the Plain English Campaign.[5] It had its origins in a consumer advice centre Maher and Cutts had set up three years earlier in Salford, near Manchester.

During the 1980s, the Plain English Campaign worked with the National Consumer Council to begin to review thousands of government forms which were badly worded and poorly designed. The National Consumer Council published several booklets on plain language writing, including *Gobbledegook* (1980), *Plain Words for Consumers* (1984), *Plain English for Lawyers* (1984), *Making Good Solicitors* (1989) and *Plain Language – Plain Law* (1990).

Sweden In 1976 the Swedish government appointed a linguist to the Cabinet Office. His task was to modernise legal language in laws and ordinances. Since 1980 there has been a team of language experts who revise written material before it reaches the parliament, prepare writing guidelines and run training courses.

---

5   Since 1994, Martin Cutts has operated his own plain language and document design consultancy, the Plain Language Commission. His web site is <www.plainlanguage.demon.co.uk>. The Plain English Campaign's web site is <www.plainenglish.co.uk>.

In many ways, Sweden has been way ahead of the rest of the world in the plain language movement. It was as early as 1713 that King Charles XII dictated this ordinance:

> His Majesty the King requires that the Royal Chancellery in all written documents endeavour to write in clear, plain Swedish and not to use, as far as possible, foreign words.

The US plain language laws

In 1978, President Carter issued an order that "regulations should be as simple and clear as possible".[6] He followed this up in 1979 with an order that government forms "should be as short as possible and should elicit information in a simple straightforward fashion".[7]

In 1978 the State of New York introduced its plain language law (often called the "Sullivan Law" after the politician who introduced it) which required that all residential leases and consumer contracts be written in understandable language. The exact requirement is that they have to be "written in a clear and coherent manner using words with common and everyday meanings". It applies to agreements involving amounts of $50,000 or less "primarily for personal, family or household purposes".[8]

Since then, nine other US states[9] have passed laws which require either plain, clear, conspicuous, accurate or understandable language to be used in certain consumer transactions. Many other state and federal laws and regulations govern the language to be used in a variety of documents, including life-insurance policies, ballots and utility bills. Some use the Flesch Reading Ease Test[10] to measure readability.

---

6   US Executive Order 12044, 23 March 1978.
7   US Executive Order 12174, 30 November 1979.
8   NY Gen Obl Law 5-702.
9   The 10 states are: Connecticut, Hawaii, Maine, Minnesota, Montana, New Jersey, New York, Oregon, Pennsylvania and West Virginia. Texas has recently legislated (Tex Fin §341.502, beginning September 2001) to require plain language contracts to be used for certain consumer loans covered by the Texas Finance Code.
10   Named for the person who devised the test, Rudolph Flesch: see Flesch, R, 1974, *The Art of Readable Writing*, revised 25th anniversary edition, Harper & Row, New York. See p 297 and following for more information about, and criticism of, readability formulas.

The Law Commission and Committee Reports

Several Law Commission and Committee reports proved to be catalysts for much of the progress made in the plain language movement in the last 30 years or so.

United Kingdom In the early 1970s, the Renton Committee was appointed to investigate and report to Parliament on the process of formulating statutes. On 7 May 1975 the *Renton Report*[11] was published. It highlighted examples of convoluted drafting in British statutes and recommended improving the explanatory materials that accompany statutes. This Report provoked discussion, but its full fruits would not be harvested until the late 1990s, when two major projects began in the UK. One was the project to rewrite UK tax laws,[12] and the other was the review of the format of UK legislation.

New Zealand The New Zealand Law Commission (established in 1985) has a brief to "propose ways of making legislation as understandable and accessible as practicable and of ensuring that it is kept under review in a systematic way". It must also "ascertain what changes, if any, are necessary or desirable in the law relating to the interpretation of legislation".[13]

In its Report No 17, issued in December 1990, the Commission made suggestions aimed at improving the form and style of laws and prepared a draft Interpretation Act, subtitled with its purpose: "to avoid 'Prolixity and Tautology'". In 1993 the Commission published Report No 27, called "The Format of Legislation",[14] in which it recommended changes to the design and typography of legislation. Report No 35 is called "Legislation Manual, Structure and Style". It gives guidelines for drafting legislation, and recommends plain language principles. These Reports paved the way for the project to review and simplify New Zealand's tax laws.[15]

Australia One of the major catalysts for the plain language movement in the law in Australia was the Victorian Law Reform Commission's report, called *Plain English and the Law*, published in

---

11   *The Preparation of Legislation*, 1975, Cmnd 6053, Chapter VI, Appendix B, HMSO, London.
12   See p 69.
13   Law Commission Report No 17, December 1990, *A New Interpretation Act to Avoid "Prolixity and Tautology"*, Law Commission, Wellington, p ix.
14   Law Commission Report No 27, December 1993, Law Commission, Wellington.
15   See pp 68-69.

June 1987. That report made 15 recommendations and included a drafting manual which it recommended be adopted by the government as the official drafting guide for government departments and agencies for Acts, regulations, forms and explanatory material.

Canada In 1988 the Justice Reform Committee of British Columbia issued its report, called Access to Justice. It recommended establishing a plain language committee to develop a strategy for introducing plain language into the justice system. Then in 1990, the Canadian Bar Association and the Canadian Bankers' Association issued a report called The Decline and Fall of Gobbledygook: Report on Plain Language Documentation. It recommended ways to promote the use of plain language in the legal profession and in banking. The Canadian Bar Association adopted these recommendations by resolution in 1991, urging banks (and governments and other organisations) to draft their documents in plain language. Ironically the first word of the resolution was "Whereas". The Report and the resolution continue to have effect in Canada, with the banks resolving in 2000 to move towards plain language in mortgage documents.[16]

Ireland The Irish Law Reform Commission called for plain language in legislation in its report *Statutory Drafting and Interpretation: Plain Language and the Law*, published in December 2000. The Commission recommended:

> a comprehensive programme of plain language reform in Irish statute law. In this regard we support the initiatives currently being undertaken by the Office of the Parliamentary Counsel to the Government and the Statute Law Revision Unit.[17]

One of the initiatives of the Office of Parliamentary Counsel is the legislative Drafting Manual prepared for drafters in that Office. It was published in November 2001, and advocates plain language principles "in so far as that is possible without giving rise to ambiguity".[18]

---

16 See pp 76-77.
17 Report LRC 61-2000. Recommendation at para 6.23.
18 The description is that of Brian Hunt, a research officer in the Office of Parliamentary Counsel, in "Plain Language Developments in Ireland: An Overview", *Plain Language Association International (PLAIN) Fourth Biennial Conference Proceedings Toronto, Canada, 26-29 Sept 2002*, <http://www.nald.ca/PROVINCE/ont/PLAIN/sweden/index.htm>.

Government departments and agencies

United Kingdom The UK government adopted a plain English policy for government forms in 1982. Many thousands of forms were reviewed, redesigned or abandoned altogether. In 1994 the Secretary of State for Wales announced a program to simplify, and reduce the number of, government forms and circulars. Since then, simplification has occurred in local government, small business, the arts, the Ombudsman's service and other areas.

United States – The Executive Memorandum One of the most encouraging developments in the plain language movement came on 1 June 1998 when President Clinton issued his Executive Memorandum on plain language. This was sent to the heads of executive departments and agencies, directing them to:

- By October 1, 1998, use plain language in all new documents, other than regulations, that explain how to obtain a benefit or service or how to comply with a requirement you administer or enforce. For example, these documents may include letters, forms, notices, and instructions. By January 1, 2002, all such documents created prior to October 1, 1998, must also be in plain language.
- By January 1, 1999, use plain language in all proposed and final rulemaking documents published in the *Federal Register*, unless you proposed the rule before that date. You should also consider rewriting existing regulations in plain language when you have the opportunity and resources to do so.

Even after the end of the Clinton administration, there is still US government support for this initiative. A volunteer group of federal government employees has formed "PLAIN" – the Plain Language Action & Information Network. PLAIN works to improve communications from the federal government to the public. PLAIN has a web site <www.plainlanguage.gov> and holds workshops and seminars.[19]

Securities and Exchange Commission Another great leap forward for plain language came in January 1998 when the US Securities and Exchange Commission (SEC) announced new rules calling for plain language in prospectuses.[20] These rules apply only to the

---

19   Secretary of Health and Human Services, Tommy G Thompson, is the Bush administration's champion for plain language. Membership of PLAIN is open to non-federal government employees as well.
20   SEC Release 33-7497 (and 34-39593 and IC-23011), <www.sec.gov/rules/final/33-7497.txt>.

prospectus that a public company or mutual fund must give to prospective investors in their securities. Help for companies trying to comply with these rules is in the SEC's *Plain English Handbook,* which is available in print and online.[21]

The recent Enron corporate scandal and subsequent prosecutions have given new impetus to the SEC's efforts to encourage better disclosure by companies to their shareholders. In early 2003 the SEC ordered 350 of the Fortune 500 companies to rewrite their last annual reports or make better disclosures in future. The SEC said companies were still using "boilerplate" provisions rather than plain language.[22]

Canada There is a move to simplify securities regulation in Canada, as part of a wider national initiative to develop uniform securities legislation for Canada.

On 1 February 2000 the Canadian Securities Administration required all mutual prospectuses to be written in a standard, plain language format. And in March 2001 the Canadian government released four model plain language loan disclosure documents.

Reform is also underway at the British Columbia Securities Commission. It aims to reduce the burden of regulation on investors and other market participants, and it wants a clearer and simpler regulatory system. In 2001 it launched a plan to simplify and write all its rules in plain language. Ontario, Alberta, and Manitoba Securities Commissions have all joined the effort, with the common goal of achieving plain language throughout the Canadian regulatory system and securities industry.[23]

Various provincial and federal government offices and agencies, including the Office of the Auditor-General of Alberta,[24] Alberta Agriculture, Food and Rural Development[25] and the Canada Customs and Revenue Agency have redesigned and re-written various forms and other documents in plain language.

---

21   <www.sec.gov/news/extra/handbook.htm>.

22   Reported in "English, Not Legalese", *Washington Post*, 2 March 2003.

23   For more information, see Maykut, J, "Plain language: a case study at the British Columbia Securities Commission", *Plain Language Association International (PLAIN) Fourth Biennial Conference Proceedings Toronto, Canada, 26-29 Sept 2002*, <http://www.nald.ca/PROVINCE/ont/PLAIN/bcscprog/1.htm>.

24   For more information, see Saher, M, "The plaining of writers", *Clarity* No 49, May 2002, p 27.

25   See p 37.

Australia Federal and state government departments have been working towards plain language since 1983, when the Australian government launched its "Plain English and Simpler Forms" program. Much work was done by the Department of Administrative Services to produce model documents and guides to better, simpler writing.

A recent example is the Independent Commission Against Corruption (ICAC). It has had a plain language program for several years. ICAC was established in 1988 to expose and minimise corruption in the New South Wales public sector. ICAC realised early on that to communicate effectively with the public, they had to do so in plain language. They brought in plain language consultants, organised training programs and developed a plain language style guide. And they are reviewing their web site and their archive of publications to ensure they are written in plain language.

Tax law rewrite projects

In the 1990s, three major projects were launched in three different countries, all with the aim of improving existing tax laws.

Australia The Tax Law Improvement Project (TLIP) was established in 1993 to restructure, renumber and rewrite the existing Income Tax Assessment Act 1936. The TLIP team produced three substantial instalments of rewritten law, dealing with the core provisions of tax law and some specific areas such as capital gains tax. These were enacted in the Income Tax Assessment Act 1997. But after a change of government the priority shifted to tax policy reform, and by 1999 the resources and expertise of the TLIP had been reallocated to the new tax reform effort. Since then some further sections of the old Act (dealing with thin capitalisation and dividend imputation) have been rewritten and placed in the 1997 Act. Those rewrites, and other "stand-alone" tax legislation resulting from the continuing tax reform process, continue to use the new style developed by the TLIP.

New Zealand In 1994 New Zealand undertook a five-year project to review and simplify its tax laws. The first part of the rewrite process involved reorganising the structure of the Income Tax Act 1976, so that it is more logical and accessible. That resulted in the Income Tax Act 1994. The next stage involved the rewriting of "core provisions" of the old Tax Act. That became law in 1996, with effect from the 1997-98 tax year. The third stage of the project involves rewriting Parts A to E and Y of the old Act. At the time this book was written, submissions on the rewrite were still being received. The new Act should come into force on 1 April 2004, and apply to income for the 2004-05 tax year and following years.

United Kingdom On 28 November 1995 the Chancellor of the Exchequer announced a five-year project to rewrite the existing direct tax legislation.

Inland Revenue's stated aim for the project is "to rewrite the United Kingdom's primary direct tax legislation to make it clearer and easier to use, without changing the law".[26] The five-year project is now in its eighth year. Inland Revenue publishes annual reports on its progress and its plans for the next year.

The first two Bills produced by the project are now law: the Capital Allowances Act 2001 and the Income Tax (Earnings and Pensions) Act 2003. Inland Revenue plans two further income tax Acts. According to Inland Revenue, both Parliament and potential users of the legislation have been receiving it warmly. Planning continues into 2007.

Other major law rewrites

Tax law is not the only area that has been targeted for a major rewrite.

Australian corporations law In 1993 the Australian government announced another major project to simplify law: the Corporations Law Simplification Program.[27] The First Corporate Law Simplification Act commenced on 9 December 1995. A key feature of this Act is to make company law more accessible through improved layout.[28] This is achieved by navigation aids such as including running headers with chapter, part, division and section, and using tables and diagrams. The drafting approach also adopts shorter sentences, careful use of definitions and explanatory notes. The

---

26   Inland Revenue Annual Report, *Tax Law Rewrite: Plans for 2003/2004*, or see <www.inlandrevenue.gov.uk>.

27   Announced in April 1993.

28   See *Drafting Issues Designing the Law*, Corporations Law Simplification Program Task Force information paper June 1995, <www.pc.gov.au/plain/docs.htm>.

project team conducted document testing of the proposed structure of the changes and of the text, on focus groups.[29] The team considered that it received "generally good press" for the project.[30]

The Second Corporate Law Simplification Bill was introduced into Parliament on 3 December 1997 and enacted as part of the Company Law Review Act 1998. But by this time, the federal government had established the Corporate Law Economic Reform Program (CLERP) to take corporate law reform beyond simplification into the area of policy reform and economic development.[31] Corporate law continues to be rewritten to simplify procedures.

Other Australian laws Other Australian Commonwealth Acts, beginning with the Social Security Act 1991, have been rewritten in a "reader-friendly" form. That Act pioneered a number of drafting and design innovations that would later become standard legislative drafting techniques. It has a better structure than the old law, and uses shorter sentences. It has a "Reader's Guide", notes, "method statements" and examples to help readers find information and use it.

In the years from 1992 to 1999 the Australian Office of Parliamentary Counsel rewrote legislation in the following areas:

- sales tax (1992)
- offshore mining (1994)
- corporations (1995-2000)[32]
- income tax (1995-2000)[33]
- aged care (1997)
- incentives for export market development (1997)
- public service (1999).

Canadian projects In 1995 the Canadian government chose a portion of the Explosives Regulations (the Consumer Fireworks Regulations) for a pilot project to rewrite government regulations in plain language.

---

29   See p 289.

30   Robinson, V, 2001, *Rewriting Legislation – Australian Federal Experience*, paper presented to a conference in Ottawa, Canada in March 2001, Appendix A, Corporations Law Rewrite team report, p 21, <www.opc.gov.au/plain/docs.htm>.

31   Company Law Advisory Committee Second Interim Report, Parliamentary Paper No 43, p 6.

32   Described on p 69.

33   Described on p 68.

Then in 1997 the Canadian government decided to rewrite the Employment Insurance Act in plain language, and test it on potential users.[34] As at this book's press-time the rewriting process was close to completion and the plain language Bill was almost ready.

European Union In 1993, European Council of Ministers passed a resolution on the quality of drafting of European Community legislation,[35] which began by stating:

> 1. the wording of the act should be clear, simple, concise and unambiguous; unnecessary abbreviations, 'Community jargon' and excessively long sentences should be avoided;

and went on to specify other ways of helping make legislation more accessible. Unfortunately, the spirit of the resolution is not always reflected in the material the Eurocrats publish.

On 5 June 2002 the European Commission presented the Seville European Council with an Action Plan for simplifying and improving the EU regulations. The Plan contains 16 specific actions for better European regulation.[36]

South Africa In 1995, as the South African government began to dismantle the legal legacy of Apartheid, it decided to reflect the transformation to a democratic state in the language of its legislation. It also wanted to improve the people's access to justice, encourage participation in the new democratic system, and to demystify government.

The government faces two other problems in communicating with its citizens. The new South Africa has 11 official languages, and more than that number are spoken there. Nearly half the population is functionally illiterate.[37]

---

34   See p 291.

35   93/C 166/01.

36   Communication from the Commission of the European Communities: Action plan "Simplifying and improving the regulatory environment", p 13, <http://www.cabinet-office.gov.uk/regulation/Europe/Successes/commissionActionplan.htm>.

37   Viljoen, F, "Baring the nation's soul through plain language", *Clarity* No 46, July 2001, p 15.

The government called on international plain language experts[38] to help it kick-start its plain language work. Plain language experts helped to draft the Labour Relations Act 1995 and the Constitution of 1996. Since then, plain language principles have been applied in a variety of Bills, though drafters have not always been as successful as they may have wished.[39]

Plain language in the courts

United States federal court rules A major achievement in the US is the effort to "restyle" all the rules of procedure in the federal courts. In 1991 the formidably named Judicial Conference of the United States' Style Subcommittee of the Standing Committee on Rules of Practice and Procedure began a monumental job: reviewing and rewriting the federal court rules for clarity, simplicity, and consistency. So far the Federal Rules of Appellate Procedure, and the Federal Rules of Criminal Procedure, have been restyled. There is no *shall* left in any of the restyled rules. Now work continues on the Federal Rules of Civil Procedure.[40]

UK Civil Procedure Rules 1998 There has been a radical review of the Civil Procedure Rules of England and Wales based on the recommendations of Lord Chief Justice Woolf. The Civil Procedure Rules 1998 came into force on 26 April 1999. The primary purpose of the review was to reduce the cost and duration of litigation.

The new Rules combine the rules for most county courts, the High Court and the Court of Appeal in a single set of rules. They are written in plain language and are intended to streamline civil litigation. They also introduce certain changes in terminology: for example, "pleadings" becomes "statement of case", "writ" becomes

---

38 The Plain English Campaign (UK), Christopher Balmford (Australia), Philip Knight (Canada) and Professor Joseph Kimble (US). See *Clarity* No 33, July 1995, pp 8-10.

39 See the critique of the Promotion of Equality and Prevention of Unfair Discrimination Act 2000 in Nienaber, A, "A search for clarity in South Africa's new equality legislation", *Clarity* No 46, July 2001, p 11.

40 Two leading lights of the plain language movement are key figures in this work: Bryan Garner was the initial drafting consultant to the project, and Professor Joseph Kimble is the current drafting consultant. For more information, see Garner, BA, "The Substance of Style in Federal Rules", *Clarity* No 42, Sept 1998, p 15 and Garner, BA, 2002, *Guidelines for Drafting and Editing Court Rules*, Administrative Office of the US Courts, Washington DC.

"claim form", "plaintiff" becomes "claimant", "subpoena" becomes "witness summons" and "discovery" becomes "disclosure". Latin is out and more familiar, everyday words are in.

Australia The courts of Australia are attempting to deal with a vast increase in the number of litigants representing themselves in court.

The Family Court of Australia and the Judicial Commission of New South Wales began several years ago to work to improve judicial communication. The Family Court of Australia has a Judicial Development Program, which has two-and-a-half days of seminars and lectures on judgment writing. Writing in plain language is an integral part of that course. Every judge does the program once every three years – that's one-third of the judges each year.

The Federal Court of Australia is also aware of the increasing number of self-represented litigants, and has begun a program to review all of its brochures and guides to make sure they are in plain language and to make them more reader-friendly. The Federal Court's Judicial Education Committee runs education days with sessions on better judgment writing.

The Judicial Commission of New South Wales organises and supervises the continuing education and training of judicial officers. It runs a half-day session on judgment writing in its orientation program for judges, and does a similar session for magistrates. As Ruth Windeler, the Commission's Education Director, told me: "No one would dare to suggest that judges should be writing in anything other than plain English."[41]

Lawyers and other groups promoting plain language in the law

United States There are many organisations and committees in the US that are devoted to reviewing legal practice and procedure to simplify legal language. One of the longest running organisations is what is now the Plain English Subcommittee of the State Bar of Michigan's Publications Committee.)[42] This group was formed in

---

41 Telephone interview with M Asprey, 2 September 2002.
42 The Committee is chaired by George H Hathaway. Professor Joseph Kimble is a committee member and an eloquent advocate of plain language in the law.

1979 and for 20 years has published the monthly "Plain Language" column for the *Michigan Bar Journal*. Another long-standing organisation was the Information Design Center of Washington DC (formed in 1979 as the Document Design Center, but closed in the late 1990s). Both organisations have done much to increase our knowledge of how lawyers can use plain language techniques (including improved document design) in their daily work.

At its 1992 conference, the Legal Writing Institute adopted a resolution which, among other things, declared that legalese was "unnecessary and no more precise than plain language", and that "plain language is an important part of good legal writing". This resolution was significant, because most of the members of the Legal Writing Institute teach legal writing at law schools, and influence the writing styles of future lawyers in America.

Canada From 1973-92, the Canadian Law Information Council ran a Plain Language Centre in Toronto. It provided resources to those interested in plain language and designed and ran training courses in plain language drafting. There was a Plain Language Institute in Vancouver, which played a similar role there from 1990-93. Then a new Plain Language Society was formed in British Columbia in 1993, and a BC Plain Language Section of the Canadian Bar Association was formed in 1994.

The Alberta Law Reform Institute organised a demonstration project to draft several model plain language documents, including a guarantee. They were published in 1992 as part of its Plain Language Initiative.[43] And for over 20 years the Canadian Institute for the Administration of Justice has held courses on legal drafting and judgment writing. Those courses incorporate plain language principles.

Australia From 1990-97, the Centre for Plain Legal Language operated within the University of Sydney. It began by developing and running successful training programs for lawyers and others in plain legal writing. It formed a library of plain language resources. It did valuable research into various aspects of plain language drafting, and provided consultancy services. In 1995 it was involved in

---

43   The suite of documents included a will, a guarantee, an enduring power of attorney, minutes of settlement, a restraining order and a parental consent form.

a major research project with the Centre for Microeconomic Policy Analysis at the University of Sydney.[44]

The Law Societies of New South Wales and Queensland both established plain language committees in the 1990s. The Law Society of Western Australia has had a Clear Writing sub-committee since 1996. The Queensland Committee published a book on plain language that is now used in law schools.[45] Unfortunately, the New South Wales Committee was subsumed into another committee after a few years of doing interesting work, including running plain language seminars and doing a survey of the attitudes of New South Wales solicitors to plain language in the law.[46]

One of the greatest success stories of plain language in Australia is that of Australian law firms.[47] They were early adopters of plain language. From the late 1980s, they began to revise and rewrite their forms and precedents in plain language, and train their staff in plain language techniques. Some have even established plain language units, which provide plain language rewriting services.

With Australian lawyers enthusiastically embracing plain language, we can now see it reflected in documents in the marketplace. And as that continues, plain language will become the norm – or at least the benchmark – for legal drafting. As plain language expert Christopher Balmford puts it:

> After all, today, commercial clients of Australian law firms are prepared to pay for legal services that are plain. One day, clients everywhere will refuse to pay for legal services unless they are plain.[48]

---

44 See p 37.

45 Clark-Dickson, D and Macdonald, R, 2000, *Clear and Precise*, Queensland Law Society, Brisbane.

46 See Asprey, M, "Trend Overwhelmingly in Favour of Plain Language, Survey Shows" (1994) 32(9) *NSW Law Society Journal* 70 and "Lawyers Prefer Plain Language, Survey Finds" (1994) 32(10) *NSW Law Society Journal* 76.

47 Including Mallesons Stephen Jaques, Phillips Fox, Freehills, Minter Ellison, Allens Arthur Robinson, Deacons, Corrs Chambers Westgarth, and many others.

48 See Balmford, C, "Plain Language: beyond a 'movement'", *Plain Language Association International (PLAIN) Fourth Biennial Conference Proceedings Toronto, Canada, 26-29 Sept 2002*, p 6, <http://www.nald.ca/PROVINCE/ont/PLAIN/movement/1.htm>.

UK Law Society In March 2003 the UK Law Society published a new set of Customer Guides to various legal transactions and issues, and a Clients Charter. The Law Society says they are written in plain English (though there are versions in other languages) and the Plain English Campaign has given "Crystal Marks" to the versions in English. The Clients Charter promises that a solicitor will "make every effort to explain things clearly, and in terms you can understand, keeping jargon to a minimum".

The Charter so far only applies to solicitors in England and Wales, but there are calls to extend the reach of the Charter to Scotland.

Clarity In 1983 in the United Kingdom, an enthusiastic group of lawyers and others formed "Clarity", an international movement to promote plain legal language.[49] Clarity's journal, also called *Clarity*, is a mine of information both on the plain language movement in the law, and on drafting techniques. It is published twice a year. It has a web site,[50] and it gives its own awards – the Clarity Awards.

PLAIN Two Canadians, Cheryl Stephens and Kate Harrison, were the founders of what is now called PLAIN (the Plain Language Association International).[51] PLAIN is a group of "professionals who plan, write, design and create communications projects to better serve the needs of the public, clients, customers, students, and staff".[52] PLAIN has a web site,[53] a lively internet discussion group,[54] and it holds an international conference every other year.

Recent developments in the business sector

Canada It seems that the financial sector is the most recent leader in the move to plain language in Canada. In March 2000 the Canadian Bankers Association followed up on the "Decline and Fall of Gobbledygook" report and subsequent resolution. It announced

---

49 Clarity's President is Peter Butt and the *Clarity* journal Editor in Chief is Michèle Asprey. Both are Australian lawyers. US Professor Joseph Kimble takes over the Presidency from 1 January 2004.
50 <www.clarity-international.net>.
51 This PLAIN is a different PLAIN from the organisation mentioned on p 66.
52 Quoted from PLAIN's web site: <http://www.plainlanguagenetwork.org/networkindex.html>.
53 <http://www.plainlanguagenetwork.org>.
54 <plainlanguage@yahoogroups.com>.

that its members were "committed to providing customers with banking information which they can easily understand and use". And it promised to begin the process of "translating" existing mortgage documents into plain language, and to apply plain language principles when revising or developing new mortgage documents.[55]

It is up to the individual financial institutions to decide how they will adapt their mortgage policies and documents to reflect that commitment.

Also in the financial services sector, the insurance company, Clarica, embarked on a major plain language program in 1999. From that date its policy is to write all new documents in plain language. At the same time it began to rewrite its existing insurance policies and related documents in plain language.[56] Now there are legislative incentives for other financial services sector companies to follow Clarica's lead.[57]

Ireland The private sector has taken the lead in moving towards plain language in Ireland. The largest telephone company, Eircom plc, has a policy of using plain language. So has a major life assurance company, Irish Life, which began working with plain language consultants in 1998. The Bank of Ireland also uses plain language.

South Africa A landmark was reached on 1 April 2000 when all the major banks of South Africa adopted a Code of Banking Practice. Under the Code, all banking contracts were to be revised in plain language before October 2000. This timetable proved to be overly ambitious, but most major retail banks had at least complied to some extent by the deadline. The Office of the Banking Adjudicator, which enforces the Code, announced on 11 November 2000 that, to avoid injustice, "unfair terms" and "legal and technical language" would be "disregarded unless the bank could show it was explained to the client".[58]

---

55   See Canadian Bankers Association web site, <http://www.cba.ca/en/ viewdocument.asp?fl=3&sl=11&tl=127&docid=296&pg=1>.

56   For more information, see Milne, S, "Plain language at Clarica", *Clarity* No 45, Dec 2000, p 19.

57   See p 67.

58   Lane, W, "South African banks must use plain language", *Clarity* No 46, July 2001, p 6.

New Zealand There are definite moves towards consumer-oriented reform in the banking and insurance industries. The New Zealand Bankers' Association's Code of Banking Practice promises, with a little equivocation: "We will provide information to you from time to time using plain language where we can."[59]

In 1994, the Rugby rulebook was rewritten in plain language so that the rules would be easier to understand for referees, players and spectators.[60] Surely there could be no stronger evidence that plain language has really begun to take hold in New Zealand.

They are just a few of the areas in which there have been significant plain language developments throughout the world. You can explore them in more detail at <www.federationpress.com.au> by clicking on Book Supplements and then *Plain Language for Lawyers*.

But despite the almost 30 years of experience in many jurisdictions around the world, many lawyers are still cautious about or suspicious of plain language, often for the wrong reasons. There is no way to address those fears by using generalisations or speaking in the abstract. Even all this evidence of what is happening around the world is not enough. The only way to understand what plain language can do to legal writing is to begin to use it. So let's learn what to do, and see what happens. That is what the rest of this book is about.

---

59   New Zealand Bankers' Association, Dec 2002, *Code of Banking Practice*, 3rd edition, para 2.2(a).
60   "Rugby in plain English", *New Zealand Herald*, 31 August 1994, Section 3, p 1.

Chapter 5

Fundamentals

Consider your reader

If I could give you only one guideline to follow it would be just that. Consider your reader. That's the secret of plain language drafting in three words.

And who is your reader? Your client? The lawyer acting on the other side of the transaction? The judge? Your barrister? A clerk working in the claims department of a corporation that you act for? That clerk's supervisor? That supervisor's manager? That corporation's board? Or all of these people? It is an important question.

When lawyers draft in the traditional style for clients, their main aim is to protect their client. They must accurately and completely document what the client wants to do. They must not leave anything out. They must anticipate what might happen and do their best to cover that too. If they do that well, they feel they have done their job. They always have in the back of their minds the possibility that a court might have to interpret the contract, and so if they get it technically right they believe they will be beyond criticism and their clients will be safe and secure.

In plain language drafting, that is not enough. There is more to it than getting it technically right.

Play to your audience

Even the most accurate and elegantly drafted document can be completely ineffective if it misses its mark. Here is a proclamation issued by Sir George Arthur (1784-1854), when he was Lieutenant-Governor of Van Dieman's Land (Tasmania). It reads:

> And I do hereby strictly command and order all Aborigines immediately to retire and depart from, and for no reason, and on no pretence, save as hereinafter provided, to re-enter such settled districts, or any portions of land cultivated and occupied by any

person whomsoever, on pain of forcible expulsion therefrom, and such consequences as may be necessarily attendant on it.[1]

Unfortunately, this meant nothing to the Aboriginal people, who could not read it. They kept on returning to the "settled districts" and kept on suffering the "pain of forcible expulsion", which was probably considerable, as well as "such consequences as may be necessarily attendant", which no doubt included death.

The proclamation did not do anything but give the authorities an excuse to punish the Aboriginal people for breaking a law they couldn't possibly have understood.

If a client has instructed you to prepare a document, the client has a right to be able to read the document. The client is your primary audience and so the document should be drafted so it can be understood by that client. If it is something more "public" you are drafting, like a prospectus or a piece of legislation, then regardless of who instructed you to draft the document, your primary audience is the general public, and the general public should be able to understand it.

By saying that, I don't mean to imply that you have to explain *in the document* all its legal ramifications. A contract to sell goods should not be a textbook on the law of sale of goods.

What I am saying is that the client (or member of the public) should be able to read the document from cover to cover, if he or she wants to, and comprehend it as a document. The client may have questions and need to ask you to explain some things, or to give more details or examples, but the client should have been able to get through the document with a feeling that he or she understood all the words, if not all the concepts or the reasons why all the words were there.

If the client is the primary audience, is there a secondary audience? There may well be. It depends what the document is and what happens in the future. Even if the contract you are drafting or the letter you are writing is for or to your closest friend, the secondary audience is lurking in the background. It might be your friend's partner, that partner's lawyer, a judge, a jury, future business rivals, future shareholders, or even the executor of a will in 50 years time. All these people will need to be able to read and

---

1   Quoted in Hughes, R, 1987, *The Fatal Shore*, Collins Harvill, London, p 419.

understand the document without having you around to explain what you really meant, or how the parties would have understood what you wrote.

How much should we be writing for them?

Earlier in this chapter I said that lawyers in the past have been content to write to get things technically correct: as if accuracy was their only goal. The audience that style of writing is aimed at is the secondary audience – the judges. But plain language says we must write for the primary audience as well. We need to be accurate, precise *and* able to be understood by all our likely readers.

How do we strike a good balance?

This is an important decision to make, because, for example, if your client is thoroughly experienced in the sort of matter you are advising about and documenting, you may not need to spell things out in the same way as you would for someone less experienced. You may be able to take short-cuts, use technical terms, and leave things unsaid.

What if we are not sure how sophisticated or knowledgeable our readers are? What do we do then? The experts recommend that in that case we write for the audience that is *least* likely to understand what we are writing,[2] or *least* familiar with the subject matter.[3] But then that brings with it the worry that it might, as Charrow and Erhardt put it, "damage your credibility with a more sophisticated audience",[4] or force you to leave out material that is too complex for some of your readers.

Charrow and Erhardt offer three useful suggestions to deal with this problem. Whether any or all of them are suitable depends on what your document is, what its purpose is and what its readership will be. The three suggestions are:

1. Consider dividing your document up into different sections addressed to different audiences. Or include a glossary explaining terms and concepts that some audiences might not understand.

---

2   Charrow, VR and Erhardt, MK, 2001, *Clear & Effective Legal Writing*, 3rd edition, Aspen Law & Business, New York, p 104.

3   Redish, JC, 1991, *How to write Regulations (and Other Legal Documents) in Clear English*, American Institutes for Research, Document Design Centre, Washington DC, p 8.

4   Charrow, VR and Erhardt, MK, 2001, *Clear & Effective Legal Writing*, p 104 (cited at note 2).

2. Consider creating two or more versions of the document.

3. Consider carefully which is your most important audience, and write primarily for them.[5]

Plain language writer George Clark recently offered his own suggestion – he calls it "multi-layering":

> Some plain language materials deal with huge topics for huge audiences [for example, UN system publications for global distribution]. These materials have to be multi-layered. On the surface they are simple and limited to the basic ideas but underneath they have to point to the complexity of the issues and to some of the more subtle points. In these situations you can think of the material having a 'core' with 'extensions'. The 'core' is aimed at the less sophisticated end of the audience and the 'extensions' at the more sophisticated end.[6]

He proposes two techniques for doing this: "cute phrasing" and text boxes. Cute phrasing involves using what seems like an ordinary phrase, but one that can stimulate a wide range of thoughts in someone who is already familiar with the topic.[7] Text boxes can be explanatory or can contain quotes, which themselves can be supportive, contrary, philosophical or in the voice of the ordinary person, for example.

The question of who is the audience for legislation is an interesting one. It was considered by the Victorian Law Reform Commission in its 1987 report *Plain English and the Law*. The report said:

> The plain English movement does not require that laws always be drafted in such a way as to make them intelligible to the average citizen. However, it does require that every effort be made to make them intelligible to the widest possible audience.[8]

---

5   Same work, p 104.

6   Clark, G, Feb 2003, *Multilayering in plain language texts*, <http://www.hakikazi. org/plain_language.htm>.

7   His example, in the context of the UK government's Millennium Development Goals: "One of the central challenges for the future is to help poor people to work more efficiently and to be better paid for their work". This, he says, not only sets topics for discussion but also alludes to a more sophisticated idea: what the International Labour Organisation calls "Decent Work".

8   1987, Victorian Law Reform Commission Report No 9, *Plain English and the Law*, p 45.

The Australian House of Representatives Standing Committee on Legal and Constitutional Affairs Report, *Clearer Commonwealth Law,* also considered this question and concluded:

> The Committee accepts that there are often many different groups in the readership of legislation. Nevertheless, the Committee considers that it is essential that the drafter bear the readership in mind when drafting.
>
> The Committee believes that the problem of multiple audiences should be overcome as far as possible by placing primary importance on drafting for the people who may be affected by a particular piece of legislation.[9]

The Corporations Law Simplification Taskforce attempted to deal with the problem of multiple audiences for legislation with its "Small Business Guide" within the rewrite of the Australian Corporations Law.[10] Representatives of small business had told the Taskforce that they wanted a separate part of the law for small corporations. But there is a great deal of overlap in the provisions that apply to all corporations, no matter what size they are.

The Taskforce came up with a compromise: draft for all corporations in the usual way, but gather together the provisions that relate to small businesses and repeat them in a more convenient format in a separate part of the law, which doesn't have operative effect. That has two benefits:

- The operative sections of the Act can deal with *all* corporations, regardless of size, and none of this is repeated in other operative sections. That eliminates the possibility of having two conflicting laws on the same topic.
- The non-operative section – the "Small Business Guide" – can be published separately in a convenient format for those who need to read and use those sections and no others.

The Small Business Guide is part of the first Corporations Law Simplification Act, which commenced on 9 December 1995. Before the Act commenced, a member of the Taskforce said that the reaction of small business to the Guide had been overwhelmingly positive. But some lawyers have thought it inappropriate to include

---

9   1993, Commonwealth of Australia, p 95.

10   Now Part 1.5 of Chapter 1 of the Corporations Act 2001 (Cth).

material in a law if it doesn't have legal effect. They were concerned that it might be "misleading" in some way. So far, though, the contrary seems to be the case. Small business people have told the Taskforce that reading the Guide has been the first time they have understood their obligations.[11]

One of the senior members of the Taskforce, First Assistant Parliamentary Counsel Vince Robinson, has worked on several other projects to rewrite laws in plain language. He recently described the way his office views the audience for legislation:

> Our rewrites have been pragmatic rather than ideological. We have aimed, by and large, to make the legislation more readable and easier to use for its actual current users. We have not tried to make the legislation accessible to people who, from a practical point of view, we believed were highly unlikely ever to read the legislation. We have sometimes factored in people who did not currently read the legislation but were likely to do so if it were easier to read ...
>
> We have not aimed to make the legislation readable by the average citizen. It is unusual for the average citizen to encounter a scheme through the legislation itself. The average citizen is more likely to encounter the scheme through brochures, notices, forms or websites.
>
> The average citizen who does wish to look up the legislation for himself or herself has a number of difficulties to overcome quite apart from the readability of the text ...
>
> This suggests that, as well as it being unlikely that the average citizen will consult the legislation itself, it may also be inadvisable.[12]

This view is obviously a pragmatic one born of experience. But plain language has never held that the reader must be able to understand all of the law behind a law, or behind a document. And with more and more legal material becoming available on the internet, access to the law is getting easier. So the potential audience for law – even tax law – may well be getting larger.

In so much legal writing, both public and private, we can't be sure about where our writing will end up. So we will often need to *assume* that there will be a secondary, wider audience. But that does

---

11   Unpublished interview of Taskforce member Claire Grose by M Asprey on 18 August 1995.

12   Robinson, V, *Rewriting legislation: Australian Federal Experience* (paper presented to a conference in Ottawa, Canada, March 2001), pp 8-9, <http://www.opc. gov.au/plain/docs.htm>.

not mean that we must write *primarily* for the secondary audience. After all, the secondary audience knows that there was a primary audience, and it wasn't them. It just means that we should also keep the secondary audience in mind. We are not writing *to* them, but they might need to understand what we have written.

In short, our first duty is to satisfy the needs of our primary audience, but we must also make sure that what we write can be understood by our secondary audience. Fortunately, our secondary audience can take into account the fact that we were writing with our primary audience in mind.

The New South Wales Parliamentary Counsel's Office considers it has at least three audiences for its drafting:

- Parliament itself
- the public or the section of the public to whom the legislation is directed
- the courts and the legal system

and each has different requirements.[13]

If we always keep our likely audience (or audiences) in mind when we write, and adjust our writing style to be appropriate for those audiences, then there is no need to ask ourselves whether we should adopt a particular writing style for particular *types* of documents. We are writing for the people who read our documents, not for the documents themselves. If we bear the people's needs in mind, our documents will be exactly tailored to the circumstances for which they were written, no matter what "types" of documents they are.

Tone and formality

Without being conscious of it, most of the time when we speak we are pretty adept at adjusting our tone. If we speak to a child, we adjust more than just our vocabulary so that the child can understand us. We adopt a different tone.

When we write privately, we can also adjust our tone to the appropriate setting. When we accept an invitation from people we don't know very well, we write differently from the way we would

---

13   NSW Parliamentary Counsel's Office *Policies relating to Plain Language and gender-neutral expression*, <http://www.pco.nsw.gov.au/about.html>.

write to a good friend. A letter to the editor of a newspaper would be different in tone from a love letter. But when we write letters in the course of our work, we tend to adopt only one tone. Where is all the subtlety we show when we write when we are not at work? Why don't we use it?

Perhaps it is because we think it is appropriate to adopt a "formal" tone in all our work. And so it may be. But there are different levels of formality. And, as Professor Joseph Kimble has pointed out, formality can be dangerous: it can degenerate into pomposity. Simple and straightforward writing need not be undignified or informal, he says, and to illustrate the point he has rewritten the orders on articles of impeachment for the US President.[14] Here's the order that ended President Clinton's impeachment trial in 1999:

Original order

The Senate, having tried William Jefferson Clinton, President of the United States, upon two articles of impeachment exhibited against him by the House of Representatives, and two-thirds of the Senators present not having found him guilty of the charges contained therein: it is, therefore, ordered and adjudged that the said William Jefferson Clinton be, and he is hereby, acquitted of the charges in this said article.[15]

And here's how Professor Kimble rewrote it:

Rewrite

After a trial on two articles of impeachment against the President, William Jefferson Clinton, fewer than two-thirds of the Senators present have found him guilty. Therefore, it is ordered that he be acquitted.

The original order is a model of legalese: one long sentence, embedded clauses, archaic and inflated words, even a "doublet" (*ordered and adjudged*): all things that we will encounter later in this book. Professor Kimble describes his rewritten version as "whittled down". It might even be capable of more "whittling". But is it undignified or informal? Is it inappropriate for such a grave document? I say no. I say the clarity of the words actually emphasises

---

14   "How to Write an Impeachment Order", *Court Review*, Vol 36, Issue 2, Summer 1999, p 8 or *Clarity* No 44, Dec 1999, p10.

15   145 Cong Rec S1459 (daily ed 12 Feb 1999).

the gravity of the order. We are faced with the stark reality of the alleged crime and the acquittal, and there is no padding to get in the way of that message.

But tone is not just about formality and dignity. There are also questions of the relationship you have with the person you are writing to, and what they need from you. They may need quick, sharp incisive legal advice on a difficult matter, or they may need hand-holding. You should adjust your tone to provide that. And what do *you* need to convey? Are you warning the client of dire consequences? Are you showing that you mean business, and have a lot more up your sleeve, or are you being conciliatory? Good writers adjust their tone to convey that.

Unfortunately (or perhaps fortunately), there are no rules to guide us about the levels of formality we should adopt in our writing. Each time we pick up the pen or the dictaphone, or sit at the keyboard, we need to decide what is the appropriate degree of formality for that piece of writing, remembering to base that decision on who our audience is, not what the document is. But even if we decide that less formality is required in a particular case, we should always take a professional approach to our legal writing, no matter how familiar we may be with our primary audience. Remember the secondary audience.

Once we realise that we don't have to adopt an unduly stiff or formal tone in legal writing, we can even begin to enjoy our writing. And we can use it to cement our relationships with our clients.

In Chapter 3, I mentioned a survey done by an Australian advertising agency in April 1994 of corporate executives, and their views about law firms.[16] One of the things the corporate executives said they wanted was a true business partnership with a law firm that understood their business. That has to involve good communication – as equals. A simple thing like adjusting the tone of your writing in letters to clients can really make a difference.

After one plain language seminar I gave for a large law firm in Sydney, one of the partners told me that he had made an effort to write letters of advice to clients in a more natural tone, using their names, less formal language, and being more direct. He was

---

16   See p 55.

delighted with the results: clients had been telephoning him to say they had noticed a change. They had begun, they said, to receive letters of advice from the person they knew and spoke to often!

Taking a professional approach: don't patronise

Taking a professional approach involves recognising the duty we have as lawyers to assist our readers to understand the law as it affects them. It involves being sensitive to the difficulties the reader may be experiencing; recognising the level of understanding the reader has and supplying whatever additional information the reader might need. But it does *not* mean patronising the reader.

For example, there is a formula of words that we often see in lawyers' letters of advice which introduces an explanation. It is:

> As you are no doubt aware ...

But *is* the client aware? How do clients react to being told they are "no doubt" aware, especially if they aren't aware? Could you blame the clients if they came storming into your office and said, "Of course we're not aware – that's what we pay *you* for".

Think about those little phrases. It could be that the ones we use all the time – the ones we don't even think about – could cause great offence. Even starting a sentence with the word "obviously" could be offensive. Think about it. Is it really that obvious?

If you need to explain something, explain it. But don't tell clients that it is "obvious". If you don't know what the client's level of understanding is, then ask, *before* you begin to write.

Remember, too, that you are writing a letter of advice to a client – not an essay for a university professor. Your client wants to know the answer to the question that he or she asked you. It is a letter of advice, not a thesis. So cut out all those formulas of words like those you see in undergraduate essays – things like:

> Before we can discuss the question you have asked, we need to examine the history of the legislation in this area ...

The first (and probably the *only*) thing the client wants to read is the answer to the question. Anything else is detail. The client doesn't want to read an essay – no matter how clever. The client wants an answer – and as briefly as possible. Of course, if there are qualifications and exceptions which the client needs to understand, you must explain them, but first give the client your advice, and then explain the qualifications and exceptions. The client needs to know what you recommend, before the client can grasp the rest of the relevant material. And don't give the client a survey of all the relevant laws unless that's been asked of you. Give an answer to the question, and qualify it as you must. But make sure it *is* an answer.

The way you arrange the information you have to convey should be governed by the needs of your readers – not by the information itself or the way you stumbled on the answer. I'll be dealing with this issue in more detail in Chapter 6.

Courtesy

Taking a professional approach also involves courtesy. No matter how acrimonious the dispute is, our writing should always reflect the fact that we are professionals conveying our client's instructions. We should not identify ourselves *personally* with the client's position. We should never write anything in anger. Our client's opponent's lawyer is our colleague, not our enemy. We are our client's professional advisors, not an extension of our client. Again, remember that secondary audience which may scrutinise our writing outside the context in which it was written. We must do our best for our client, but we can do that and at the same time keep cool and maintain professional control.

Courtesy has always been a fundamental principle of good drafting, and is not unique to plain language drafting. But the reason I mention it is because I want to make it clear that using plain words does not mean rudeness. There is plenty of room in plain language for courtesy, and the struggle to be brief does not require that all signs of courtesy be deleted from our writing. But always remember the distinction between courtesy and pomposity. Formulas such as:

> We beg to remain, dear sirs, your faithful servants

add nothing and do not even sound sincere. They can be safely omitted and no one will miss them.

Pomposity

Pomposity is an intangible quality, harder to describe than most of the other concepts in this book. Still, it is a quality that the general public strongly associates with legal writing.

On the other hand, one of the common criticisms lawyers make of plain language is that it is not "dignified enough". It seems to be this search for "dignity" that leads us away from simplicity and clarity and into pomposity. We choose language which is more remote and less personal than ordinary everyday language.

The interesting thing about pomposity is that, unlike most of the other characteristics of legal writing that I've described in this book, pomposity often appears in speech as well. Mellinkoff quotes a judge of a US federal court saying to a group of students at Harvard:

> I give it to you as my considered opinion, gentlemen, that this is a government of checks and balances.[17]

I have a favourite example of my own. Some years ago at a legal conference I attended, the delegates were given this instruction:

> I have to advise, ladies and gentlemen, that available outside the door to my immediate left are facilities for the making of coffee, and indeed, tea.

Pompous statements are usually wordy as well, and that contributes to their dullness. We all agree that important subjects demand serious treatment, but there is no need to clothe our writing with ponderous trappings and adopt a remote or inflated drafting style. Clarity and simplicity contribute much more to the dignity of our writing than a forced or artificial tone of respect.

So that is a brief rundown of some of the threshold issues in plain language drafting – things that you have to bear in mind long before you put pen to paper. Here they are again, in summary.

- Consider your reader. There is more to good legal writing than just getting it technically right.
- Remember that your writing will probably have both a primary and a secondary audience, so you need to keep the needs of both those audiences in mind.

---

17   Mellinkoff, D, 1963, *The Language of the Law*, Little Brown, Boston, p 27.

- If unsure, write for the audience that is *least* likely to understand.
- Decide on your tone and the appropriate degree of formality. Don't be afraid to use your own voice in your writing. But always take a professional approach. Remember that secondary audience.
- Arrange your information with the reader's needs in mind, not yours. Give your client an answer, not an essay.
- Never write in anger. You are an advisor, not a party.
- Always be courteous. Plain words do not require rudeness.
- Don't be pompous. Clear and simple writing can be dignified too.

In the next chapter, we actually begin the writing process. We examine how the structure you choose for your writing can affect its clarity and readability, and talk about how, and where, to begin writing.

Chapter 6

Structure

Planning

All good writing begins with a plan. But even before the plan there is the thinking stage. The stage when you begin to analyse the problem you have to deal with. This is the stage when you should ask yourself questions. What am I trying to achieve? What does the client want? What information do I need before I start? Has the client given me all the information I need? Perhaps I didn't understand all the ramifications of the client's problem when the client first came to me. Should I now contact the client again and get the additional information I need or clarify anything that I don't understand?

Once you have assembled all the information you think you'll need – read it! You may read something which changes your mind about your approach, or tells you that you need still more information. Don't begin work on the document until you think you have a clear idea of all the issues. You might make notes as you are reading, but resist the temptation to start work on the document until you think you've covered all the research you need to do.

One question you might ask yourself is: do I really need a document at all? Mark Adler points out in his book, *Clarity for Lawyers*,[1] that putting something in writing is sometimes unnecessary and a waste of time and money.

Sometimes the best document for the job is not the one you think it is. Lawyers are so used to producing the same types of document over and over again – just cranking out the precedents – that they often miss the opportunity to give their client a document in a form that will do the job better that the more traditional form. We should ask ourselves: is there better a way to achieve the result the client wants? Is it a deed I need, or would a contract which

---

1   Adler, M, 1990, *Clarity for Lawyers*, The Law Society, London, pp 11-13.

looks more like a form or a checklist suit the client better? A document like that will do more than just record the transaction as a matter of law. It will also show your creativity and your interest in how client's business works. It will be a marketing tool.

The time to ask these questions is *before* you begin to write. Answer them first. *Then* take up the pen and paper or to sit at the keyboard. But it is not yet time to write "Dear Sirs" or "This Deed". It is time to write a plan.

Even quite simple letters should follow a plan. The more complex the document, the more detailed the plan.

Your plan may be a diagram, a list, a flow chart, or a series of headings and points. Find whatever it is that suits you. I usually use the headings and points method, but that is just what suits me.

Put down every aspect of the research that you thought was important, and arrange them in the order that suits your purpose, your client. Don't leave them in the order they occurred to you, or the order that the textbooks had them or the order the last person who drafted a similar document used. Arrange them in the best order for the purpose. For example, it might be best to put the most important points first, or the basic answer first, and all the exceptions and detail later.

As you write, your views about order may change. It doesn't matter: that's the beauty of a plan. You can easily shuffle things around later, because you aren't locked in to any particular structure. It is much more difficult to do this if you are working with a first draft of a document. There is something about the structure of a document that looks permanent, and we are tempted to stay with the existing structure and try to fit our own ideas in here and there.

When you use a plan you can set your own structure, tailored for the particular task at hand. Your ideas can set the structure; they shouldn't have to fit an existing structure if it isn't the best structure.

Again, this sort of approach is simply good drafting practice. It is not unique to plain language drafting, but it is essential for plain language drafting. I said earlier[2] that plain language drafting looks not only at the words being used and what they mean, but also at

---

2   Page 13.

the organisation of the words in a sentence, the sentences in a document and the design and layout of the document itself.

The combination of all these things governs how effective the document is at communicating information and helping readers understand and use it. A document written in the simplest words and arranged in short sentences will still be difficult to understand if the information is poorly organised or presented. This is particularly so if the document is long or complex.

Organisation

So what is the best way to organise information? To a degree, it depends on what the document is, what its purpose is and what the reader requires from it. A letter of advice on a complex question might need to be arranged so that the reader is carefully taken, step by step, through a logical sequence that will help the reader to understand why you are giving the advice you are giving. A document such as a mortgage or lease is not susceptible to the same sort of logical arrangement as a letter of advice, but the provisions can still be arranged in the order which best draws the parties' attention to the clauses that are most important for them. Acts, and other laws, can be set out so that their main points aren't hidden among their procedural and mechanical aspects.

Important things first

In each of these cases, there is one common factor governing the best way to organise the information: the most important parts should be put first. And when we are deciding what is the most important part, we look at it from the reader's point of view – not ours. That is a very important distinction to make. Again we fall back on that fundamental of plain language drafting: consider the reader.

What is the most important part of a document for a reader? It depends on what the reader is looking for in each particular case – but here are a few general guidelines.

Letters of advice: the most important part of a letter of advice is the answer to the client's question. Everything else is secondary.

Loan and security documents: in a document such as a mortgage, the most important parts are *the loan amount, the security, the interest rate* and *the repayment dates.* There are other very important aspects of a mortgage, but these four things are the very essence of the transaction. There are other matters, like events of default, that are extremely important for the parties to understand, but they are not as important as the four things I've listed. You could not have a mortgage without those four things.

Leases: in a lease, the most important things are *the property leased, the term of the lease, the rent amount* and *the rent payment dates.* Other things, like the obligations of the tenant, and even the termination provisions are less important. It stands to reason: the four things I've listed are what the bargain is all about. The landlord and tenant are interested in the parts of the lease that are peculiar to *their* agreement: names, addresses, amounts and dates. Other things might also be very important, but when the landlord and tenant are reading the documents for the first time, their main concerns are the beginning of the lease and all the details that relate to that.

Legislation: in a statute, the most important thing is what it is about – not when it commences, who administers it, what other legislation is affected by it, and so on. Of course, it does depend on who is reading the Act and what they are looking for. For example, a particular bureaucrat may only be interested in the provision dealing with the power to make regulations. But the main purpose of laws is to regulate behaviour, and so that is the point of view that we should take when assessing the relative importance of different parts of Acts and other laws.

To organise your material in this way means that you have to look at it from the reader's point of view. Once you have this knack, you will probably find that your legal drafting style is completely transformed. You will no longer organise material in the form that is most convenient for you, or most familiar to you. Let me illustrate this with a hypothetical letter of advice.

Here is a letter of advice about whether a floating charge can be created simply by means of a minute of a meeting of directors recording a resolution passed to create the floating charge. It was written quite a few years ago, so pay no attention to the detail of the law and just focus on the structure. Why did the writer structure it this way? Think about it while you read.

Dear Sir,

1. We are asked to advise as to the sufficiency of the creation of a floating charge over the entire assets and undertaking of a company by use of a Minute of a Meeting of the Directors of such company recording the passing of a resolution to that
5. effect. We advise as follows:

10. 1. *Stamp Duty Liability*

In New South Wales, the relevant duty imposed is payable on a "loan security". A loan security is defined to mean a mortgage, bond, debenture or covenant (Section 83(1) of the Stamp Duties Act). Mortgage is further defined to mean a security by way of
15. mortgage or charge for the payment of a certain sum of money lent at the time or previously or repayment of money to be thereafter lent upon an account current (Section 3(1)). Mortgage is further defined in Section 83(1). For relevant purposes, the extended definition includes:

- A Security by way of mortgage or charge given in
20. consideration of the transfer of property;
- An agreement, contract or covenant for the making of a mortgage accompanied by or relating to documents of title;
- Any instrument of mortgage for the purpose of securing repayment of debentures.

25. Nothing in the above (except perhaps the definition incorporating the word "instrument") specifically excludes *oral* transactions creating a "loan security". Presumably, the classic legal definition of "bond and covenant" would also exclude those from the definition as each would require instruments or agreements under seal. However, this is not necessarily the case as regards "mortgage" which security can be created orally.

30. The learned authors of *Stamp Duties Legislation* (Tolhurst & Ors) state at paragraph 1.20 that in the absence of express reference to a memorandum, there is no general rule that a document which is evidence of an unwritten or oral transaction is dutiable as if it were a written document. The authors go on
35. to refer to some exceptions to the rule and state that there is authority to indicate that a document which is brought into existence as part of the transaction is dutiable as if it effected the transaction.

40.   In the present case your "Minute" evidences a resolution by the company through a meeting of its directors to accept moneys and in return to give a floating charge (as security) upon certain terms.

        We do not think that, on any view, a resolution to do

45.   something could be said to constitute the doing of that act. Further, as regards a Minute prepared exclusively for one party in relation to the prior entry into a transaction it has been said:

…

Do we have the answer yet? The suspense is killing me! Nearly 50 lines and it looks like it will be a while yet. And so it was. The answer to the stamp duty question took another 40 lines. Even then it was hidden in the middle of a paragraph. And the writer went on to say that in any case the security risk was too great and they'd be better off to create the charge the usual way. This revelation came after 75 lines. After that there were four more pages of advice dealing with other problems associated with a charge evidenced by a minute, with the various pitfalls scattered throughout the paragraphs.

This letter is a good example of the point I'm making here. It is actually quite well written if you look only at the language. It uses reasonably simple words, quite short sentences and paragraphs and follows a careful logical sequence. It explains a fairly technical area of the law with care, and it shows considerable respect for the intelligence of the reader.

But what is the *answer*?

That is what the client is asking while pacing up and down with the letter.

It is unlikely that the writer wanted to hold the client in suspense. It is just that the structure of the letter is a reflection of the thought processes the writer had to go through to get to the answer. The writer takes the reader through all those steps as well, whether they like it or not, before the writer yields up the answer.

See how the writer first repeats the question that the client asked (lines 1-5). This might be of some benefit to a client who has forgotten what they asked their solicitor, but it is really there for the writer's benefit: so the letter stands on its own as a record for the writer's file.

Next, the writer takes the reader through the legislation: the reader has to learn about "loan securities" (lines 7-10), the various definitions of "mortgage" (lines 10-29), what various commentators say about oral transactions (lines 30-38). It is not until line 39 that we even get a mention of "the present case". And no conclusion is drawn by the author until line 43. Even then it isn't the one the reader is looking for.

Is it fair to inflict that kind of torture on the reader? We may think it is important that the reader understands why we have come to the conclusion that we did, and be aware of the assumptions that we've had to make, and that the answer isn't cut and dried. Of course, those are all important, both for the client, and for the writer. But isn't the client entitled to the answer *first*? It's what they're paying for.

Then, by all means, take the reader step by step through all the nooks and crannies of the law. But do it *after* you've given the client what they have asked for.

Sometimes, it is better to put all the detailed explanation of a complex advice into a separate memorandum. Then you can make the main point in a short covering letter and tell the reader that the rest of the detail is attached. That way the reader can come to grips with the basic advice first and deal with the rest when it suits.

Once we have given the reader the most important part of the advice, we should continue to arrange the rest of our material in the order that we think will best suit the reader. As I said before, this might depend on the document, its purpose and what the reader requires of the document. There are no hard and fast rules, but your guide should always be the best interests of the reader.

Arranging things so that the reader gets the answer to the question or the most important material first has two other advantages:

- It gives the reader a context in which to read all the subsidiary information. That makes it easier on the reader. It is likely that the reader will understand the material better because they have a context – they know where it is all leading.
- It makes the information more useable by the reader. That in turn shows that you are sensitive to the reader's needs and – if the reader is your client – you are presenting

material in a way that makes your client more efficient in his or her business. Again, your writing becomes a marketing tool.

Put related material together

The other guiding organising principle is to put related material together. If the reader can see a pattern in your logic, it will be easier for them to grasp. This might seem simple, but it requires discipline to identify and classify material in this way. It also requires you to be willing to rewrite and reclassify material if new relationships between parts of the material occur to you as you are writing, or as you collect new material.

This is where the plan we discussed at the beginning of the chapter comes into its own. If you have the skeleton of your document in a plan before you begin to write, then it is not much trouble to reorganise the bones. It is only when you begin to put flesh on the bones that it becomes more work to rethink, reorganise, reclassify and reorder your document.

If the plan you are using has headings, you need to rethink those headings too as you rework the plan. In the final document, the headings will be for the reader – both to help them find the material they are looking for, and to help them grasp the structure of the document.[3] But at this stage the headings can be part of the organisation process.

And don't neglect the headings as the document evolves. Remember to look at them from time to time as you write – to make sure that they change if the text below them changes. Too many times I have seen headings that no longer relate to the text they are supposed to describe. Too many writers write their headings once, and never look at them again.

So now that we have slabs of related material, with good descriptive headings, how do we deal with them? We divide them again.

---

3   See pp 254-256 for more on headings.

Paragraphs

As readers, we know instinctively that it is easier to cope with material that is divided into "bite-sized chunks". We like to see lots of "white spaces" around what we're reading. It makes it look easier to read, and more inviting.

So why, when we come to write, do we write paragraphs that go on and on without a break? It looks as if we have adopted the "stream of consciousness" technique of writing.

When we write we usually start slowly, collecting our thoughts and sifting them. Then, if we're lucky, we start to pick up some momentum and it all begins to flow. This is particularly so when we write by dictating. We pick up on an idea and run with it and before we know it, it runs away with itself. A huge unbroken paragraph is the result.

What causes this run-on effect? The writer is dealing with too much information at once, and hasn't taken the time to organise like thought with like, or to separate different aspects of the same topic from each other. If your paragraphs are too long, it is probably because you are dealing with more than one idea in each paragraph.

Plain language consultant Elizabeth Murphy has said that a paragraph should be a unit of thought, not of length. She suggests having one main topic sentence and perhaps several supporting sentences, plus a final sentence leading the reader to the next paragraph.[4]

And one other thing. Don't be afraid of the one sentence paragraph. If you use it sparingly, and in the right place, it can be very effective as a device for emphasis.

It will catch the reader's eye.

See?

Sub-paragraphs

Sub-paragraphs help to divide the material up so that it is more easily digested, but they can also be used for emphasis, or to draw the reader's attention to a similarity in the subject-matter. For example:

---

4   "Plain English – Style of Choice" in the Australian Government Department of Finance and Administration publication *Stylewise* Vol 7 No 1, 2001, p 2.

The trustees may invest in:
(a) shares;
(b) debentures;
(c) bills of exchange; and
(d) certificates of deposit.

makes a *list* for the reader. Next time they want to know what to invest in, the trustees can go back to the list and check off the items they are interested in. It is much easier to follow, even just visually, than:

> The trustees may invest in shares, debentures, bills of exchange and certificates of deposit.

This is particularly so when the list is long, or the individual items have to be described in more than a few words.

But a word of warning about sub-paragraphs: don't use them instead of paragraphs. Remember that a sub-paragraph works best as part of a paragraph. If you use sub-paragraphs instead of paragraphs then you'll force yourself to use sub-sub-paragraphs, and *they* should really be reserved for emergencies. Here is what I mean; it is an example from a traditional form sale of business agreement:

5. *Assignment of Leases*

5.1 (a) The Vendor agrees to use its best endeavours to procure the assignment of the Leases to the Purchaser. The Purchaser agrees to accept such assignment and to keep the Vendor indemnified against any claims made under the Leases in respect of the period after the Completion Date and the Purchaser acknowledges that it has inspected copies of the Leases and is aware of their terms.

(b) Consent to assignment of the Lease to the Purchaser or its nominee on terms acceptable to both parties shall be a condition precedent to this sale and purchase of Business. If the terms of the landlord's consent to the assignment of the Leases are not acceptable to the parties then this Deed shall be at an end and all moneys paid by the Purchaser shall be refunded forthwith.

(c) In consideration of these presents the Covenantors jointly and severally agree:
    (i) to indemnify and keep the Vendor indemnified against any and all claims made under the Leases

assigned by or at the request of the Vendor to the Purchaser pursuant to this Deed in respect of the period on and from the Completion Date; and

(ii) to notify the Vendor of any such claims made or threatened as soon as they are notified to the Covenantors.

What has happened here? First, and most obviously, the text has moved right across to the right side of the page because of all the "tabs" the typist has had to insert to cope with the paragraph structure. Of course, there are layouts that minimise this problem, but it should not be necessary to resort to them. The real problem is that the writer went straight to the sub-paragraph (that is, 5.1(a)), to break up the material. The writer could simply have used a paragraph (that is, 5.1)).

Without even attempting to change the language – although it is very tempting, because there is so much to work with in that example – we can make the text more manageable by reorganising the paragraphs like this:

5. *Assignment of Leases*

5.1 The Vendor agrees to use its best endeavours to procure the assignment of the Leases to the Purchaser. The Purchaser agrees to accept such assignment and to keep the Vendor indemnified against any claims made under the Leases in respect of the period after the Completion Date and the Purchaser acknowledges that it has inspected copies of the Leases and is aware of their terms.

5.2 Consent to assignment of the Lease to the Purchaser or its nominee on terms acceptable to both parties shall be a condition precedent to this sale and purchase of Business. If the terms of the landlord's consent to the assignment of the Leases are not acceptable to the parties then this Deed shall be at an end and all moneys paid by the Purchaser shall be refunded forthwith.

5.3 In consideration of these presents the Covenantors jointly and severally agree:

(a) to indemnify and keep the Vendor indemnified against any and all claims made under the Leases assigned by or at the request of the Vendor to the Purchaser pursuant to this Deed in respect of the period on and from the Completion Date; and

(b) to notify the Vendor of any such claims made or threatened as soon as they are notified to the Covenantors.

See how much easier the text is to cope with. We've moved more type over to the left and we're left with the roman numerals up our sleeve in case we need them. We've saved a couple of lines, even though we haven't deleted a word, and we haven't lost *any* of the "white spaces".

One other difficulty to avoid with sub-paragraphs is what is sometimes called "shredding". This is when writers over-enthusiastically divide up information into unnecessary or irritating sub-paragraphs, which sometimes return to the margin several times, as in:

1. If a person:
   (a) is aged over 75 years; and
   (b) is in good health,
   the person may apply for a discount card for travel on:
   (c) State government transport; and
   (d) private buses,
   unless they already hold a Gold Pass.

This kind of structure interrupts the sentence in order to force items into categories that don't really help the reader. When the sub-paragraphs are longer, the whole paragraph becomes even more difficult to handle. This is usually because there is more than one idea being dealt with in the paragraph. In this example, the material might be better divided into two groups, but using only one list, as in:

1. A person may apply for a discount card for travel on state government transport and private buses if that person:
   (a) is aged over 75 years;
   (b) is in good health; and
   (c) does not already hold a Gold Pass.

But this is not the only approach. There are several other ways of tackling the information. The structure and order you choose should depend on the emphasis you want to give. And the question to ask is: which parts of the information are more important than others?

Document "Add-ons": schedules, appendixes, annexures

It is often convenient to be able to "hive off" material that is not of vital importance to the main body of the document. That material can be put in schedules, appendixes or annexures.

Some people draw distinctions between these things, saying that they are all for different purposes. Some say that a schedule is for short details, like the parties' names and addresses, the address of the leased property, the rent payable and the termination date. Some say an appendix should be reserved for documents, and annexures might be for unwieldy things like maps and computer printouts. There is also the theory that schedules are part of an agreement itself, and therefore come after the "testimonium" (the "In witness whereof …") but before the execution clauses.

Whatever the validity of these views and the authority for them, there is little purpose in making those distinctions. There might be agreements which have all three – schedules, appendixes *and* annexures – and that would be very confusing for the reader who probably doesn't know all those theories.

It is better to pick *one* of these labels, put all your "hived off" material into it, and use numbering (eg Schedule 1, 2, 3 etc) to separate the different items.

What sort of material should be hived off? There are two types of material that I think go best in schedules (or annexures or appendixes).

1. Details that make up the essence of a document – details which, if you read them apart from the rest of the document, give you a feel for the most important parts of the transaction. In an employment contract, for example, you might have a schedule which sets out:

    - the names of the employer and employee
    - their addresses
    - the job title and description
    - the period of employment
    - the starting date
    - the annual salary
    - other benefits.

Anyone reading the schedule would then know the essence of the contract. The same sort of thing can be done for any common sort of document or transaction: leases, loans, share and business sales and the like.

2. Material that is secondary to the main body of the agreement. Things that the reader can assume while reading the document, keep in the back of their mind and look at later. Things like maps, computer printouts, lists, secondary documents and other matters of less important detail.

Where should the schedule (or annexure, or appendix) go?

Now that we are considering putting very important details in our schedule, we don't want anyone telling us it isn't really part of the rest of the document – even if we call it an appendix or an annexure. We want to ensure that the signatories acknowledge that too. So there are two possible places for the schedule: at the beginning of the document or at the end of the substantive clauses of the document.

If it is the type of schedule that summarises that transaction (as in the example I just set out), then it stands to reason that it should be the first page of the document. Schedules of this kind should have plenty of visual help for the reader – headings, bold type and so on, so that the reader can see what kind of information is being summarised.

If the schedule contains only secondary material, or if there is more than one schedule, the schedule or schedules should be at the end of the document, just before the testimonium and the execution clauses. There is no reason to use a schedule to separate the testimonium from the execution clauses. After all, the testimonium, when translated, is the bit that says "I am signing here to show I agree with everything in the document". That should include the schedules. So the testimonium's logical place is just before the signatures, and after any schedules.

Sentence structure

So far in this chapter I've concentrated on the more mechanical matters of the structure of a document. The framework, so to speak. Now we need to focus on the material we will use to fill in the framework: the sentences. In the next chapter we will focus in even closer – we'll look at the words that make up the sentences. But before we do that, a few words about the way we string words together in coherent units.

We need to look at sentence length, sentence structure, and the way we join sentences and the words in them: punctuation.

Sentence length

We all know that we should avoid writing long sentences. We know that we find them difficult to read. Unfortunately, the "stream of consciousness" that I mentioned earlier[5] can intervene and we end up with not only long paragraphs but also long sentences.

The mind, it seems, processes written information in short "bites," basically clause by clause. It can handle only a couple of clauses at a time, depending on their length. If we pile up the clauses in a sentence and embed them one in the other, we virtually ensure that what we write won't be understood on the first reading.

Out of consideration for our readers, and in the interest of efficiency, we should learn to write in relatively short sentences. As to how short – I think it is probably counterproductive to specify a length. Some authorities suggest 20-25 words is an appropriate average length.[6] A well known Australian journalist has said[7] that his editor's view was that 24 was the optimum number of words, but his personal aim was for a maximum of 17 words. The New South Wales Parliamentary Counsel's Office aims for sentences with a maximum length of five lines (in their B5 legislative format).[8] The US Federal Court's Committee on Rules of Practice and Procedure recommends aiming for fewer than 25 words, and 30 at most.[9]

---

5   Page 100.

6   Statistic quoted in 1987, Law Reform Commission of Victoria, Report No 9, *Plain English and the Law*, Appendix 1, p 33 – Drafting Manual.

7   Gareth Powell of the Sydney Morning Herald, speaking at a meeting of the Society of Business Communicators on 27 November 1990.

8 · NSW Parliamentary Counsel's Office *Policies relating to Plain Language and gender-neutral expression*, p 2, <http://www.pco.nsw.gov.au/about.html>.

9   Garner, BA, 2002, *Guidelines for Drafting and Editing Court Rules*, Administrative Office of the United States Courts, Washington DC, p 13.

Few of us have the time or inclination to count the number of words per sentence in our writing. And, of course, not *all* long sentences are difficult. Those constructed with care can be a joy to read. In 1931, the Fowler brothers put it this way:

> No sentence is to be condemned for mere length; a really skilful writer can fill a page with one and not tire his reader, though a succession of long sentences without the relief of short ones interspersed is almost sure to be forbidding. But the tiro,[10] and even the good writer who is not prepared to take the trouble of reading aloud what he has written, should confine himself to the easily manageable.[11]

However, by 1986 the commentators were harder on long sentences. Greenbaum and Whitcut said in their revision of Gowers's *The Complete Plain Words*:

> The two main things to be remembered about sentences by those who want to make their meaning plain is that they should be short and should have unity of thought.[12]

I think the point to be made is that short sentences are not an end in themselves, but that habitually using long sentences can be tiring for the reader. And they require extra time and care with punctuation and other aspects of structure.

There are plenty of examples of long sentences in legal writing and we are only too familiar with them. Long sentences appear both in laws and in private documents, especially, it seems, in leases, loan documents, security documents and trust deeds.

All that needs to be said about long sentences has probably already been said. No amount of punctuation and care can save a sentence of 368 words (which exists in the Credit Act, 1984 (New South Wales)).[13]

It is sometimes said that sub-sections or sub-clauses should only be one sentence long. Some people even say this rule applies to sections and clauses. It seems to have been a rule of legislative drafting, perhaps designed to stamp out long sub-sections and sub-

---

10   Means *beginner*.
11   Fowler, HW and FG, 1931, *The King's English*, 3rd edition, Oxford University Press, Oxford, p 309.
12   1987, 3rd edition, Penguin Books, London, p 175.
13   Section 24(2): defences available to a "linked credit provider" against liability for misrepresentation.

clauses. Whether or not this ever was a valid principle of drafting, it is far too restrictive to follow as a general rule. The subject-matter will always have to govern the number of sentences, and no rules about numbers can guarantee good drafting.

Punctuation

The only thing that actually controls sentence length is the full stop. But for the long sentences we all have to use from time to time, punctuation can make them manageable.

This is not the place for a grammar lesson, and there are plenty of grammar and other texts that give guidelines on how to punctuate. The Australian government's *Style Manual*[14] gives all the conventions in detail. But remember to use punctuation to help readers. It can help avoid confusion and ambiguity. Use it as you would in non-legal writing – in a natural way.

The best advice I've seen about the full stop (or period) comes from William Zinsser. He said:

> There's not much to be said about the period except that most writers don't reach it soon enough.[15]

There is no rule of legal construction that says that punctuation is to be disregarded. There is a legal myth to that effect, which has persuaded some lawyers that documents must be written so they can be understood without punctuation, if it were to be deleted. This is nonsense. It harks back to the days when punctuation was the printers' responsibility. That was hundreds of years ago, and for many years now the courts have taken punctuation into account when construing legal writing.

It is true that over the years the courts have hedged their bets on punctuation. Adler points out[16] that the House of Lords came down clearly in favour of punctuation in 1918 – in *Houston v Burns*, when Lord Shaw said:

> Punctuation is a rational part of English composition, and is sometimes quite significantly employed. I see no legal reason for

---

14 2002, *Style Manual for Authors, Editors and Printers*, 6th edition, John Wiley & Sons Australia Ltd, p 95 and following pages.

15 2001, *On Writing Well,* 6th revised (25th anniversary) edition, HarperResource Quill, New York, p 72.

16 Adler, M, 1990, *Clarity for Lawyers*, p 67 (cited at note 1).

depriving legal documents of such significance as attaches to punctuation in other writings.[17]

But the courts aren't keen to be constrained by punctuation. Mellinkoff has been able to compile a long list of conflicting pronouncements on the significance of punctuation by different state and federal courts in the United States.[18] Richard Wydick has made his own list in an article in *The Scribes Journal of Legal Writing*.[19] This ambivalence was repeated in a decision of High Court of Australia, when Justice Dawson said:

> Whilst punctuation may sometimes be helpful as an aid to construction, in these circumstances it would be wrong, in my view, to allow the presence of a comma to control the meaning of the sub-section.[20]

Clearly the judges like to keep their options open. This is also true in Canada, where in a recent case the Supreme Court refused to believe that the absence of a comma in a revised statute indicated that the legislature intended to give a different meaning to the section. The court construed the statute by looking at the purpose of the law instead.[21]

So should lawyers punctuate? Richard Wydick says "yes, but carefully". He gives three reasons:

1. Punctuated documents are less puzzling to other lawyers and judges.
2. They are easier for clients and other non-lawyers to understand.
3. They are easier to translate into other languages – an especially important consideration in Europe these days.[22]

All the leading commentators on legal writing agree: lawyers should punctuate. Everyone else does. Unfortunately, there is no guarantee that a court will always read every comma and dash the way we intend it. But that is a hazard of all drafting. Punctuation is not exempt.

---

17 [1918] AC 337 at 348.
18 Mellinkoff, D, 1963, *The Language of the Law*, Little Brown, Boston, pp 368-371.
19 Wydick, R, 1990, "Should Lawyers Punctuate?" (1990) 1 *The Scribes Journal of Legal Writing* 7 at 21-22.
20 *Chew v The Queen* (1992) 173 CLR 626 at 639 (a casual observation only).
21 *Nanaimo (City) v Rascal Trucking Ltd* 2000 SC 13.
22 Wydick, R, 1990, "Should Lawyers Punctuate?", pp 23-24 (cited at note 19).

Quirk[23] points out that when we write we don't have all the communicative advantages of the spoken language, like intonation and facial movements. So, he says, we have an obligation to give the reader all the help we can, by punctuating. We have to try to anticipate what might cause the reader difficulty.

Even so, we should try not to over-punctuate. Otherwise we can lose our reader along the way, because we have forced them to stop and pause too often. Perhaps the best advice is to try to punctuate only where a reader would naturally need to pause if the writing were read aloud.

One particular area of punctuation has caused problems for lawyers in the past is punctuation in lists. Does a list of items have to be punctuated as one sentence, like this:

> Here is my list:
> (a) a paragraph;
> (b) another paragraph; and
> (c) a final paragraph?

I don't believe it does. You may notice that throughout this book I am quite relaxed about the punctuation for lists. Sometimes I use a broken sentence to introduce a list of full sentences, like this:

> A broken sentence, introducing full sentences, such as:
> (a) This complete sentence has a capital letter, a verb and a full stop.
> (b) This one does too.
> (c) And so does this. In fact it has two.

At other times, I don't use punctuation after each item in the list, especially if they are not full sentences. For example:

> When I use bullet points to list short sharp items, such as:
> • this item
> • that item
> • the other item.

The reasoning behind this relaxed attitude is that the *list itself* shows that one item is finished by beginning text on a new line. A letter or symbol indicates the start of the new item. So we don't

---

23   1968, *The Use of English*, 2nd edition, Longman, London, p 239.

need to fuss over punctuation to help our reader make sense of the list.

The second list has complete sentences which help the reader make sense of the material within the individual items in the list. But we are not necessarily helping the reader if we always try to pretend (as in the first list) that a list is one full sentence, and each item in a list has to be a series of clauses separated by semi-colons. We are forcing the reader to connect all the items in the list together, instead of allowing them to read them individually.

The third list has no punctuation at all between the individual items. But this does not hinder the reader. The bullet points and new lines give all the signals the reader needs.

There is more about lists in chapter 11, when we discuss *and* and *or*.

Building a sentence

I mentioned Gowers's view that we need unity of thought in our sentences. That is a principle that is easier for lawyers to bear in mind than a grammatical theory about clauses, sub-clauses and subordinate clauses and adverbial, adjectival and relative clauses.

Try to keep to one thought per sentence. If you do this, it is easy to keep control of your sentence length and complexity.

Commas are sometimes a good indicator of a sentence that is too complex. If you find yourself putting in commas after every few words in your sentence and never quite getting to a full stop, it is likely that your sentence is becoming entangled in a mess of clauses which are out of control. Stop: break the sentence up into the various different thoughts you are expressing, and separate them into separate sentences.[24]

Cases and conditions: Coode's rules

Many lawyers are hampered by some old rules of legal drafting called "Coode's rules".

George Coode was an English barrister who wrote a famous analysis of legal drafting in 1843. His work, *On Legislative Expression* was probably the first attempt ever made to analyse

---

24 See also Interrupting a sentence with phrases and clauses, pp 146-147.

what happened in the legal drafting process. [25] He set down what he said were "natural" rules of drafting.

Coode's idea was that there are four basic elements in legislative drafting: the legal subject, the legal action, the case and the conditions. He said that they should appear in this order (my examples alongside):

1. *Case:* "Where a person owns more than one property ..."
2. *Condition:* "... and if application has been made for a dispensation ..."
3. *Legal Subject:* "... the Commissioner ..."
4. *Legal Action:* "... may exempt one property from liability to duty."

Coode thought that confused drafting resulted from a neglect of these rules. That may well be true. But the problem is that clear drafting does not always result from following these rules.

Coode has been criticised by a number of commentators, among them Dr EA Driedger QC,[26] and Robert Dick QC,[27] both of whom are well respected Canadian authorities on drafting. Piesse[28] allows that there are times when Coode's rules cannot be followed, or when it is not the most effective means of communication. Other commentators recommend adhering to Coode's rules.

I think it is a mistake to accept Coode's analysis as gospel, appropriate for all forms of drafting today. Following the sort of rigid structure that Coode recommended can create problems. For example, as the Law Reform Commission of Victoria pointed out,[29] putting a condition at the beginning of a sentence can create a problem for the reader, and if there is more than one condition, the

---

25 It was an extract from the introduction to the Appendix to the *Report of the Poor Law Commissioners on local taxation to Her Majesty's Principal Secretary of State for the Home Department*: House of Commons papers 1843, vol XX; set out in full in Robinson, Dr S, 1973, *Drafting*, Butterworths, Sydney, Appendix A, p 335.

26 1976, *The Composition of Legislation, Legislative Forms and Precedents*,2nd edition, Department of Justice, Canada and 1982, *A Manual of Instructions for Legislative and Legal Writing*, Department of Justice, Canada, pp 3-4.

27 1995, *Legal Drafting in Plain Language*, 3rd edition, Carswell, Toronto, p 60 and following pages.

28 Aitken, JK, 1995, *Piesse: The Elements of Drafting*, 9th edition, Law Book Company, Sydney, pp 33-34.

29 1987, Law Reform Commission of Victoria, Report No 9, *Plain English and the Law*, Appendix – Drafting Manual, p 35.

reader has to keep them all in mind, while still in a state of suspense as to what the core of the provision is about.

All this difficulty is compounded when you add a "case" up-front as well, as Coode's Rules would require.

Here's what I mean. It is an example taken from the Conveyancing Act 1919 (NSW), section 81(1):

> Whenever, in any deed of mortgage which is expressed to be made in pursuance of this Act [case], or in any mortgage under the Real Property Act, 1900 [case], the mortgagor employs the form of words contained in the first column of Part I of the Fourth Schedule, and distinguished by a number therein [condition], such form of words [legal subject] shall imply a covenant by the mortgagor for himself, his executors, administrators, and assigns, with the mortgagee, his executors, administrators and assigns, in the terms contained in the second column of the said schedule, and distinguished by the corresponding number [legal action].

The writer certainly followed Coode's Rules. But is it really clear? It is intelligible – if you read it slowly with the help of the words in brackets, and look over it a couple of times – but is it clear?

Lawyers are used to this sort of structure, because it follows step by step the thought processes that the lawyer went through to get to the main point. But for general readers it is most unusual.

Normal people say things like: "You can come with me if you are on time". The action is stated up-front, and the condition comes later. Of course, putting the condition first really isn't confusing if there is only one condition. But even just two conditions (or cases) at the beginning of a sentence can make a sentence difficult.

Let's try redrafting section 81(1) of the Conveyancing Act with the conditions and cases at the end and see if it improves things:

> The form of words contained in the first column of Part I of the Fourth Schedule, and distinguished by a number therein, [legal subject] shall imply a covenant by the mortgagor for himself, his executors, administrators, and assigns, with the mortgagee, his executors, administrators and assigns, in the terms contained in the second column of the said schedule, and distinguished by the corresponding number [legal action], whenever, in any deed of mortgage which is expressed to be made in pursuance of this Act [case], or in any mortgage under the Real Property Act, 1900 [case], the mortgagor employs the form of words contained in the first column

of Part I of the Fourth Schedule, and distinguished by a number therein [condition].

The language is still difficult, but at least now we know what we are talking about before we have to run off at a tangent into cases and conditions.

Today, not too many lawyers know about Coode and his rules. They couldn't imagine themselves drafting in that fashion. But there is a common structure that has the same problem for the reader as Coode's structure. It is one we probably use every day, thinking it is quite logical and simple. It is the *If ... then ...* structure. For example:

> If a person who has no criminal record makes an application, pays the scheduled fee and waits for the statutory cooling off period, the Commissioner may issue a gun licence.

It is nice and logical. It follows the format for mathematical formulae. But it keeps the reader waiting for far too long to get to the action. Our sentence is much better in this format:

> The Commissioner may issue a gun licence to a person who has no criminal record, makes an application, pays the scheduled fee and waits for the statutory cooling off period.

In that form, it is easier to follow and it is much more positive and lively as well.

Not all *if ... then ...* sentences are difficult to follow. You'll notice that in the example I chose there are several requirements that a person must satisfy to get a gun licence. If there is only one condition, then an *if ... then ...* structure can be quite straightforward. Like that one. But when the conditions start piling up, the sentence becomes more difficult. And then it is time to start thinking about breaking your sentence into paragraphs.[30]

The Australian Office of Parliamentary Counsel puts it this way:

> In drafting, you often need to put the conditional clauses first because they spell out all the facts, and the main clause would be meaningless without them. However, if the main clause is very simple and the conditional clauses are long and/or numerous, put

---

30   See p 100.

the main clause first. This way, the reader knows what it's about before ploughing through the paragraphs.[31]

I might quibble with the word "often" there. But as is frequently the case in matters of plain language, it is a question of judgment for the writer. How much complication is too much for the reader to cope with?

So that's structure: the framework on which we hang our words, and the way we arrange the paragraphs, sentences, words and thoughts in our documents. In the next chapter, we leave behind the way we put words together, and focus on the words themselves.

---

31 *Plain English Manual*, para 54, p 14, online version as at 11 March 2003, <www.opc.gov.au>.

Chapter 7

Words

Technical terms

I said in Chapter 2 that plain language can be used to express highly technical or otherwise complex concepts far more effectively than convoluted drafting. I said that plain language writers may choose to use an uncommon or technical word in their writing if they know the readers will be specialists, who are familiar with the word.

Technical terms can be really useful for lawyers. They can be a shorthand way of expressing a complicated idea: "expressio unius" for example. It is shorthand Latin for the legal maxim "Expressio unius est exclusio alterius" – which means "the expression of one is the exclusion of the other". It refers to the doctrine that if a general statement is made, and a list of examples follows, the general statement may be ignored and the list of examples treated as a complete list.

It is helpful for lawyers to write "expressio unius" and know that other lawyers will know all the detail that goes with it. But it doesn't help general readers. It is precise, but unintelligible to the public at large.

Using technical terms in legal writing is acceptable if the writer either explains what they mean or is sure that *all* the likely readers will be able to understand.

In fact, it is not really the technical terms that cause problems for readers of legal documents. The main problems are more to do with long sentences and unfamiliar, complex sentence structures. Using the occasional technical term will not mar an otherwise well written document

But if you suspect the technical term might cause difficulty, explain it. Better still, unless it really works well as shorthand for a long explanation that you'd have to make over and over again, don't use it at all! Your client probably only wants the facts, not technical jargon. Especially if the client needs lessons in Latin to understand it.

For example, if the point you are explaining to your client is that the phrase "everything in my garage, including my toolbox, tools and workbench" won't necessarily include *everything* in the garage (because a court might restrict it to mean only the items that have been listed) then *say so*. Explain that there is a legal doctrine that has that effect. Don't even mention "expressio unius". It is not necessary.

There are some technical terms, though, that really are useful labels. Things like *affidavit, withholding tax, hearsay, injunction* and *subpoena*[1] that don't really have a neat alternative. There is no problem in using these words, even when they are unfamiliar to your reader, as long as their meaning is explained. Depending on the document (and the intended readers), you might even consider putting the explanation in a box alongside the text.[2]

Terms of art

I've used a separate heading for this, because lawyers are inclined to say about a word: "Ah, but that is a term of art – I can't change that". And sometimes they are right. There are some special terms, such as the word *indemnify*, that are "loaded" with meaning and might be difficult, or even dangerous to do without. Very often, though, there are alternative words that are easier and more common, and it may not be necessary to use the term of art at all.

Another example is the word *estoppel*. Lawyers generally say that it is a term of art, which must be used because it is loaded with meaning. And that might be so, *if* you are pleading estoppel as part of a cause of action or making a submission to a judge, referring to the doctrine of estoppel. But if you are just referring to the *effect* of estoppel, there is nothing to stop (or estop) you from using *stop* or *prevent* instead. So, you could say:

> Because of what Mr Smith said to you at the time, the law prevents him from denying it now.

---

1   See p 162 note 1.
2   See p 264.

In fact in the 5th Australian edition of one of the major Australian texts on contract law, *Cheshire & Fifoot's Law of Contract*, the word *estopping* was relegated to brackets in favour of the word *stopping*:

> *Waiver, estoppel.* Statements or other conduct which suggest that a party will not terminate the contract, though entitled to do so, may be considered as waiving the right or as stopping ("estopping") the party from going back on his or her apparent intention.[3]

Be careful, too, when using terms of art that have a different meaning for the general public. We may completely overlook the fact that although the technical meaning is familiar to us, it might be unknown to our readers, or the word may mean something quite different to them. For most readers, words and phrases such as *execute, good faith, demise, instrument, satisfaction* and *dishonour* mean something different from the meaning lawyers give to them. They might be completely misunderstood.

Just because something is a term of art doesn't mean we have to use it. If there is an easier alternative, use that. But of course we should make sure the alternative is a true alternative. It is our responsibility as lawyers to know when we must use particular words. As Professor Mellinkoff says:

> Correct use of his terms of art marks a lawyer.[4]

We must know why we are using terms of art, and any other words for that matter. The classic excuse for continuing to use old formulas and old forms and precedents is that there is a reason every word is there and if we alter any we take too great a risk. But if we don't know why each word is there, how much greater the risk? And how can we consider ourselves professionals? It is our job to know. If we know why we use a term of art, or a particular formula of words, then we know if alternatives do the same work.

---

3   1988, 5th Australian edition, Butterworths, Sydney, para 2114. In the 8th edition, the concept of estoppel has its own chapter. Unfortunately there is no plain language translation of *estoppel*, although it is described (at p 63) as an "old-fashioned word": 2002, 8th Australian edition, LexisNexis Butterworths, Australia, Chapter 2, p 61.

4   Mellinkoff, D, 1963, *The Language of the Law*, Little Brown, Boston, p 391.

Legal buzzwords

There is another class of words that lawyers use that isn't technical, and isn't composed of terms of art – it is more like the secret language of a club. We seem to pick it up at law school, perhaps from reading cases, perhaps from talking to other lawyers. We pepper our conversations with these odd words and phrases: expressions such as *on all fours with*, *cover the field*, *at first blush*, *jointly and severally*, *a fortiori*, *otiose*, and *nugatory*.

Many lawyers would say that they use these expressions as a kind of legal shorthand, and that it helps them to communicate efficiently. But when you really look at the words, you see that they do not involve complex legal descriptions and that they all have equivalents in everyday language. There are no valid technical reasons for using them, but we continue to use them almost as a badge of our legal status. Even though we may recognise that they are potentially confusing for non-lawyers, it is tempting to think that there is no real harm in lawyers continuing to use those sorts of expressions among themselves.

But I wonder about the wisdom of doing that. The expressions slip too easily into our conversations with and writings to people who have not been initiated into the legal club. We have to watch that they don't set up barriers in communication. Otherwise we may find ourselves asking our friends for "further and better particulars" of the restaurant they have "jointly and severally" chosen for tonight's dinner, accusing them of "negligent mis-statement" when it turns out to be dreadful, and demanding "aggravated damages" for the "nervous shock" the meal induced.

Colourful language

Lawyers do use some wonderfully colourful phrases to describe particular legal concepts. I would not suggest that we should get rid of them. Things like the *eggshell skull*, the *fertile octogenarian* (and her friend, the *precocious toddler*), the *man on the Clapham omnibus* (or in Australia, the *Bondi tram*, or in Hong Kong, the *Shau Ki Whan tram*). Then there is the *snail in the ginger beer bottle*, and the verb to *Mirandise*[5] (or should it be *Mirandize?*). And even though that latter

---

5   *Miranda v Arizona* 384 US 436 (1965).

one is only used in the United States, Australians, Britons and others can now be *Marevaed*[6] or even, perhaps, *Anton Pilleried*.[7]

These colourful expression are not only fun, they also help to make legal principles easier to remember. They are descriptive and they enliven legal communication.

Word strings

How we lawyers love to use words. They are our tools of trade. But how difficult we find it to use only one word if we can use two. Or three. Or more.

It isn't that we're naturally long-winded, or that we like using paper. It is just that we are afraid to leave anything out. It is our job to imagine all the possibilities and make sure that they are covered. So we pile up words to cover each individual case.

But that can be dangerous.

I've already mentioned the "expressio unius" rule,[8] which means that lists can be dangerous if they are tacked on to the end of more general words which are intended to cover the topic. For example, "everything in my garage, including toolbox, tools and workbench" may not include the car, because the list sets out particular items and the car was not in the list.

There is also the "ejusdem generis" rule. This operates when a document has specific words followed by more general words – in other words, the other way round from "expressio unius". The "ejusdem generis" rule restricts the meaning of the general words to the same class or category as the specific words. For example, "My toolbox, my tools, and my workbench and the other things in my garage" may not include my car, because the general words may be read down to refer only to things in the tool/workbench category.[9]

---

6   *Mareva Compania Naviera SA v International Bulk Carriers SA* [1975] 2 Lloyd's Rep 509.

7   *Anton Piller KG v Manufacturing Processes Ltd* [1976] 1 Ch 55. However, under the Civil Procedure Rules introduced in England and Wales in 1998, Mareva injunctions became "freezing orders" and Anton Piller orders became "search orders".

8   Meaning explained on p 116.

9   The New South Wales Court of Appeal has recently held that using the *ejusdem generis* rule in statutory construction is rarely justified: *Deputy Commissioner of Taxation v Clark* [2003] NSWCA 91 at [127].

In both these cases, the writer would have been better off leaving the general description to stand on its own. "Everything in my garage" is quite clear on its own and doesn't attract any strange rules of construction – although the writer should probably also specify a time at which the items are to be counted.

The alternative, to get around both the "expressio unius" and the "ejusdem generis" rules is to use a phrase like "including, but not limited to", which shows that the list is not meant as a complete one. This works, but it is the word string that caused the problem and so it would be better to leave out the word string and rely on some suitable general words, as long as they are clear and precise. Lists of words can be trouble, unless you are absolutely certain that they are complete.

But is also important to bear in mind that both of these rules are merely rules of construction which courts use to help them interpret a document if it is ambiguous or unclear. If the intention of the parties or the legislature is clear from the document or law, it is not necessary to apply the rules of construction.[10] So there is no need use the phrase "including, but not limited to" as a magic incantation in every document which contains a list.

Synonyms

Even worse are strings of synonyms. If they really are synonyms, the string of words can be avoided altogether. One word should do. One of my favourite strings of synonyms is the magical phrase:

> release, remise and forever quitclaim unto ...

It is amazing how many times that ancient phrase crops up in modern release documents. Of course, *release* does exactly the same work in one word.

Often these synonym strings come in pairs ("doublets") or threes ("triplets"). Professor Mellinkoff has explained how this came about.[11] When French, which used to be the language of the law, declined and English took over, lawyers and others were

---

10   The High Court of Australia has confirmed that "expressio unius" is not automatically applied. See *PMT Partners Pty Ltd v Australian National Parks and Wildlife Service* (1995) 184 CLR 301 at 311 and 320. See also Chapter 12.

11   1963, *The Language of the Law*, p 121 and following pages (cited at note 4).

reluctant to choose between two words, and sometimes kept both. So we have:

> fit and proper
> free and clear
> goods and chattels
> had and received
> keep and maintain
> save and except
> will and testament.

Mellinkoff says that doubling became a habit and we now have doublets where both words came from Old English:

> each and every
> from and after
> have and hold

to name just a few.

Sometimes Latin got into the act as well. And so, at the end of the 20th century, we still have the doublets – and the triplets:

> give devise and bequeath
> null void and of no effect
> rest residue and remainder
> remise release and quitclaim.

Robert Dick describes this as killing one bird with three stones.[12]

This problem is simply another example of what happens when writers do not select their words with care, but just follow the old formulas. They assume that there must be a reason for using two or three similar words.

As I said before in the context of terms of art, it is a lawyer's responsibility to know when to use particular words. If a word adds nothing, we shouldn't use it.

Rarely are two similar words needed, much less three. Rather than assuming that more than one word is needed, and straining to find reasons why one word is not enough, we should make sure we know the limits of the words we use. We should select additional words only if they really add to the meaning.

---

12   1995, *Legal Drafting in Plain Language*, 3rd edition, Carswell, Toronto, p 128.

For a list of some of the doublets and triplets where the second and third words are probably unnecessary, see the lists set out in Dick's book *Legal Drafting in Plain Language*.[13]

Word clusters

There is another way that lawyers (and others) pile up words. They usually do it at the beginning of a sentence, when they are circling around and winding themselves up to say what they have to say. It is the "word cluster" – a kind of throat clearing ritual. Here are some examples:

> It is important to note that ...
> It should be remembered that ...
> We should point out that ...
> At this point in time ...
> Before we answer your question it is necessary to refer to ...
> You should take great care to ensure that ...
> We refer to previous correspondence and now advise as follows ...
> Having regard to (or notwithstanding) the foregoing ...

All of these are meaningless and could be deleted. They are just a cascade of words that don't mean anything, or to the extent they do, are so insincere or such a familiar formula, as to be practically worthless. They are simply a waste of time and effort, both for the reader and the writer.

Archaic words

We all know what these are and we know we shouldn't be using them. If they aren't technical terms and they aren't terms of art, that is, if there is no reason to cling to the archaic language, then why do so? The only possible reason is habit. It isn't much of a reason, is it? Especially when it can interfere so drastically with our ability to communicate with non-lawyers.

All you need to do to make a list of archaic words is picture in your mind's eye the bare bones of a deed, and write down the words in the deed that you never use in everyday speech. Here are a few favourites:

---

13   Same work, pp 127-129.

hereinafter, witnesseth, these presents, the premises (in the sense of "the matters") hereby, herein, herewith, hereafter, heretofore, above-mentioned, aforesaid, in witness whereof, the day and year first hereinbefore written, hereunto, unto and upon.

They really speak for themselves, don't they? Many of them, such as *heretofore, hereinafter, abovementioned* and *aforesaid* are imprecise. For instance, what precisely does *abovementioned* or *aforesaid* refer to? Where is *above*? Where is *afore*? The "time" words, such as *heretofore* and *hereinafter* have a similar problem. I'll deal separately with that in Chapter 9.

There are perfectly good alternatives for all of them.

Then there are *whatsoever, wheresoever, whosoever* and *howsoever.* These words are archaic too. We rarely see them outside legal writing. Other writers use them – if they use them at all – only for emphasis. In or out of legal writing they rarely, if ever, add meaning.

Compare, for example, these two definitions of "Secured Property". The first is a shortened variation of the classic mortgage definition :

> "Secured Property" means all the assets and undertaking of the Mortgagor whatsoever and wheresoever situate

and

> "Secured Property" means all the assets and undertaking of the Mortgagor.

Is there a difference? If there is, what is it?

Unfortunately, in legal writing many words that might be useful have been overused and abused and have lost much of their impact. But if, like the archaic words I have listed, they have lost most of their impact *and* their meaning, we should not be using them.

Many legislative drafters have long since abandoned these archaic words. Unfortunately, they still seem to pop up in private documents. Perhaps this is due to our reliance on forms and precedents which still contain archaic language. If so, even if there is no time for us to review all our old forms and precedents, we should at least make time now to search for and destroy all the archaic words.

Definitions

Words pose a particular problem for lawyers because their meanings can change. Lawyers are concerned with making their writing last, and making sure it reflects the intentions of those involved at the time of writing.

One of the ways that lawyers try to keep words under control is by using definitions. A good proportion of the documents that lawyers write (and even some letters) have definition sections. If there isn't a separate section for definitions, there'll probably be some definitions scattered about the text. Most legislation has a definition section at or near the beginning.[14]

These definitions do several things:

1. they enable the writer to use a convenient shorthand label for complicated concepts, so that the writer doesn't have to repeat the long explanation each time the writer wants to use the concept. (For example, "'Tax Act' means the Income Tax Assessment Act 1936 (Commonwealth) as amended" or "'Land' means the land situated at 44 Northern Highway, North Beach, New South Wales, and described in certificate of title volume 4444 folio 555");

2. they can clear up ambiguity by allowing the writer to give details of what was meant by a particular word (eg "'Stock' means all the stock in the factory at the close of business on 30 June 1991");

3. they can also clear up ambiguity by allowing the writer to specify one of several common meanings (eg "'month' means calendar month");

4. they allow the writer to be intentionally flexible about what a word means (eg "'Business Assets' *includes* the plant, fixtures, fittings and stock of the Business");

5. they allow the writer to stretch the word a little to include things that would not usually be encompassed in the normal meaning of the word (eg "'sell' includes offer to sell")

---

14   But not all – in Australia, older Acts had the definitions at the end, and the Income Tax Assessment Act 1997 has its "Dictionary" at the end of the Act. See p 133.

The one purpose that lawyers rarely use a definition for is the dictionary-type definition. The one that tells us what an unfamiliar word means.

Rarely do we write in our documents that "'writ of execution' means a document issued by a court under its own seal, commanding a sheriff or bailiff to take the property of a debtor to satisfy what the debtor has been judged liable to pay". It would be most unusual to see a definition like "'scheme of arrangement' means an arrangement made between a company and its creditors or shareholders, which is approved by the court under section 411 of the Corporations Act 2001, to enable the company to reorganise its affairs".

Now of course I'm not suggesting that we should use the definition section of the documents we write to explain to the lay person all the unfamiliar or technical terms we use in the document. As I said before,[15] there is no need to explain all the legal ramifications of a document *in the document itself*. I am just making the point that we lawyers use definitions in a different way from the way some of our readers might expect. That is why I do not favour the technique of using the word "Dictionary" for a definitions section. Generally the definitions are not the ones you would find in a dictionary.

We can see this in the long title of the Acts Interpretation Act 1901, an Australian Commonwealth law. It is: "An Act for the Interpretation of Acts of Parliament and for Shortening their Language".

What does that tell us about the way lawyers use definitions?

It tells us that lawyers use definitions more for their own convenience rather than for their readers'. Definitions can allow them to use a kind of shorthand in their documents. But what it means for readers is that they have to keep flicking back to the definition section to see what particular words might mean, and then try to keep all those meanings in their mind as they read the whole document.

This process is sometimes made even harder in the documents which don't use any kind of signal (like capital letters, for instance) to point out which words have a special meaning. Yet lawyers

---

15   Page 80.

don't often see this as a defect in their writing style. Perhaps that is because they see that it is economical to use definitions – they can use fewer words but still be as precise.

Lawyers are often happy with a document which begins or ends with scores of definitions – especially if it means that the rest of the document is very short. A document like that is almost invariably unreadable. But the lawyers who draft like that don't see the unreadability as a problem, perhaps because they prize the brevity it gives them in the main clauses of a document.

But with definitions, we should remember that the longer way round is sometimes the shortest way out. Even though definitions are a useful way of shortening a document, they can often interfere with the flow of meaning in a sentence. The aim is not to use definitions to create a "code" that the reader must know by heart to read a document.

For example, a sentence like this:

> The Covenantor is liable for the Primary Obligations under any Secondary Security except the Excluded Obligations.[16]

conveys no concrete meaning on its own. We have to look up four definitions to understand it. But if those defined words are not often repeated in the document, it would have been better to forget about defining them altogether. Not defining them might mean we have to pay more attention to drafting the main clause, to make sure that the information is manageable and clear. But then the main clause will be meaningful on its own.

A few pointers

Means and *includes*

In the examples of definitions I gave, some used the word *means* and some used the word *includes*. Using the word *means* in a definition limits the meaning of your defined word to the meaning you give it. The defined word means *only* what you specify and nothing else. Look at the examples of definitions on page 125. Examples 1, 2 and 3 are quite definite. The defined word means only one thing.

---

16   Defined words indicated with a capital letter.

Using the word *includes* in your definition leaves your definition open-ended. You have not closed off your definition. The defined word means what you've described, *and* anything else that the defined word would normally mean.

In the first example I gave of an "inclusive" definition (example 4), the plant, fixtures, fittings and stock of the Business are all "Business Assets", but other things might also be Business Assets as well. Maybe the books and records of the business, for example. The writer didn't want to close off the definition so it could include things that weren't specified.

Of course, this looseness can create difficulties as well: what if the writer didn't want the book debts of the business to be included. Would they be? What about the leased assets? Are they included? You need to be sure that your inclusive definition won't work against you.

Sometimes you see a definition that mixes both *means* and *includes*. For example:

"Company" means ABC Limited and includes its employees.

The writer wanted to be definite, and then extend the definition a little. This method works well if you use it correctly (as in "*means* X and *includes* Y"), but it should never be used in the "*means and includes …*" format (as in "'Company' *means and includes* ABC Limited"). As you can see, the word *includes* there did no extra work and was only confusing. It leaves the reader querying. Did the writer mean to say that Company only meant ABC Limited? Or could it mean something else? It is not clear.

Once only definitions

Never define a word or phrase if you only use it once. If you define a word or phrase and then use it only once, you don't need to use a definition at all. Put the full details in the text, where the reader needs it. Don't impose a definition on the reader unless it is going to be helpful.

Misleading definitions

Don't define so as to mislead the reader. Try to choose a label which is consistent with the full definition, so that the defined word can sensibly stand in the place of the full definition. There was a good example of a misleading definition in the New Zealand Poultry Act 1968,[17] which said in section 2:

> For the purposes of this Act "day old poultry" shall be deemed to be any poultry of an age of 72 hours or less.

Or take a definition like "'Furniture' includes computer equipment". You might find it in a business sale agreement. Most people would not automatically assume that the word "Furniture" would be used to include computer equipment, so when they see the word "Furniture" in the text, they probably won't even bother to check the definition. They will assume it means the things that people normally speak of when they use the word "furniture". The writer should have chosen a better label, like "Movable equipment", for instance, which at least is flexible enough to include both concepts. In fact in this case, it probably would be clearer to refer to the computer separately.

Useless definitions

Don't define things that are obvious. For example, "'Animal' includes dog". Was there ever any doubt? Or "'Agreement' means this agreement". That's a common one, and people persist in using that definition because they say there might be more than one agreement referred to in any document. They forget that whenever they refer to "this agreement", they *write* "this agreement"! And if they have to refer to a different agreement, they describe it, either by using its name and perhaps its date, or in terms of its function.

The Workplace Relations Act 1996 is an Australian law that contains what would seem to be two rather unhelpful definitions:

> "employee" includes any person whose usual occupation is that of employee ...
> "employer" includes:
>   (a)   a person who is usually an employer ...[18]

Elegant variation

This is an expression that is used to describe the way writers can vary the words they choose to avoid repeating themselves. This is

---

17   Repealed in 1993.
18   Section 4.

most often done in fiction writing to make the writing interesting and lively. The writer selects many different words for similar concepts. The classic example is all the different ways of saying *said: replied, asked, cried, shouted, sighed* and so on.

There is no place for elegant variation in legal drafting. We are in the business of being precise and so if we choose to use a word to refer to a particular concept, we should continue to use it whenever we refer to that concept. Otherwise we deceive our readers.

We should make sure that if we refer to a person by their name – even if we haven't used a definition – we *always* refer to them by that name. For example, if we are talking about Mr Smith and the proceedings he is taking, we should not suddenly call him "the plaintiff" or "the appellant". The reader may not be used to that sort of terminology and might think that we are now referring to someone else. It is clear to lawyers, because we know that as soon as the proceedings (or the appeal) comes to court Mr Smith will "become" the plaintiff (or the appellant). But our client may not know that. To our client, his name is Mr Smith, we called him Mr Smith at the beginning of the document, and Mr Smith he should remain.

Confusing labels

When you are choosing your labels for the words you are defining, don't choose confusing ones. Even lawyers mix up similar words like *lessor* and *lessee*, *mortgagor* and *mortgagee* and *chargor* and *chargee*. Try to find something less confusing, like *landlord* and *tenant* or *borrower* and *lender*. Or better still, use the parties' names, in a shortened version if necessary. Remember that readers don't want to have to keep checking the front page to find out who's who. Give them some help so they can keep the parties' names in their minds. But be careful not to make the names themselves too cryptic. If you use abbreviations for company names, don't make them too similar. For example if ABC Limited sells land to ABC Holdings Limited with finance provided by AIBC Limited and leases it to ABCD Pty Limited, you begin to get an alphabet soup.

Have another look at some of the other labels you use. What about something like *vendor* and *purchaser*? They are very familiar words to lawyers, but some readers would say that *vendor* is an unfamiliar word: it has the ring of an icecream seller about it. The English Law Society has obviously recognised this problem: in the 1990 version of their *Standard Conditions of Sale of Land* they decided to start using the terms *buyer* and *seller* instead. This document is now in its third edition,[19] but there is still some resistance to it. A British colleague[20] tells me that more than once he has seen a special condition added to the Standard Conditions which read:

> In this contract, "Seller" shall mean "the Vendor".

Too many definitions

As I have mentioned, nothing is more tiresome in a document than being confronted with scores of definitions, all appearing in the first clause of a document. Not only are we forced to read all the definitions before we get to the main point of the document, so they make little sense until we get the gist of the document, but we are also forced to keep flipping back and forward to check the definitions to decode the message.

Of course, definitions can be extremely useful and without them documents would be much longer. But if we want to write in plain language, we must balance that advantage against the disadvantage that the reader suffers when faced with a very long list of definitions. Finding that balance is most difficult for a writer of a long and complex document, but here are a few suggestions to soften the blow.

- Put the definitions at the end of the document, but clearly mark the defined words, each time they appear, with a sign that shows they are defined (I'll mention this again shortly).

- Make sure you've used each defined term more than once. If not, don't use the defined word – put the concept directly in the text.

- Look at the defined words you've used only twice or three times. Would it be easier on the reader if you abandoned the defined term and put the concept in the text? Even if it

---

19   A 4th edition is expected later in 2003.

20   Mark Adler, author of *Clarity for Lawyers*, 1990, The Law Society, London.

makes the document slightly longer, it could end up being easier to read.

- Have you defined anything that is obvious? If so, cut the definition out.

Where should the definitions go?

In statutes, the definitions have traditionally (though not always) appeared at the beginning. In documents, some writers put the definitions at the beginning and some at the end. Where is best?

The prime rule of plain language – consider your reader – would tell us that they should go at the end, because the definitions are one of the "technical" parts of the document. They are detail. The detail is important for our full understanding of the document, but not vital to our first reading of the document when we want to find out the basics of the transaction. We need to use the definitions to understand the document properly, but we can't use them properly until we know what the transaction is all about.

If the definitions are at the end of the document, then we get to them when we've got through the document. Then we are ready for the detail.

That was the view of the Australian Tax Law Simplification Project team. It considered definitions to be "mechanical" provisions. The team gathered together those definitions which are used regularly throughout the Act and placed them in a Chapter called "Dictionary" at the end of the Act.[21]

The Corporations Law Simplification Project team suggested another possibility: publishing the definitions in a separate volume. That way, readers could look up a definition and at the same time keep the page of the relevant section open.[22] This seems a very practical benefit – but of course it is only feasible for reasonably long laws or documents, and it does not work if the Act is viewed on a computer screen.

---

21 Section 995-1 of the Income Tax Assessment Act 1997. See also Tax Law Improvement Project, 1995, Information Paper No 2: *Building the New Tax Law*, Australian Government Publishing Service, p 13.

22 Corporations Law Simplification Task Force, 1995, *Drafting Issues: Organising the Law*, p 6. However, as enacted in the Corporations Act 2001, most definitions appear towards the beginning, in the "Dictionary" in section 9, and some appear at the beginning of the chapters, parts, divisions, subdivisions or sections to which they relate (see Corporations Act 2001, section 7).

It is important, though, that we warn our readers that some words have special meanings and they can find them in the definition section. Traditionally, this has been done in private documents by using a capital letter for each defined term. In statutes, though, this has not always been the case. Failing to warn people that a term is defined allows people to miss defined terms and so it is not a good drafting practice.

But are capital letters a good enough symbol? I think not. Capital letters are used for another purpose: for proper nouns. So we risk misleading people into thinking that the proper nouns are defined or that the defined words are proper nouns. And there is another problem: lawyers (and others) love to dignify words by giving them a capital letter. So we have Directors and Companies and Partners and Shareholders and even Shares and Loans and Mortgages. More confusion! Are they defined or aren't they?

Clearly we should be using another signal.

The Law Reform Commission of Victoria suggested that italics or bold type, combined with a footnote on each page referring the readers to the definition might do the trick.[23] When they came to their report on the structure and format of legislation[24] they actually adopted the practice of marking the defined term each time it appears with a "plus" symbol (+) to show it is defined, with a corresponding footnote pointing the way to the definition section. *And* the first time the defined word appears it is put in italics to alert readers to the special meaning, and footnoted with the whole definition at the foot of the page.

The Tax Law Improvement Project used a similar system, with most defined words appearing with an asterisk and a footnote telling the reader that the word is defined in the "Dictionary" starting at section 995-1. However, there are other defined words that are not indicated by an asterisk, including those that are defined within the Division or Subdivision they are used in, and some other "basic" terms used often throughout the Income Tax Assessment Act 1997. So the system is something of a hybrid. The details of the system are explained in Subdivision 2-C of the Act.

---

23   1987, Law Reform Commission of Victoria Report No 9, *Plain English and the Law*, p 55.

24   1990, Law Reform Commission of Victoria Report No 33, *Access to the Law: the structure and format of legislation*.

The Australian Office of Parliamentary Counsel's *Plain English Manual* specifies that defined terms should be printed in bold type when they're first defined. However, it also says that they have not found a way to mark definitions throughout the text without "distracting the eye from the main text or causing other problems". Instead the *Manual* suggests alerting the reader to important definitions by putting an explanatory note below the provision.[25] This is the system used in the rewritten New Zealand tax legislation, with lists of defined terms at the end of various segments of the Act.[26]

Martin Cutts considered this issue carefully in his review of the UK Timeshare Act.[27] He, too, worried that using footnote symbols throughout the text might be "visually intrusive". So he proposed a three-part solution:

- The first time the defined word appears it is in italics.
- All defined words are listed in the margin of every page – and readers are directed to the definitions section.
- The definitions are grouped together and listed in one section at the end of the Act.

This system might not work too well for a long Act, with many definitions (although Martin Cutts says it would have been possible for him to include as many as 65 definitions in his margins if he'd needed to, and after that he'd consider listing only the definitions used in that particular section of the Act).[28] Even if this seems to be too elaborate a system for private documents, it should at least be possible to select one symbol which indicates that a term is defined. Whatever it is, it should be unique. So if we use capital letters for proper nouns and bold type for underlining, perhaps we should use something else to indicate that a term is defined.

I have tended to use an asterisk or a footnote reference because it is not a "style" applied to the word itself, and so it doesn't distract the reader too much, and doesn't make the text look too

---

25   *Plain English Manual*, para 147, p 30, online version as at 11 March 2003, <www.opc.gov.au>.
26   See Income Tax Act 1994 (NZ) section AA3(2).
27   See Cutts, M, 2000, *Lucid Law*, 2nd edition, Plain Language Commission, High Peak, England.
28   Private correspondence with M Asprey, 17 November 1995.

busy. I prefer to see one system applied consistently throughout the whole document, if possible. And I do like Martin Cutts' system of listing defined words in a margin. But that system may not always work. As with most plain language principles, there is no one "right" answer that applies to every document. We need to think about what works best in the particular context. Remember that the main thing is to alert the reader that they should be checking the definition.

When to draft the definitions

It is very tempting to begin drafting a document by drafting the definitions. I don't think it is good drafting practice at all.

I've already pointed out how important it is to begin with a plan. If you do that, you won't get to the definitions until you've mapped out the structure of the document and listed everything that will go in it. Then you will be better able to select and fine tune the words you will be using.

But you will be even better placed to think about the definitions when you are putting the text in place. That is the time to work on the definitions. If you do that you will never waste time on defining words that you don't need. You also won't saddle yourself with unhelpful concepts that are hard to discard when you've been playing with them for a while. You'll only work on the concepts and words that you actually need. So working out the definitions at that later stage is much more efficient.

Now we have seen some of the problems there are with the words lawyers use. In the next chapter, we look at what we sometimes do to our words – by means of grammar – and see how it can make our writing turgid and tiring to read.

Chapter 8

Grammatical structures to avoid

About grammar and its place in legal drafting

Very few lawyers are also linguists. But they do use language all the time. That means they are using grammar all the time. Grammar deals with words, their inflexions (the variations on the root of a word that allow us to use it in different ways) and the arrangements of words.

In Chapter 2 I asked the question whether lawyers were different – whether they were stuck with having to use unusual words and strange and complex sentence structures because of the nature of the law and its practice. I answered *no* to that question. Lawyers can write as simply as other writers and still be accurate. But we all know that much legal drafting looks different from other writing. Why is that?

In the last chapter we dealt with the words that lawyers use, and there is no doubt that lawyers can use very strange words, but there is something else that can make legal writing look strange, and that is the grammatical structures that lawyers use.

Even if you don't know anything about grammar, you are using it all the time when you write. This chapter isn't intended as a grammar lesson, but I do need to explain some of the unusual grammatical structures that lawyers use, so that we can recognise and avoid them.

The future tense

Why do many lawyers slip into the future tense when they write? Why don't they write in the present tense? Why do they write:

> *Future*
> "Company" shall mean ABC Ltd.
> The Company shall sell and the Buyer shall buy ...

This agreement shall be governed by the laws of ...

If A shall learn that B shall have granted an easement ... (future tense followed by future perfect tense)

instead of:

Present

"Company" means ABC Ltd.

The Company sells and the Buyer buys ...

This agreement is governed by the laws of ...

If A learns that B has granted an easement ... (present tense followed by perfect tense)?

Maybe it is because they think that, as they are writing for the future, they should write about things as if they will occur in the future. But this only makes the document sound stilted. And of course, the document operates in the future, but by that time the future will be the present! So it is much more sensible to draft in the present tense.

Another concern some lawyers have is that the present tense might not cover things that happen "in the future" (after the document is drafted and signed). For example, in a provision like:

The Company indemnifies the Distributor against any loss it suffers because of claims by the Customers.

they worry that a court might allow only one claim, and only if it is a current claim at the date of the document.

That is not so.

There is a general principle of interpretation which says that the law can be regarded as "constantly speaking". This means that we can apply the relevant provision again and again to different circumstances as they arise.

This principle that the law speaks constantly was recognised long ago by Coode in the context of legislation.[1] Some jurisdictions have decided to spell it out as it applies to legislation. For example, section 8 of the Interpretation Act 1984 of Western Australia says:

A written law shall be considered as always speaking and whenever a matter or thing is expressed in the present tense, it shall be applied

---

1   Coode, 1843, *On Legislative Expression*, set out in full in Robinson, Dr S, 1973, *Drafting*, Butterworths, Sydney, pp 392-396.

to the circumstances as they arise, so that effect may be given to every part of the law according to its true spirit, intent, and meaning.

The corresponding provision in the South Australian Acts Interpretation Act 1915 says:

> Every Act will be considered as speaking at all times, and every enactment, whether in the present or the future tense, will be applied to the circumstances as they arise, so that effect may be given to each Act and every provision according to its spirit, true intent, and meaning.[2]

There are similar provisions in the interpretation Acts of other countries, including Northern Ireland and Canada. New Zealand's Interpretation Act 1999 says:

> An enactment applies to circumstances as they arise.[3]

These sections are strictly speaking unnecessary, but they do enunciate the "constantly speaking" principle quite clearly as it relates to legislation.

How does it apply to private documents?

The leading drafting commentators seem to agree that there is no doubt that the principle *does* apply to private documents: that we are safe to draft in the present tense in the knowledge that our documents can be read as "constantly speaking".

Piesse notes that the objections to *shall* in statutes apply also to business documents, and then says:

> There may be doubts whether the courts would hold that a document between parties in which cases, occasions, circumstances, conditions and the like were expressed in the present or perfect and not in the future should be interpreted as applying whenever (within the words of the document) the case, occasion, or circumstance arose or the condition had to be satisfied. Although a general formal statement to this effect may not be found in the reports there can be no doubt that this is correct. If in a particular clause there seems any room for doubt whether a statement in the present tense will be so interpreted, the doubt can usually be avoided by introducing it with some such phrase as *if at any time*.[4]

---

2   Section 21.

3   Section 6.

4   Aitken, JK, 1995, *Piesse: The Elements of Drafting*, 9th edition, Law Book Company, Sydney, p 67.

Dick agrees. He refers to Piesse's analysis when he suggests that drafters of private documents might like to use the phrase *if at any time*, if they feel that the present tense doesn't express the time relationship that applies to the circumstances they are describing in their document. He says:

> An equally effective method of ensuring correct interpretation would be to specifically insert an interpretation section at the beginning of the document. However, this is unnecessary. As an Australian authority has pointed out, the courts will hold that circumstances, conditions and stipulations expressed in the past or present and not in the future, will be interpreted as applying whenever the circumstances arose or the condition or stipulation has to be satisfied or performed.[5]

This point is also nodded to with approval by Dr Robinson, who says in a footnote to some comments he makes on the use of the present tense for conditions:

> remember that documents are treated as if continually speaking.[6]

I, too, have been unable to find any pronouncements by the courts which confirm that private documents are "constantly speaking", just like statutes. But perhaps that isn't surprising. It would be very difficult for a court to frame a blanket rule on that subject. After all, it does depend on the context of the document and the intention of the parties. For example, a provision such as: "I agree to sell my house to you" is intended to apply just once. But a provision like the example I gave a few paragraphs ago: "The Company indemnifies the Distributor against any loss it suffers because of claims by the Customers" must be intended to apply again and again, each time a customer makes a claim. It will always be a matter of looking at the words in their context. That is why both Piesse and Dick suggest the occasional use of words such as *if at any time*, in case things need clarifying.

Common sense, of course, and ordinary language use would say that something written in the present tense is intended to operate in the present, whenever that may be. That is certainly true for statutory interpretation.

---

5   Dick QC, RC, 1995, *Legal Drafting in Plain Language*, 3rd edition, Carswell, Toronto, pp 88-89.
6   Robinson, Dr S, 1973, *Drafting*, p 42 (cited at note 1).

Maxwell[7] points out that the present tense in the words of a statute will be read as indicating the present at the time the section is *applied*, not the time it was *enacted*. For example, Maxwell quotes, among others, a case in which a section enabled a minister to make an order if a school "is being administered" in contravention of the relevant law. The court held that the minister could only consider the *present* conduct of the school at the time the minister was making the order, and not the past.[8]

Maxwell makes these points when he is discussing the "rule of literal interpretation". His point is that the literal meaning of the present tense is that it applies to the present – when the words are being interpreted. I discuss the "literal" rule in Chapter 12.[9] The "literal" rule applies to private documents as well as statutes. Therefore, if the context allows, and it is consistent with the intention of the parties, the present tense in a private document applies to the time it is read, and each time it is read.

All this demonstrates that there is no need to anticipate the future by drafting in the future tense. The present tense is not only adequate and appropriate, but also leads to simpler sentence structure and easier comprehension.

The principle that the law constantly speaks is also important to remember when we draft provisions that relate to time. I deal further with this in Chapter 9.

One other thing before we leave the topic of the future tense: lawyers like to use the word *shall* not only to express the future, but also in one of its special senses – to express an obligation. This is the "imperative" sense of *shall*: *shall* as a command. If lawyers want to use the imperative *shall* and also draft in the future tense, things can become very confused indeed. It is better to avoid those problems by drafting in the present tense.

It is also possible to avoid the imperative *shall* altogether, as we'll see in Chapter 11.

---

7   Langan, PStJ, 1969, *Maxwell on the Interpretation of Statutes*, 12th edition, Sweet & Maxwell, London, p 31.

8   *Maradana Mosque (Board of Trustees) v Mahmud* [1967] 1 AC 13.

9   See p 207.

The passive voice

The difference between the next two sentences illustrates the difference between the active and passive voices:

> *Active:*   The lawyer sat on a chair.
> *Passive:*   A chair was sat on by the lawyer.

See how the active is more direct, more lively, less complicated (and shorter) than the passive? The structure is simple: subject, active verb, object, rather than object, complex verb, subject. The subject of the sentence is the "actor" – the person acting (which is the lawyer) and the object (which is being "acted on") is the chair. The structure is simplest if the actor-subject comes first. The vast majority of all writing follows that formula: subject verb object.

Lawyers seem to love the passive. Here are a couple of common examples of the passive voice from legal writing:

> Shares may *be* issued *by* the Directors.
> Application must *be* made *by* the Tenant to the Landlord in writing.

These two sentences can be rewritten in the active voice as:

> The Directors may issue shares.
> The Tenant must apply to the Landlord in writing.

The subjects, who do the action, come first, and the objects, who have something done to them, come later.

But this guideline is not an absolute rule against using the passive voice. Occasionally we might want to use the passive for a particular reason. For example:

- if we do not have a subject: we do not know (or do not wish to state) who is doing the action, as in:

  > Trespassers will be prosecuted.
  > The victim was robbed in the park.

  In each case the only possible structure is the passive; or

- if it is more important to stress something other than the subject of the sentence, as in:

  > Even though it was late, the notice was *served*.
  > To acquit the accused, the jury must believe the accused's alibi. The *alibi* must be confirmed by the evidence.

One way to recognise the passive voice is by using the *be/by* test: look for some form of the verb *to be*, and then the preposition *by*, as in these examples:

> You must *be* seen *by* the Dean.
> The witness *was* called *by* the defence.

But this test does not work for sentences that do not have a subject, as in:

> Trespassers will *be* prosecuted.[10]

Subjunctive mood

This structure isn't much of a problem, simply because the subjunctive mood is not used very often, even by lawyers. But it still occasionally crops up in legal documents. Some of us use it without being aware that we are doing so, and without knowing what its function is.

The subjunctive mood is another form of the verb, which is used to express a wish, a command, a hypothetical circumstance or an anticipated event. Its use is rare now – and has been rare for many years, except for a few specific examples. Here are some. You can see the unusual verb inflections reflecting the fact of the subjunctive mood.

> God *save* the Queen!
> If I *were* you …
> *Come* Monday, I'll be gone.
> I suggest that he *leave*.
> I move that standing orders *be* suspended.
> If the court finds that the evidence of the witness *be* false …
> If it *should appear* to the court …

These uses still crop up in speech and writing, but there's no telling how long the subjunctive will last. Most grammarians seem to agree that the subjunctive is dying, but some suggest there is a last-minute revival coming from America.[11] Some of the examples I have given will probably stay around longer than others, but the last three, which are the sort we are most likely to encounter in legal

10   See the explanation on p 141.
11   See the comments of Greenbaum and Whitcut (eds), 1987, *Gowers's The Complete Plain Words*, 3rd edition, Penguin Books, London, pp 138–139.

drafting, could easily be rewritten in the indicative mood (which is the one we normally use in everyday speech and writing) as:

> I move that standing orders are suspended.
> If the court finds that the evidence of the witness is (or was) false …
> If it appears to the court …

It looks a little less formal that way, and is a more natural form for most readers.

Negatives

It is easier to read something that is written in a positive way. In other words, it is not as easy to read something that is not written in a positive way.

Do you see the difference?

Of course, as lawyers we deal with negatives all the time: some things can only be expressed in the negative. For example, some of the ten commandments would be pretty strange if they were expressed as positives. Imagine the 6th and 8th commandments:

> 6. You must keep everything alive.
> 8. You may only keep what you have rightfully acquired.

The 7th, on the other hand, has a nice ring to it in the positive:

> 7. Always be faithful to your spouse.

A negative statement can often be rewritten as a positive statement and that usually makes it easier to comprehend. For example:

> The Secretary may not register shares without the consent of the Directors.

could be rewritten as a positive statement:

> The Secretary may only register shares with the consent of the Directors.

May only

The sentence:

> The shareholders may not transfer shares to persons who are not shareholders unless the Foreign Investment Review Board has approved the transfer.

is even more difficult, because it already has a negative in it which is difficult to make into a positive. But we can make the first negative into a positive, so that the sentence becomes:

> The shareholders may only transfer shares to persons who are not shareholders if the Foreign Investment Review Board has approved the transfer.

It is often a matter of giving permission to those who follow the rules, rather than denying it to those who break them, as in the example:

> Persons without a licence may not ...

which could be rewritten as:

> Only persons with a licence may ...

The words *may only* were considered in 1995 by the High Court of Australia, in a case involving legislation which set a time limit for taking action. Now we have authority from the High Court for the proposition that when the words *may only* are used in a statute, they mean exactly what they say. In *David Grant & Co Pty Limited (Rec Apptd) v Westpac Banking Corporation*,[12] the High Court was considering sections of a statute (sections 459G(1), (2) and (3)) which read:

> (1) A company may apply to the Court for an order setting aside a statutory demand served on the company.
> (2) An application *may only* be made within 21 days after the demand is so served.
> (3) An application is made in accordance with this section *only if*, within those 21 days: ...[13]

The court found that the word *only* in that context means what it says – that it excludes all other possibilities. Justice Gummow said:

> The force of the term "may only" is to define the jurisdiction of the court by imposing a requirement as to time as an essential condition of the new right conferred by section 459G. An integer or element of the right created by s 459G is its exercise by application made within the time specified ... it is a condition of the gift in subs (1) of s 459G that subs (2) be observed and, unless this is so, the gift can never take effect. The same is true of subs (3).

12   (1995) 184 CLR 265.
13   Emphasis mine.

This consideration gives added force to the proposition which has been accepted in some of the authorities that it is impossible to identify the function or utility of the word "only" in s 459G(2) if it does not mean what it says, which is that the application is to be made within 21 days of service of the demand, and not at some time thereafter and that to treat s 1322 as authorising the court to extend the period of 21 days specified in s 459G would deprive the word "only" of effect.[14]

The words *may only* appear in another section of the (now) Corporations Act 2001 (Cth). Section 588FF(3) says:

An application under subsection (1) may only be made:
    (a) within 3 years after the relation-back day; or
    (b) within such longer period as the Court orders on an application under this paragraph by the liquidator within those 3 years.

In both *Greig v Australian Building Industries Pty Limited*[15] and *Star v National Australia Bank Limited*,[16] the court applied the reasoning of the High Court in *David Grant* to construe *may only* in section 588FF(3) in the same way: you can *only* apply in the relevant period. Other sections of the Act, giving the court a discretion to extend the time for doing things, do not apply.[17]

Double negatives

Negatives are difficult enough, but two negatives are worse. The US Securities and Exchange Commission, normally praised for its efforts to introduce plain language to the securities industry, recently blotted its copybook with a double negative. It approved a rule that specified when lawyers who notice that their client companies are breaking securities laws have to report them to the authorities. The relevant part of the definition within the rule reads:

Evidence of a material violation means credible evidence, based upon which it would be unreasonable, under the circumstances, for

---

14   (1995) 184 CLR 265 at 277.
15   (2003) 21 ACLC 324.
16   (1999) 30 ACSR 583.
17   But section 588FF(3) may ultimately be destined for the High Court: the judges in *Sutherland v Dexion (Australia) Pty Limited* (2003) 21 ACLC 341 and *Brown v DML Resources Pty Limited (No 6)* (2002) 40 ACSR 669 felt that there was power to extend time, and that the reasoning in *David Grant* did not apply.

> a prudent and competent attorney not to conclude that it is reasonably likely that a material violation has occurred, is ongoing, or is about to occur.[18]

That sentence has many ideas going on in it. It is complicated enough already without the double negative *unreasonable ... not to conclude*. There was an earlier, simpler version that read:

> Evidence of a material violation means information that would lead an attorney reasonably to believe that a material violation has occurred, is occurring, or is about to occur.

That version is not only simpler, but it is also a stricter obligation on the lawyer. After much lobbying and discussion with lawyers and other interest groups, the SEC adopted the more complicated, more difficult to prove version.[19]

Interrupting a sentence with phrases and clauses

This sounds technical, too, but it is a really common problem for lawyers. We have so much to say and so many digressions to make that we often try to do it all too quickly in the one sentence.

Here is an example of a problem sentence:

> The Tenant may, with the prior written consent of the Landlord, which consent shall not be unreasonably withheld, and which consent, if it is to be given, must be given within 14 days of application, assign the Lease.

What has happened to the verb in this sentence? It has been split down the middle and several clauses have been stuck in between the auxiliary (may) and the main verb (assign). So we lose track of what it is the Tenant can or can't do until we get to the end of the sentence.

The best way to keep up the interest of the reader through all the conditions and requirements that surround the main idea of the sentence is to give the reader the verb up-front. Then they know

---

18   SEC Release No 33-8185, 29 Jan 2003, *Implementation of Standards of Professional Conduct for Attorneys*, Release No 34-47276, IC-25919, File No S7-45-02, effective 5 August 2003. This will be a new Part 205 to Title 17, Chapter II, Code of Federal Regulations.

19   See Norris, F, "No Positives in this Double Negative", *The New York Times*, 24 January 2003.

what the sentence is about before they have to deal with the detail. So, one rewrite of the sentence would be:

> The Tenant *may assign* the Lease with the prior written consent of the Landlord, which consent shall not be unreasonably withheld, and which consent, if it is to be given, must be given within 14 days of application.

But still the sentence is not perfect, because the writer has tried to pack three ideas into the one sentence. The ideas are:

1. The Tenant may assign the Lease with the prior written consent of the Landlord.
2. The Landlord may not unreasonably withhold consent.
3. If the Landlord gives consent, he or she must give it within 14 days of application by the Tenant.

Arranged as three separate sentences, they are simpler to grasp. Depending on what else is in the document, we might need to refine this draft further. But the new arrangement makes the logic much more apparent than before.

Incidentally, there was another way we could have put the auxiliary and the verb back together in this example. We could have written:

> The Tenant, with the prior written consent of the Landlord, which consent shall not be unreasonably withheld, and which consent, if it is to be given, must be given within 14 days of application, *may assign* the Lease.

This way isn't as effective because it keeps the reader in suspense. The auxiliary and verb are together, but at the end, rather than at the beginning, of the sentence. The problem here is that the subject and the verb are still separated by too large a gap. The reader needs to know not only what is happening, but also who is doing it. These are the things that keep a reader reading. The rest are details which the reader can deal with better once the reader has the primary information needed to make sense of the sentence.

Making verbs into nouns

I like this concept because the word that describes it is an example of the very phenomenon it describes: *nominalisation*.

Lawyers, and many other writers, seem to want to make their writing sound more important by multiplying the number of words they use to say exactly the same thing. So they make verbs into nouns. They never *state*, they always *make a statement*. They never *apply*, they always *make an application*. They never *consider*, they always *give consideration to*. They never *provide*, they always *make provision*. They never *pay*, they always *make payment*.

You can see how much weaker the noun-based phrase sounds. It sounds removed, indifferent, uninvolved. The verb sounds more active and positive. It makes the sentence more readable.

Provisos

Most lawyers know that they shouldn't use provisos. But many still do. A proviso is nearly always an afterthought. A clause is drafted, and then later the writer remembers something else and tacks it on as a proviso. Even if the proviso is not an afterthought, it *looks* like an afterthought because it is tacked on after the main statement, instead of being integrated with it.

The problem with a proviso is its tendency to put information in the wrong place: most provisos are exceptions or modifications of a statement that has just been made, and often they contradict the preceding statement. So drafting by using provisos can often mislead the reader.

The proviso-user must recognise this – at least sub-consciously – because the hallmark of a proviso is that its introductory words are nearly always in capitals:

> PROVIDED THAT …
>
> AND PROVIDED THAT …
>
> AND PROVIDED FURTHER THAT …

The writer seems to feel the need to draw attention to the provisos, in case they are missed.

In these days of computers, there is no excuse for using provisos to cope with afterthoughts. It is just as easy to amend the text to cope with the extra material.

How can we rewrite provisos? It depends on what is in them and how long and complex they are. Here are a few hints.

- If the material in the proviso is a short statement of an exception to a preceding statement, the exception can be linked to the statement by the word *but*. For example:

  > The Lender may demand payment of the loan PROVIDED THAT it may not do so unless the Borrower has failed to make an interest payment.

  can be rewritten as:

  > The Lender may demand payment of the loan, but it may not do so unless the Borrower has failed to make an interest payment ...

- If the material in the proviso is really a condition, rather than an exception, the link word should be *if*. For example:

  > The Purchaser may pay the lower price PROVIDED THAT it pays on or before 1 January 2004.

  can be rewritten as:

  > The Purchaser may pay the lower price if it pays on or before 1 January 2004.

- If there is a series of exceptions or conditions, they are better divided up into a series of separate paragraphs, all linked with *and* or *or*, depending on whether they are alternatives or all operate together. For example:

  > The Trustee may distribute funds PROVIDED THAT it has a surplus of funds AND PROVIDED THAT the beneficiaries are over 21 AND FURTHER PROVIDED THAT no loans to beneficiaries are outstanding.

  can be rewritten as:

  > The Trustee may distribute funds if:
  > 1. it has a surplus of funds; and
  > 2. the beneficiaries are over 21; and
  > 3. no loans to beneficiaries are outstanding.

because all three conditions operate together. If they had been alternatives – that is, if the fulfilment of only one condition is enough to allow the Trustee to distribute, the clause would have been rewritten like this:

> The Trustee may distribute funds if:
> 1. it has a surplus of funds; or
> 2. the beneficiaries are over 21; or
> 3. no loans to beneficiaries are outstanding.

Other rules of grammar

There are many other rules of grammar that we know, or used to know. Many people fuss about things like the problem of whether it is acceptable to split an infinitive, or end a sentence with a preposition, or whether we should say "It is I" or "It is me", and so on. How important are they?

The first thing to bear in mind about these rules is that they can't be said to come naturally any more. Many of us were taught them and told that to break them was "bad English". Yet how often do we hear people breaking the rules and how much of this "bad English" has been written – even by our most admired writers?

Many of these rules are slipping out of general language use. It is reaching the point where staying with the "correct" version can sound stilted, or even wrong.

The second thing to bear in mind is that many commentators on language take a flexible approach to the bending or breaking of these rules. And it is not a new flexibility. For example, in 1962, Randolph Quirk wrote:

> On points like these, where there is divided usage, we find a good deal of controversy, and much energy is fruitlessly expended in attempting to prove that one or other is "correct". Two issues which are particularly notorious in this way are illustrated in the sentences "I am sure we will succeed" and "It is me", some people being strongly of the opinion that "It is I" is the only acceptable form and that only "we shall succeed" is correct when we want to indicate the future ... it should be made clear that disputed points of this kind are small in number and that their importance has been exaggerated beyond all measure by the distorted judgment of those whose feelings run high on the subject. It is surely time we rid ourselves of the idea that *they* are what grammar is all about. The very fact that usage is divided, that we are all aware that some say one thing and some another in these disputed areas, should itself make it obvious that it is impossible to say one is "correct" and the other "incorrect". One might as well argue about whether *begin to work* is more correct than *start to work* or whether a plain tie is more correct than a striped one ...[20]

Samuel Johnson, too, recognised the power of spoken language usage. He said:

---

20   1968, *The Use of English*, 2nd edition, Longman, London, pp 113-114.

The pen must at length comply with the tongue.[21]

Respected writers have lampooned the inflexible adherence to these rules. Winston Churchill said that the practice of ending a sentence with a preposition was "the type of arrant pedantry, up with which I shall not put".[22] And James Thurber had fun with *who* and *whom:*

> The number of people who use "whom" and "who" wrongly is appalling. Take the common expression "Whom are you, anyways?" That is of course, strictly speaking, correct – and yet how formal, how stilted! The usage to be preferred in ordinary speech and writing is "Who are you, anyways?" "Whom" should be used in the nominative case only when a note of dignity or austerity is desired. For example, if a writer is dealing with a meeting of, say, the British Cabinet, it would be better to have the Premier greet a new arrival, such as an under-secretary, with a "Whom are you, anyways?" rather than a "Who are you, anyways?" – always granted that the Premier is sincerely unaware of the man's identity. To address a person one knows by a "Whom are you?" is a mark either of incredible lapse of memory or inexcusable arrogance.[23]

George Orwell was generous in recognising the need to be flexible in our approach to writing-even to the point of breaking his own rules. His essay "Politics and the English Language" begins with the proposition that the English language is in a bad way. At the end, he gives us six rules to follow "when instinct fails", and we are in doubt about whether to use a particular word or phrase. The last rule is:

> Break any of these rules sooner than say anything outright barbarous.[24]

In summary, we should respect the rules of grammar, but never become their slaves. And the same is true for these plain language guidelines as well.[25]

---

21   Quoted in Zinsser, W, 2001, *On Writing Well*, 6th revised (25th anniversary) edition, HarperResource Quill, New York, p 42.

22   Quoted in Flesch, R, 1974, *The Art of Readable Writing*, revised 25th anniversary edition, Harper & Row, New York, p 163.

23   Thurber, J, 1931, *The Owl in the Attic and Other Perplexities*, Harper & Bros.

24   Orwell, G, "Politics and the English Language", in 1985, *The Penguin Essays of George Orwell*, Penguin Books, London, p 365.

25   See p 161.

The gender problem

The gender problem in writing is this: our language doesn't cope very well with the fact that both men and women participate in society. Most of our older laws are written on the basis that laws only apply to men. Unfortunately, this is not the case.

Our private documents have traditionally followed the drafting style of our older laws, and so *she* and *her* are not often mentioned.

It is not always a simple matter to fix this problem, for two reasons:

1. our language doesn't make it easy to refer to both male and female genders together (or to neither); and

2. some people don't see this as an issue in the first place. They either consider it unimportant, or they think that attempting to deal with the problem does "violence" to the language.

I think that those who hold the second view will soon be overtaken by the rest of us who recognise the need for our language to adapt to fit a changing society. Language has always done this: it is hardly a radical view to suggest that it should continue to do so.

Years ago, when the word *Ms* as a form of address was new, some people said it was "stupid" and "unnecessary": that no self-respecting woman would use it because it would be a sign that she was ashamed of her marital status. The word *Ms* was often said with a sneer. These days it is the rule, not the exception, to address a woman as *Ms* if you don't know her preferred form of address.

In the future, Mrs and Miss might be considered "stupid" or "unnecessary" – who knows?

It seems pointless to try to resist the trend to gender-neutral language. Who can tell whether their readers will be male or female? Why should we write assuming that the world is male when we risk offence by doing so? It is not always *easy* to make your writing gender-neutral, but it is always *possible*.

I have come up against the problem a few times in writing this book. I wonder if you noticed. It might help to illustrate a few of the "tricks" of gender-neutral writing if I point out those parts of the book to you.

Here are nine ways to be gender-neutral in your writing. Choose whichever achieves the most harmonious result in your context.

- *Use "he or she" instead of "he"*

  The common criticism of this technique is that it is tiresome. So is anything, if it is overused. I have been writing in this book about *lawyers* and *writers* and *clients* and *readers* who can be male or female and I have used *he or she* several times – twice in this paragraph from p 80:

  > What I am saying is that the client (or member of the public) should be able to read the document from cover to cover, if *he or she* wants to, and comprehend it as a document. The client may have questions and need to ask you to explain some things, or to give more details or examples, but the client should have been able to get through the document with a feeling that *he or she* understood all the words, if not all the concepts or the reasons why all the words were there.

  and once in a paragraph on p 88:

  > Remember, too, that you are writing a letter of advice to a client – not an essay for a university professor. Your client wants to know the answer to the question that *he or she* asked you.

  If this seems tiresome, don't forget how tiresome it is for some of us to read writing which refuses to deal with the gender problem!

- *Repeat the noun*

  For example, on p 112 I wrote:

  > putting a condition at the beginning of a sentence can create a problem for *the reader*, and if there is more than one condition, *the reader* has to keep them all in mind, while still in a state of suspense as to what the core of the provision is about,

  rather than:

  > putting a condition at the beginning of a sentence can create a problem for *the reader*, and if there is more than one condition, *he* has to keep them all in mind, while still in a state of suspense as to what the core of the provision is about.

- *Drop the pronoun*

  For example, on p 118 I quoted Professor Mellinkoff, who said:

Correct use of his terms of art marks a lawyer.[26]

Because I was quoting, I couldn't make the language gender-neutral. But if I had written that sentence, I would have dropped the pronoun and expressed it like this:

Correct use of terms of art marks a lawyer.

Or in a case like:

The President may, if *he* is of the opinion that …

we could rewrite it as:

The President may, if of the opinion that …

which avoids the problem by dropping both *he,* and the verb *is.*

- *Use something other than a pronoun*

In the example before the last one, I could have written:

Correct use of legal terms of art marks a lawyer.

which uses an adjective to tie the *terms of art* to the lawyer.
Or we could replace the pronoun with *a, an* or *the*. For example, in a case like:

A trustee who abuses the authority of *his* position may be replaced.

we could replace the *his* with *the,* so that it reads:

A trustee who abuses the authority of *the* position may be replaced.

We could also replace a noun with a verb, like this:

A lawyer who gives *his* undertaking to provide a document.

becomes:

A lawyer who *undertakes* to provide a document.

- *Write in the plural*

For example, on p 14 I wrote:

In summary, lawyers who write in plain language try to put themselves in the reader's shoes. They think about what they are writing and what it will mean to the reader – how the reader will react and how they can help the reader to understand what they have written.

---

26   Mellinkoff, D, 1963, *The Language of the Law*, Little Brown, Boston, p 391.

My first thought had been to write: "in summary, the lawyer who writes in plain language tries to put himself in the reader's shoes. He thinks about ...". I caught myself so quickly that that version never reached the paper. I simply converted the same words to the plural. It is not always appropriate to use the plural, but it is one of a range of options to consider.

- *Use "you" or "one"*

  For example, see p 158:

  > The particular solution you pick is less important than the fact that you have addressed the problem.

  This could be also be written with *one* instead of *you*.

- *Change the phrasing*

  If ... then clauses which are gender-specific can be changed to avoid the pronoun. For example:

  > If a member applies for a dispensation, *he* must do it in writing.

  becomes:

  > A member *who* applies for a dispensation must do it in writing.

  Similarly,

  > If a director decides to vote on a resolution, he must disclose all relevant interests.

  might become:

  > On deciding to vote on a resolution, a director must disclose all relevant interests.

- *Select neutral words*

  This book is about *writers, drafters* and *authors* – not *draftsmen* or *authoresses*. The implication of a word like "poetess", for example, is that she is not a *real* poet. And using the suffix *–man* can imply that women are excluded or invisible. As the Australian government *Style Manual* points out:

  > With women now routinely undertaking roles once performed exclusively by men, the use of 'man' in such titles seems out of step.

  and:

The principle of avoiding gender-specific occupational terms means that those that specify women should also be set aside. Thus 'actress', 'manageress' and 'waitress' are better replaced by 'actor', 'manager' and 'waiter'. The use of gender-specific modifiers, as in 'woman doctor' or 'male nurse' should only be used where the information is essential to the context.[27]

There is almost always a perfectly acceptable alternative word. Etymological arguments about whether the suffix –*man* is a generic term for both sexes don't address the real problem, which is the question of how the reader perceives the word.

- *Use "they" with a singular noun*

Did you notice on p 97 when I wrote:

> The writer takes the reader through all those steps as well, whether *they* like it or not, before the writer yields up the answer?

I used the plural pronoun *they* with the singular subject *the reader*. This is a fairly common usage in spoken English, and it is a structure that has been approved by the United States Council of Teachers of English for written usage. Before it is too quickly dismissed as "ungrammatical", we should remember that at some point in our language's past we switched our second person singular pronoun from the "grammatical" *thou* to the "ungrammatical" *you*. I wonder if there was as much justification for that "error".

Most people don't realise that they are already using *they* as singular pronoun, in speech and perhaps in writing. When we don't know the gender of the subject we are referring to, we might say, "If anybody wants me, tell them I'm out" or "No one can tell what lies in store for them". This usage has been recognised by the three great unabridged dictionaries of the English language: the Oxford English Dictionary,[28] Webster's Third New International Dictionary,[29] and the Dictionary of the English Language.[30] Their entries for *they* all quote this usage

---

27 2002, *Style Manual for Authors, Editors and Printers*, 6th edition, John Wiley & Sons Australia Ltd, pp 59-60.

28 (1989) 2nd edition, Clarendon Press, Oxford.

29 (2002) Merriam-Webster Inc.

30 (1987) Random House.

as far back as the 14th century. Many other dictionaries also refer to this singular use of *they*.

The Australian Corporations Law Simplification Program adopted this technique for its rewrite of the Corporations Law, and has published compelling evidence, including the dictionaries I've just mentioned, to support the move.[31] The paper supports the technique with references to dictionaries, literature, HW Fowler, research done at Sydney University and Macquarie University, legal documents and forms, and legislation already in force in Australia and elsewhere.

One of the other jurisdictions that has adopted the singular use of *they* as part of a gender-neutral drafting policy is the province of Ontario in Canada. The reasoning behind this decision has been outlined by Ontario's Chief Legislative Counsel, Donald Revell, in a paper called "'Themself' and non-sexist style in Canadian legislative drafting".[32] The article notes that they have had no negative comments from the Parliament, the press or the public about the "nonsexist" drafting policy. In fact, they say, there have been almost no comments at all. The authors of the article believe this confirms that the issue is taken for granted, even in legislation.[33]

South Africa has also adopted the technique: in the South African Constitution, section 10 reads:

> Everyone has inherent dignity and the right to have their dignity respected and protected.

Still, it takes some confidence for lawyers to "break" a grammatical "rule" like this. Some worry that their clients will think less of them for using "bad grammar". But lawyers are hardly at the cutting edge of our language's development. This technique of using the singular *they* has been standard policy for some book publishers for more than 10 years. The spoken language has already moved in that direction. Written language is following. Lawyers should not lag too far behind, just

---

31 Corporations Law Simplification Task Force, 1995, *Drafting Issues: A singular use of THEY*, Commonwealth Attorney-General's Department, (1994-95) 5 *Scribes Journal of Legal Writing* 87.

32 Article by Revell, D, Schuh, C and Moisan, M, originally published in *English Today* 37, Vol 10, January 1994 and reprinted in *Clarity* No 31, October 1994, p 27.

33 Same article, *Clarity* No 31, p 41.

because they fear being seen as ill-educated by those who believe that language cannot change.

Salutations

One of the most obvious formulas in legal and business writing that does not allow for women as participants in law and business, is the common salutation of a letter: *Dear Sirs*.

In these days when women are about to outnumber men in law schools (if that is not already the case) it seems absurd for firms of lawyers to continue to refer to each other in this way. Several possible solutions have been tried. Some are:

- Find out exactly who you are writing to and address the letter to that person by name (eg *Dear Ms Smith*).

- If that is not possible write to the organisation using its name (eg *Dear Smith, Smith & Smith*).

- If that doesn't appeal, write *Dear Sir or Madam*.

- One salutation I have seen occasionally from law firm to law firm is *Dear Partners*.

- A more radical alternative adopted by one New Zealand firm is to abandon the salutation altogether and start the letter with the heading. After all, the address appears in full immediately above where the salutation normally goes, so there is no question of confusion about the intended recipient.

The particular solution you pick is less important than the fact that you have addressed the problem.

In case there is anyone who still thinks this exercise in gender-neutral drafting is pointless, or merely an unnecessary cosmetic exercise, consider that the Australian government *Style Manual* devotes a whole chapter to "Effective and inclusive language",[34] and gender-neutral drafting is part of the policy of many governments, including the Australian, Victorian and New South Wales governments.

---

34   Chapter 4, which also deals with the need for writers to be ethnically and culturally sensitive.

In New South Wales, the Parliamentary Counsel's Office officially adopted a policy of gender-neutral drafting on 16 August 1983, making New South Wales the first Australian jurisdiction to do so. In 1994 the Office began a specific program to get rid of gender-specific language in the existing statutes. Various Statute Law (Miscellaneous Provisions) Acts have been passed to remove gender-specific language from New South Wales Acts and replace it with gender-neutral language. Gender specific language is being removed from subordinate legislation by staged repeal under the Subordinate Legislation Act 1989.

The Commonwealth Parliamentary Counsel began a gender-neutral policy in 1984, and this is enshrined in, among other places, the Acts Interpretation Act 1901 which no longer says that a reference to the male gender includes the female. It was amended in 1984 to say:

> In any Act, unless the contrary intention appears:
> (a)   words importing a gender include every other gender.[35]

There is also a section dealing with the way to refer to a Chair (or Deputy Chair) of a body. It says:

> (1) Where an Act establishes an office of Chair of a body, the Chair may be referred to as Chair, Chairperson, Chairman, Chairwoman or by any other such term as the person occupying the office so chooses.
>
> (2) If a person occupying an office mentioned in subsection (1) does not make known his or her choice of term, the person may be referred to by whichever of the following terms that a person addressing that person considers appropriate:
> (a)   Chair;
> (b)   Chairperson;
> (c)   Chairman;
> (d)   Chairwoman.

The provisions are repeated for Deputy Chairs.[36]

The corresponding section in the New South Wales Interpretation Act[37] has a subsection which allows a person whose statutory title is "chairperson", "chairman" or "chairwoman" to use "which-

---

35   Section 23.
36   Section 18B.
37   Section 19.

ever of those terms is appropriate" for the office-holder. Again, there is room for personal preference.[38]

Gender-neutral drafting is more than just a cosmetic or symbolic matter. It can actually affect the way we perceive ourselves. And it can affect the way we act, or influence others to act. This point was made forcefully at a plain language conference held in Vancouver in 1992.[39] A (female) judge told the conference how, for 10 years, she had instructed juries that they should appoint a "foreman". Then one day she decided to say instead that they should appoint a "foreperson". For the first time in her 10-year experience of instructing juries, they appointed a woman.

The drafters of the South African Constitution recognised this too. In some provisions they decided to refer specifically to gender. For example, in section 86(1) they made the point that women may also hold high office:

> At its first sitting after its election, and whenever necessary to fill a vacancy, the National Assembly must elect a woman or a man from among its members to be the President.[40]

In George Orwell's essay "Politics and the English Language",[41] he expresses the view that language can influence thought. This is a view shared by Glanville Williams in his essay "Language and the Law".[42] The linguist Edward Sapir expressed the same view in 1929. He said:

> Language is a guide to social reality ... it powerfully conditions all thinking about social problems and processes ... The fact of the matter is that the real world is to a large extent built upon the language habits of the group.[43]

Another linguist, Benjamin Lee Whorf, has described language as a "vast pattern" by which a person:

---

38 For more on "Chairs", see Asprey, M, "A 'chair' with no leg to stand on", *Clarity* No 41, April 1998, p 9 and *Australian Style*, Vol 6, No 2, December 1998.

39 *Just Language*, 22-24 October 1992, organised by the Plain Language Institute of British Columbia.

40 The same technique is used in section 174(1) concerning judicial appointments.

41 Orwell, G, "Politics and the English Language" (cited at note 24).

42 (1945) 61 *LQR* 71.

43 Sapir, E, 1929, in Mandelbaum, DG (ed), 1949, *Culture, Language and Personality; Selected Essays*, University of California Press, Berkeley and Los Angeles, pp 68-69.

not only communicates, but also analyses nature, notices or neglects types of relationships and phenomena, channels his reasoning and builds the houses of his consciousness.[44]

If language can shape thought, then it is important not to be careless with it. We should not ignore the issue of gender in our writing. Even if gender-neutral drafting requires extra effort, it is important we make that effort. As with most things, the effort diminishes with practice.

Be flexible

That deals with the most common of the strange grammatical structures that we need to avoid if we want to write in plain language. But we must be flexible.

Nearly every grammatical structure I have listed in this chapter can be used correctly, if we are selective. There are times when we must use the passive voice or draft in the negative. There are times when putting an adverbial clause before a verb is the most natural way of expressing a thought. If these things are done thoughtfully and sparingly they do not make our writing cluttered or unclear.

On the other hand, it is difficult to think of an occasion when using a proviso would be acceptable, or when it is proper to use masculine words to refer to females, or males and females together.

The point of all this is not to lay down yet another set of rules to be slavishly followed in preference to the old rules of grammar. It is that if we want to improve and simplify our legal writing style, we should at least be alive to all these problem areas and be aware of their effect on what we write.

We now come to consider some habit-forming words and phrases that seem to affect lawyers in particular.

---

44   Carroll, JB (ed), 1956, *Language, Thought and Reality: Selected Writings of Benjamin Lee Whorf*, The MIT Press, Cambridge, Mass, p 252.

Chapter 9

Legal affectations and other nasty habits

Latin

We saw in Chapter 7, in the context of technical terms, that our clients do not come to us for Latin lessons. Latin is *sometimes* a useful shorthand among lawyers, though this is less so as the years go by. And it does tend to spread into documents and letters to clients. When it does that, it ought to be translated or cut out.

The only excuse for using Latin in a letter to your client is that your client is an ancient Roman.

Of course there are some Latin phrases and symbols that have entered the English language and their meaning is well known. For example: *de facto, versus, per cent, per capita, quid pro quo, ie* and *eg*.[1] Plain language does not require these commonly used and well understood expressions to be eliminated.[2]

But there are others that lawyers tend to use, almost as if they think everyone either already knows what they mean or is dying to find out. Some of the common ones are:

ab initio	*in personam*	*re*
a fortiori	*mens rea*	*res ipsa loquitur*
bona fide	*mutatis mutandis*	*sui generis*
et al	*obiter dictum*	*sui juris*
ex parte	*per stirpes*	*uberrimae fidei*
	quantum meruit	

---

1   I am tempted to add *subpoena* to this list, but for two things: the difficult spelling, and the fact that Lord Woolf, in his recent review of the Civil Procedure Rules of England and Wales, has replaced it with *witness summons*. Against this is an anecdote I heard that a witness, when faced with a *witness summons* said, "What's this, a subpoena?"

2   "Is Magna Carta (The Great Charter) to be translated and its real name abandoned?" John Gray misguidedly asks in the introduction to *Lawyers' Latin*, Trafalgar Square Robert Hale Ltd, London, 2002.

All of these expressions, and the other Latin expressions we use when we write or talk to other lawyers, can be readily translated into English when they are going into documents that are to be read by non-Roman non-lawyers: and they should be.

Case references

How automatically case references seem to flow from our lips and pens. When you read our letters you would think lawyers are not allowed to refer to cases without giving the full citation.

It is appropriate to give a full citation when one lawyer quotes a case to another. In fact, it would be discourteous not to. But when we write to or for non-lawyers, there is no need to clutter up the letter with citations. By all means refer to the case by name. It is often helpful, and even interesting to do so. But don't bother to give the client the details that would enable them to look the case up for themselves – unless of course you know they would like to do so.

The client who sees the case reference will not be impressed, because they know it is your job to know these things. The client will probably suspect what we all know – that you are just putting the case reference down so that it is in the file for next time you want to look it up.

Don't waste your client's time by using their letters as memo pads. Use a memo pad!

Where

This is another word that lawyers love. Nearly everyone else writes *when* or *if* to describe a circumstance, but lawyers love *where*. Even worse than *where* on its own, is *in cases where* or *in cases in which.*

Legal drafting books have tried to teach lawyers the distinction that was made in the past between *where* and *when*, but there are problems with that distinction, and it just doesn't come naturally. Dick says that *where* may be used if "frequent occurrence of an event is contemplated", and *when* may be used if the event is only expected to happen once, or rarely. But Dick admits it is often hard to tell how often something will happen.[3]

---

3   Dick QC, RC, 1995, *Legal Drafting in Plain Language*, 3rd edition, Carswell, Toronto, p 145.

This sort of analysis ignores the fact that this use of *where* is drifting out of our language. And that drift has been recognised by our legislators. For example, the Law Reform Commission of Victoria reports that in 1985 the Victorian Attorney-General directed that *where* should no longer be used as a synonym of *if* to introduce a condition.[4] The Australian Office of Parliamentary Counsel, in its *Plain English Manual*, says:

> The traditional style uses "where" to introduce a set of facts, but in common usage the word conveys the idea of place. Say "if" to introduce a set of facts. But if the event is so certain that "if" is inappropriate, use "when".[5]

Speaking of conditions, there are also those who say that the distinction between *where* and *when* ought to be kept, because they say *where* is the word that should be used for a case, and *when* is the word that signifies a condition.

It was George Coode who first formulated this idea of cases and conditions. We looked at Coode's rules in Chapter 6.[6] I mentioned then that Coode's analysis had been criticised by a several commentators, including Dr EA Driedger QC[7] and Robert Dick QC.[8] Dick has summarised what Driedger said about Coode's cases and conditions:

> there is no grammatical distinction between the case and the condition that Coode describes. Each is a clause or phrase that modifies the predicate and is joined to other parts of the sentence by a conjunction or a preposition. It is often impossible to identify a particular phrase or clause as the case or condition, using Coode's definitions.[9]

What is the point of reviving such artificial concepts?

The plain language approach has been summarised by Bryan Garner this way:

---

4   1987, Law Reform Commission of Victoria, Report No 9, *Plain English and the Law*, Appendix 1, p 45 – Drafting Manual.

5   Paragraph 86, p 20, online version as at 11 March 2003, <www.opc.gov.au>.

6   Pages 111-114.

7   1976, *The Composition of Legislation, Legislative Forms and Precedents*, 2nd edition Department of Justice, Canada and 1982, *A Manual of Instructions for Legislative and Legal Writing*, Department of Justice, Canada, pp 3-4.

8   Dick QC, RC, 1995, *Legal Drafting in Plain Language*, p 60 and following pages (cited at note 3).

9   Same work, p 64.

The best word in stating a circumstance to which a statement relates is either *if* or *when*, the word *where* being archaic and legalistic to nonlegal readers ... One writer actually suggests a nuance between *when* and *where*, but actual usage has never reflected this distinction.[10]

Above and *below*

These words, when used in the sense of "clause 4 above" or "paragraph 6 below" are unnecessary. They seem to be an affectation, perhaps even stemming from the days when documents were only one page long, and there was a physical "above" and "below". Even worse, when they are used without a specific page, paragraph or clause reference (as in "see below") they are vague and unhelpful.

Any, each, every and *all*

Lawyers seem to have a fetish about these words. Most legal documents are littered with them. It looks as if the writers are afraid that unless they write *any applicant, all directors, each shareholder,* and *every person,* one member of these groups will slip through the net.

These are useful words, certainly. But if we use them all the time, they won't mean as much when we want to use them for emphasis.

Most commentators agree that the indefinite article "a" can often be used instead of these words. But sometimes it *is* appropriate to use them. For example, if you want to impose an obligation separately on each individual in a class, it is appropriate to use *each,* as in:

> each applicant must complete the prescribed form.

In that example, because you wish to emphasise that there is an obligation on each individual applicant, it is best to use the word *each.* But it would have been possible to use the indefinite article instead, as in:

> an applicant must complete the prescribed form.

---

10   Garner, BA, 1995, *A Dictionary of Modern Legal Usage*, Oxford University Press, New York and Oxford, 2nd edition, under *where*, p 928. The writer he quotes is GC Thornton in *Legislative Drafting* (an earlier, 2nd edition, 1979).

You would have achieved the same meaning, but you wouldn't have achieved the emphasis.

Two other ways you could have achieved emphasis in that sentence are:

> every applicant must complete the prescribed form

or

> all applicants must complete the prescribed form.

But consider the effect on the reader if you *always* use *any, each, every* or *all*, when *a* would do. Emphasis is only emphatic if used sparingly.

Again, some commentators have tried to analyse when is the right time to use some of those words, and have come up with some rules. The rules stated by Dickerson[11] are:

1. Use *any* to give a right, privilege or power (eg: any applicant may complete the prescribed form).
2. Use *each* to impose an obligation (eg: each applicant must complete the prescribed form).
3. Use *no* to restrict a right, privilege or power (eg: no applicant may complete the prescribed form).

That is an interesting analysis, but it seems to me that the indefinite article does just as well. Here is my version of each:

1. *An* applicant may complete the prescribed form.
2. *An* applicant must complete the prescribed form.
3. *An* applicant may not complete the prescribed form.

Is there a difference in meaning? If there is, I can't see it. The difference is in emphasis. That is all. So why not try to reserve *any, each, every* and *all* for emphasis?

The same, the said **and** *such*

These are particular legal usages of words that are rarely seen outside legal and other "official" documents. They look strange to most readers and make writing stilted. We can replace them with

---

11 Dickerson, R, 1986, *The Fundamentals of Legal Drafting*, 2nd edition, Little, Brown and Company, Boston and Toronto, p 217.

more usual words, or leave them out altogether. Here is what I mean:

The same: either replace those words with a pronoun, or leave them out and rephrase the sentence. For example, we can rewrite:

> The property may be sold by the Executor auctioning *the same*.

either as:

> The property may be sold by the Executor auctioning *it*.

or:

> The property may be sold by the Executor by auction.

The said: Replace *the said* with *the, that* or *those*. For example, we can rewrite:

> The stock must be counted and the price for *the said* stock is to be calculated using a unit price of $10.00.

as:

> The stock must be counted and the price for *the* stock is to be calculated using a unit price of $10.00

There can be no doubt about which stock we are pricing. When things get a little more complicated, you might be better to use *that* or *those*. For example:

> ABC Company may sell any shares the Borrower owns if the loan is not repaid on time and ABC Company may complete the transfer forms for *the said* shares on the Borrower's behalf.

becomes:

> ABC Company may sell any shares the Borrower owns if the loan is not repaid on time and ABC Company may complete the transfer forms for *those* shares on the Borrower's behalf.

There is no truth in the belief of some lawyers that *those shares* leaves doubt about which shares we are talking about. *Those* is a perfectly adequate referent, as is *that*.

Such: The lawyer's beloved "defining" use of the word *such*, as in:

> ... any such person must register an interest

can always be replaced by *the, that* or *those* or a
pronoun. In that respect it is a mixture of *the same* and
the said. The word *such* was traditionally used as a
reference to a category or kind of persons or things. It
can still do that job, if used carefully.[12] But less skilled
writers use *such* to refer to *any* person or thing that has
been mentioned before. In neither case is there a real
need to use *such*. For example, take the sentence:

> Recipients of the invalid pension are not entitled to
> receive unemployment benefits in addition to *such* pen-
> sion. *Such* recipients may apply for a supplementary
> benefit.

We could be said to be referring to a class of pension
and a class of recipient. But we could get rid of both
*such*es; we could replace the first with *the* or *that*, and
the second with *those*:

> Recipients of the invalid pension are not entitled to
> receive unemployment benefits in addition to *the* pen-
> sion. *Those* recipients may apply for a supplementary
> benefit.

The meaning does not change at all, and it does not
create ambiguity to do without *such*.

Whereas and recitals

Using *whereas* in the sense of *but on the contrary* is not the problem.
That sense of *whereas* is still in everyday use to show a contrast (eg
"He speaks fluent French, whereas I only remember a few words
from my high school days").

The problem with *whereas* is its archaic use in the sense of *given
the fact that*. That, and the way lawyers use it as a banner on the
front of their documents, in the recitals:

> WHEREAS ...
> AND WHEREAS ...
> AND WHEREAS ...

---

12   See, Thornton, G, *Legislative Drafting*, Butterworths, London, 1996, p 106.

In fact, before we even begin to consider *whereas,* the question that we should ask is: why do lawyers still have so many recitals in their documents?

Recitals are usually formal statements that come before the main body or "operative part" of the agreement. Recitals have traditionally been used to set out background material. Even though they are not in the "operative part" of the agreement, they are not completely inoperative. If it appears to have been intended by the parties, recitals can create a covenant.[13]

Recitals can also provide evidence of the intention of the parties in some circumstances.[14] And recitals may also be used as evidence of the existence of facts because of the doctrine of "estoppel by convention".[15]

According to Spencer Bower & Turner,[16] the doctrine is based on the proposition that justice must stop the parties to a transaction from denying what they have assumed to be the facts on which the transaction is based. There is a sub-class of estoppel by convention, called "estoppel by deed". In cases involving estoppel by deed, we usually find the assumed facts, which give rise to the estoppel, in the recitals or other "non-operative parts" of the document. This is where, so Spencer Bower & Turner tell us, the parties have agreed "to assume the facts as the conventional basis upon which they have founded their contractual obligations".[17]

For these reasons, some lawyers are reluctant to delete recitals from their drafting. In fact, some lawyers pack their documents full of facts that they think might possibly be useful, just in case they need to use them defensively. If the facts are all set out in the recitals, they say, they can use the recitals as evidence, or they can invoke the doctrine of estoppel and stop the other party to the transaction from denying those facts.

---

13 *Hill v Carr* (1676) 1 Cas in Ch 294; *Aspdin v Austin* (1844) 5 QB 671 (approved by Mason J of the High Court of Australia in *Ansett Transport Industries (Operations) Pty Ltd v Commonwealth* (1977) 139 CLR 54); *Mackenzie v Childers* (1889) 43 ChD 265; *Buckland v Buckland* [1900] 2 Ch 164; *Re Weston* [1900] 2 Ch 164.

14 For example, section 53(2) of the Conveyancing Act 1919 (NSW) states that recitals in some documents which are 20 years old can be used as evidence.

15 The word *estoppel* is dealt with on pp 117-118 of this book.

16 1977, *Estoppel by Representation,* 3rd edition, Butterworths, London, pp 157 and following pages.

17 Same work, p 159.

But if the facts are so important, why aren't they in the main body of the agreement? If we want to be able to rely on them, why aren't they warranties instead of recitals? If they are warranties, they can actually found a cause of action. The injured party can sue for breach of warranty, and it is a simple matter to point to the contract and say: "here is the promise you broke – you owe me damages".

Three Australian cases illustrate that the doctrine of estoppel by deed operates in quite limited circumstances.

Offshore Oil NL v Southern Cross Exploration NL[18] is an example of a case where the recitals of a deed *did not* stop a party from disputing the facts set out in the recitals. In the Supreme Court of New South Wales, Clarke J (as he was then) said that estoppel is only created in proceedings which arise from the particular transaction that the parties entered into on the basis of the assumed facts (as set out in the recitals in that case). In the *Offshore Oil* case, the proceedings were based on a *related* transaction, but not *the* transaction, to which the recitals related. Therefore, estoppel was not available.

A similar point is made in *Garraway v Synergy Pty Ltd*,[19] in which Nader J held that the recitals of a deed did not create an estoppel because the action brought by the liquidator was not an action on the deed which contained the recitals that the liquidator wanted to rely on. That was enough to dispose of the case, but the judge also reviewed some of the authorities on estoppel. He cited Jordan CJ, who said that, for a party to be bound by estoppel by deed, the deed must contain a "precise and unambiguous state-ment of the fact in question" and that the statement must be a statement *by* the defendants (not something from which one might infer a fact). In other words, there must be a "clear and explicit statement" made *by the defendants* that a fact exists.[20]

More recently, in *Lewis v Nortex Pty Ltd*, Young CJ in Eq of the Supreme Court of New South Wales emphasised the limitations of relying on recitals. He said:

---

18 (1985) 3 NSWLR 337.
19 Unreported, NTSC, Nader J, 13 November 1989. Extracts reproduced in (1990) ANZ Conv R 117.
20 *Discount Finance Ltd v Gehrig's NSW Wines Ltd* (1940) 57 WN (NSW) 226.

Recitals in a deed are not representations of fact on the faith of which a stranger to the deed is entitled to act without enquiry: *Trinidad Asphalte Co v Coryat* [1989] AC 587, 592. Furthermore, one only has an estoppel by a recital in a deed in an action based on the deed. In a collateral action there can be no estoppel: *Carter v Carter* (1857) 3 K & J 617, 645; 69 ER 1256, 1268.[21]

In short, as the judges in those cases were at pains to point out, the doctrine of estoppel by deed is not as useful as some lawyers seem to think.

Even if we do allow that sometimes it might be quite useful to have background material set out in recitals, so that the context of the transaction is explained at the beginning of the document, there is another pitfall to consider. The recitals can have an unintended effect on the operative provisions. Two English cases show that if the relevant provisions of the operative part of an agreement are expressed in a general way, the court may limit those general words by reference to more specific terms in a recital.[22]

And it is not just the recitals which can restrict the interpretation of the operative part of an agreement. In a 1978 New Zealand case,[23] the Court of Appeal restricted the scope of a guarantee by reference to its introductory words, which described the consideration given for the guarantee in a more limited way than the rest of the agreement did. These introductory words appeared before the first clause and, although they weren't set out under the heading WHEREAS or RECITALS, they were in that unnamed land before the main body of the agreement.

The court in that case did not draw any distinction between what appeared before clause 1 and what appeared after it. It read the agreement, and construed it as a whole. It determined the intention of the parties from the plain words of the document, introductory words and all.

Therefore, we should be careful about what we put in the recitals and the other introductory material: superfluous or loosely drafted background material can come back to bite us and should

---

21   [2001] NSWSC 511; (2001) 10 BPR 19,035 at [37].

22   *Danby v Coutts* (1885) 29 ChD 500 and *Ex parte Dawes; re Moon* (1886) 17 QBD 275 (applied recently in Australia in *Western Power Corp v Normandy Power Pty Ltd* [2001] WASC 202).

23   *National Bank of New Zealand v West* [1978] 2 NZLR 451.

be left out. Important material should really be in the body of the agreement itself, so that its status is unambiguous and it is not skipped over by the reader.

And if we *must* have recitals, it is best either to label them as recitals, by using the heading RECITALS, or, if we feel confident enough to do without the technical label, we can give the recitals a more useful label, such as BACKGROUND.[24]

For those who are worried that changing the label of the recitals to BACKGROUND might change the character of the recitals to something else, I should point out that using the heading WHEREAS for recitals does not have that effect.

Pursuant to

This is an expression we are so used to that we barely notice we are using it. Yet to most non-lawyers it is one of the hallmarks of legalese. Ordinary people say *under* if they mean to refer loosely to something (eg: "*Under* the law, you must put in a tax return"). Or, if they are being more specific, they say *according to* (eg: "You must build the model *according to* the directions on the box").

There is no reason why lawyers cannot do the same. We should be able to say "Under the contract, you must indemnify the Buyer against claims by customers" or "You must complete the share transfer form *according to* article 44 of the articles of association".

In fact, the Federal Court of Australia has indicated that *pursuant to, in pursuance of, by virtue of* and *in the exercise of powers conferred by* mean the same thing as *under*.[25] The Australian Office of Parliamentary Counsel agrees, and recommends using *under*, or *because of* in place of *pursuant to, in pursuance of* and *by virtue of*.[26]

Moneys and *monies*

What are *moneys* and *monies*? Are they different from *money*? To the rest of the community, *moneys* and *monies* are archaic forms of the word *money*. Yet to lawyers and bankers they are mellifluous

---

24   In *Lewis v Nortex Pty Ltd* (cited at note 21), Young CJ in Eq held that a section headed "Introduction" in a deed was the plain English version of "Recitals".

25   *Collector of Customs v Brian Lawlor* (1979) 24 ALR 307.

26   *Plain English Manual*, p 40, online version as at 11 March 2003, <www.opc. gov.au>.

words we won't let go of. Somehow, we think, a mortgage or a loan document doesn't sound quite right if it deals with mere *money* rather than the more abundant-sounding and richer *moneys* or *monies.*

Moneys or *monies* did traditionally have a sense of "sums of money" about it. But it is by no means clear that this will come across to the reader. It would be better, if you want to refer to "sums of money", to do just that.

The Law Reform Commission of Victoria is short and sweet on the subject of *money.* It says:

> Use the word *money.* The form *moneys* or *monies* is obsolete and should not be used.[27]

The time problem

Lawyers are always worried about time. They never have enough time to do what they have to do. They keep slipping into the future when they draft.[28] They talk about *at this particular point in time,* rather than *now.* And they worry about how to cover the future in their documents.

So they sometimes use expressions like *at any time* and *from time to time* and even *at any time and from time to time.* They use those expressions to save them from a court holding that when they refer to an action it should be read as occurring once only. For example, they may not be content with:

> If the Bank considers that the Mortgaged Property is in jeopardy it may appoint a receiver.

They worry that writing it that way might imply that the Bank can only act once. That it has one chance to consider and one chance to act. If it blows that, they think, it can't ever rely on the clause again.

So they might rewrite it as:

> If at any time and from time to time the Bank considers that the Mortgaged Property is in jeopardy it may at any time and from time to time appoint a receiver.

---

27   1987, Law Reform Commission of Victoria, *Report No 9*, "Plain English and the Law", Appendix 1, p 59 – Drafting Manual.
28   See p 136.

But do we really need the words *from time to time* and *at any time*?

I referred earlier to the principle that the law is "constantly speaking" and said that it generally applies to both statutes and private documents.[29] But several commentators have said that we can use words like *if at any time* if there is any doubt about that principle applying to those words.

The key point is to use those words *only if there is likely to be any doubt* about whether the provision should be interpreted as applying more than once. Remember that the commentators agree that, generally, anything that is expressed in the present or the past will be interpreted as applying whenever the circumstances occur and whenever the obligation has to be performed or the condition has to be satisfied.[30] They only recommend the expression *if at any time* for cases where there might be doubt. Normally it is not needed. That makes sense. Otherwise we'd have to use expressions like that constantly, and risk diminishing their effect when we really do need them. So there is no need to say:

> If at any time two or more members are present in person or by proxy, attorney or company representative and entitled to vote at a meeting of the Company, there is a quorum.

We can delete the reference to *If at any time* and simply write:

> Two or more members present in person or by proxy, attorney or company representative and entitled to vote at a meeting of the Company is a quorum.

Similarly, we don't need to say:

> If there is any inconsistency at any time between the special conditions attached from time to time to this agreement and the provisions of this agreement, the special conditions prevail.

We just say:

> If there is any inconsistency between the special conditions attached to this agreement and the provisions of this agreement, the special conditions prevail.

---

29 Page 137 and following.
30 For example, see Aitkin, JK, 1995, *Piesse: The Elements of Drafting*, 9th edition, Law Book Company, Sydney, p 67; Dick QC, RC, 1995, *Legal Drafting in Plain Language*, pp 88-89 (cited at note 3); and Robinson, Dr S, 1973, *Drafting*, Butterworths, Sydney, p 42.

If we are sparing in our use of these time expressions, we can insert them for emphasis when the normal implication would be that the provision operated once only, as for example it might be with certain kinds of payments or the giving of unusual powers. But normally, as the commentators say, that is not necessary.

Incidentally, there is another problem with the expression *at all times*. Its misuse can lead to ludicrous results. The 5th edition of *Stroud's Judicial Dictionary* dryly pointed out one example:

> A covenant in a mining lease to work the mine "at all times", is frequently incapable of literal performance.[31]

Another good example is a clause I have seen, also in a lease, under which the tenant was obliged to "make a reasonable amount of noise at all times". One wonders what sort of noise would qualify … perhaps a constant low hum?

Hereafter, hereinafter and heretofore

I mentioned these expressions earlier in the context of archaic words.[32] The problem with these three, and the other archaic "time" words, is that they are imprecise. When does *hereafter* begin? When or where is *heretofore?* Professor Mellinkoff points out that the starting point can vary. He says:

> When legislators say hereafter, it sounds as if they mean as-soon-as-we-pass-this-law, and sometimes they do. More often, the courts say they mean after-this-law-becomes-effective. And so, when a statute is amended and republished, the hereafter may refer to two effective dates, one for the old part and one for the new.[33]

Hereafter is clearly so uncertain that we should avoid it altogether. The same applies to *heretofore.*

Now

Another "time" word that creates the same sort of problem (when does it start?) is *now*. It is not an archaic or difficult word, of course,

---

31   James, JS, *Stroud's Judicial Dictionary*, 5th edition, Sweet and Maxwell Ltd, London Vol 1, A-C, p 212. Example quoted in *Clarity* Newsletter No 17, June 1990, p 9. Sadly, this observation is missing from the 6th edition, which seems to have a diminished sense of humour: Greenberg, G and Milbrook, A (2000) *Stroud's Judicial Dictionary,* 6th edition, Sweet & Maxwell, London, Vol 1: A-F.

32   Page 124.

33   1963, *The Language of the Law*, Little Brown, Boston, p 312.

but it can create difficulties in legal documents. When is *now* in a document? *Now* when I'm drafting it, *now* when you're signing it, *now* when the event we are talking about is occurring or *now* when we are in court?

We often see *now* in documents. For example in "all money" mortgages and other securities, which secure the repayment of:

> all amounts now or in the future owing to the Lender

or some similar formula. The question I always ask when I see those provisions is: when is *now*? And when, for that matter, is *the future*? When does it start? When is *the past*? Is it anything that happened before we ended up arguing in court? Or was it before we began to talk about the deal? We need to be more precise.

A starting point

In each of these cases: *hereafter, hereinafter, heretofore, now, the future* and *the past,* we are creating problems for the reader and the later interpreters of the document. We should be providing the reader with a point of reference: giving them a way to measure the time.

The State of Victoria has recognised this problem in its Interpretation of Legislation Act 1984. Section 44(7) provides:

> In a provision of an Act or a subordinate instrument the expression "now", "heretofore" or "hereafter" shall be construed as referring to the time when the provision in which the expression occurs came into operation.

We need to give the reader similar help when we draft private documents. Give the reader a starting point to count from. If the relevant starting point is the date of the document, say so. Write "at the date of this agreement" or "after this agreement is signed by the parties" or "14 days from the date of this agreement" or "by 5pm on 30 June 2004". Be exact in your time measurements. And always give a clear starting point for any calculations.

Forthwith

Another "time" word that is most imprecise is *forthwith*. Like *heretofore* and *hereafter*, it is archaic. But it is also unclear. Bryan Garner, in *A Dictionary of Modern Legal Usage*, called it "a fuzzy word with no pretence of precision".[34] Professor Mellinkoff has traced its meanings from the Middle English, when it was *forth with,* and meant "along with, at the same time with something else",[35] through various shades of meaning, from *immediately,* through *such convenient time as the court shall judge reasonable,* and *without unnecessary procrastination or delay* to *a reasonable time.*

Forthwith is not a word we should use unless we are *intending* vagueness. If we don't intend vagueness, it is better to specify a time limit if we can. For example, "By 5pm that day" or "By the close of business".

The word *immediately* is often suggested as a better alternative to *forthwith.* And it certainly is more common in general usage outside law, so it is more in keeping with the aims of plain language. But it seems it is no more precise.

Piesse[36] quotes cases that say that *forthwith* and *immediately* are synonyms, "stronger" than the expression *within a reasonable time,* and that they mean something like "without any delay" or "with as little delay as possible".

Time and again we see statements that *forthwith* means the same thing as *immediately.* But we are also told that both words mean something other than *immediately.* For example, they have been held to imply "speedy and prompt action and an omission of all delay; in other words that the thing to be done should be done as quickly as is reasonably possible".[37] Halsbury agrees, saying:

> There appears to be no material difference between the terms "immediately" and "forthwith". A provision to the effect that a thing must be done forthwith or immediately means that it must be done as soon as possible in the circumstances, the nature of the act to be done taken into account.[38]

On demand

The expression *on demand* suffers the same problem. It is a "time-honoured" expression in the law, and we can find it in countless loan and security documents, but the common law tells us that a

---

34   1995, 2nd edition, Oxford University Press, New York and Oxford, p 372.

35   Mellinkoff, D, 1963, *The Language of the Law*, p 310 (cited at note 33).

36   Aitken, JK, 1995, *Piesse: The Elements of Drafting*, pp 123-124 (cited at note 30).

37   *R v Berkshire Justices* (1878) 4 QBD 469 (Cockburn CJ).

38   45 *Halsbury's Laws of England* (4th edition Reissue) Vol 45, para 251.

loan payable *on demand* does not actually have to be repaid the minute the demand is made.

Australian law on this question has come into line with the law of the United Kingdom[39] and New Zealand.[40] All three jurisdictions apply what is called the "mechanics of payment" test, and say that the debtor who must pay *on demand* must have an opportunity to get funds from a convenient place. In *Bond v Hongkong Bank of Australia*,[41] the New South Wales Court of Appeal held that a guarantor who had to pay *on demand* had to be given the time to organise whatever "mechanics of payment" it needed to discharge the debt.

In Canada, the question of what is a reasonable time to make an *on demand* payment is a question that has to be determined on the individual facts of every individual case.[42] It seems the expression has *no* meaning that can be anticipated.

The point of all this is that some of the "time" words we use in order to be *precise*, are actually *imprecise* or *misleading*. Often they do not mean what they appear to mean. *Immediately* doesn't always mean *immediately* – it can mean *as soon as possible*. Payment *on demand* may not mean immediately on demand – the mechanics of payment need to be considered.

As lawyers, it is our job to know how the courts have bent the meanings of words in the interests of justice. We must choose our words carefully, so that they accurately reflect the aims of the parties (or the legislators) *and* so that – as far as possible – readers cannot be mislead.

The best way to deal with the time problem, if you need to be precise, is to *specify a time limit* in concrete, measurable terms. Or if you are being lenient, you can use a flexible phrase like *as soon as possible* – but don't expect it to give you speed or precision. We should avoid, if we can, those words that mean something other than they appear to mean.

---

39 *Bank of Baroda v Panessar* [1987] 1 Ch 335.

40 *Gibson v ANZ Banking Group (NZ) Limited* [1986] 1 NZLR 556.

41   (1991) 25 NSWLR 286.

42 *Mister Broadloom Corporation (1968) Ltd v Bank of Montreal* (1979) 101 DLR (3d) 713, 723; *Ronald Elwyn Lister Ltd v Dunlop Canada Ltd* (1982) 135 DLR (3d) 1.

Amounts of time and other commodities

We lawyers also have some difficulty describing numbers and amounts – amounts of time, numbers of people, amounts of things. For example, when we try to describe the number of days notice in a document like a lease, we might write something like:

> The Tenant must give not less than six months notice of its intention to terminate the lease.

What does the *not less than* do in that sentence? Does it help us with the real problem in that sentence, which is: when does the six months start and finish? No. It begs that question, and adds words that don't tell us any more than "six months" on it own told us. If you must give six months notice then you've given six months notice if you give seven months. *That* is not what is confusing about the sentence. If you want to give the reader some *real* help, tell the reader whether a month is 30 days long and so six months is really 180 days, or whether a month is counted from one day in a month to the corresponding day in the next month.

The same thing can be said if we had used the words *at least* in the last example. They too could be deleted.

Strangely enough, *not more than*, which is parallel to *not less than,* does not suffer from the same problem because those words are usually intended to prohibit the additional time or other items. For example:

> This lift is licensed to carry not more than 15 people

has a point to make, because it is when we pass the limit of 15 that trouble can occur.

But the structure *not more than* isn't easy to comprehend, and there is a plainer way to say the same thing. "This lift is licensed to carry a maximum of 15 people" is easier to comprehend, probably because it is framed in the positive, rather than the negative *not more than.*

The time between dates and times can cause similar problems. For example, if we can take up an option to purchase land *between* 30 June and 31 December, can we take up the option on 30 June? Or on 31 December? Is *from* 30 June *to* 31 December any clearer? Perhaps, but if we added the word *inclusive* it would be crystal clear.

And then, would 1 minute to midnight on 31 December be an acceptable time to take up the option?

If that is likely to be a problem, specify the time (eg 5pm on 31 December). Or if the time at which notice may be given is very important in your agreement, then you might want to put in an interpretive clause that makes it clear that notice may only be given after, say, 9am and before 5pm.

In other words, when you are drafting provisions that relate to time or dates, or provisions for which time or dates might be important, you should try to anticipate the problems that the parties might have in working out the time and dates, and clarify anything that might be ambiguous or left unsaid.

Put yourself in the shoes of the party trying to work out how much notice to give or whether the right amount of notice has been given. Make it easy to work out.

This also applies to numbers. Try to be definite if you can. If it is possible to be specific, then be specific. When it comes to numbers, some writers seem to have a morbid fear of the specific. One of my favourite clauses along these lines is this one:

> The Borrower must give more than one and less than three days notice of its intention to prepay interest.

Did the writer mean two?

Drafting by stealth

Lawyers are often accused of saying very little and making it sound like something more than it is. But there is a worse sin: saying something and making it look like nothing. Or hiding it among clauses that deal with a different issue. I call that "drafting by stealth".

The proviso is one way that lawyers sometimes intentionally or unintentionally hide provisions in documents. The afterthought doesn't fit too well into the existing structure of the document, so they put it in a proviso.

Poor organisation is another reason people unintentionally draft by stealth. They have not organised the document well enough to get all the issues that relate to each other in the same place. And they haven't given adequate cross-references and other guides to the reader. So material is hidden from the reader.

Sometimes material is hidden in unexpected places, like schedules that relate to different matters entirely. The bonus the stealthy drafter sees is that the lawyers for the other side might miss the hidden tough provisions and allow their client to sign up without asking for amendments. But these days the courts are examining documents more closely to see if the parties were aware of all their obligations. I've already mentioned several cases in which that was done: *Commercial Bank of Australia v Amadio*,[43] *National Australia Bank Ltd v Nobile*,[44] *Goldsbrough v Ford Credit Aust Ltd*,[45] *Houlahan v Australian & New Zealand Banking Group Ltd*,[46] *Karam v Australia & New Zealand Banking Group Ltd*[47] and *Garcia v National Australia Bank Limited*.[48] In that sort of climate, the person who drafts by stealth takes a great risk.

This chapter has dealt with some of the words, phrases and other habits that lawyers have adopted as their own. The next chapter looks at some ordinary words and phrases that aren't the exclusive property of lawyers, and are free to be overused by everyone.

---

43   (1983) 151 CLR 447.

44   (1988) 100 ALR 227.

45   (1989) ASC¶55-946.

46   (1992) 110 FLR 259.

47   [2001] NSWSC 709.

48   (1998) 194 CLR 395.

Chapter 10

Overused words and formulas

Accordingly

This word is useful. It is so useful that it has been worn out with overuse. It is a grander-sounding alternative for *therefore* and *so*. Gowers suggests we should prefer those two words.[1] Even if we don't give up *accordingly* altogether, we should remember that *therefore* and *so* are simpler (and shorter) alternatives.

The writer

I'm thinking here of that expression when used in this sort of context:

> Should you need any more information, please contact the writer.

How coy it sounds! "I" am the writer, if the letter is written in the first person singular, so I should say so: "please contact *me*".

If the letter is written in the first person plural (we) and the writer writes, "please contact us", the writer might not be being coy, but isn't being too helpful either. Who is "us"? How can the reader telephone or write to "us"?

Of course, pure politeness tells us that we should give the reader a name. And just a name. Not "our Ms Smith". Just Ms Smith, or Mary Smith. And while we're on the subject, how about giving the reader a direct telephone number if it is different from the one on the letterhead? The aim of the game is to help the reader to contact you … not to make it difficult. Each letter you write is a potential marketing tool. Why not make it easy for your clients to give you more work?

---

1   Gowers (Greenbaum and Whitcut eds), 1987, *The Complete Plain Words*, 3rd edition, Penguin Books, London, p 199.

Tired openings

Even though most lawyers are not writing purely for the joy of creation, there is no need for our writing to sound as if it comes from a machine. Most lawyers begin their letters in exactly the same way each time, no matter whom they are writing to or what it's about. Here are a few of the classics.

1. We act for … and are in receipt of your letter of …
2. We refer to your letter of …
3. Please find enclosed …
4. We refer to previous correspondence in this matter …

These openings are so hackneyed that it is doubtful anyone reads them. If that is the case, why use them at all?

Lawyers often say that it is necessary to refer to earlier correspondence, and it is customary to do that by referring to the date. This enables anyone looking through the file to see the string of correspondence.

That may be true, but it doesn't have to be done by using tired old formulas.

How about trying something a little livelier, like:

1. Thank you for your letter asking us to advise you about land tax. We would be delighted to help.
2. In your letter dated 17 July 2003, you asked four questions about your family trust. Here are the answers:
    1. …
    2. … [etc].
3. Here is the document you asked us to prepare …
4. Over the last few weeks we have been gathering evidence for the case …

The overwhelming impression you will give with this sort of fresh approach is not that you are unprofessional, but that you are actually interested in your client's matter or the other business to hand.

Tired endings

If we are tired when we begin a letter, by the time we get to the end we are positively exhausted. We abdicate all control of our writing and switch to automatic pilot. This is the sort of thing we like to finish with:

1. If you have any queries, please do not hesitate to contact the writer.
2. If you require any clarification of the foregoing, please let us know.
3. We trust the foregoing is of assistance to you.
4. We hope that the above meets with your satisfaction.

These phrases are not only hackneyed, they are so hackneyed that they sound insincere. Imagine the impression they make on the client.

And do we think that our clients are so shy that they need to be coaxed to call us or write back? Occasionally that might be so, but there are plenty of clients who would ring up straight away if they had questions, thought the advice was unclear (heaven forbid!), needed more help, or were unsatisfied. And what's more, clients know it is most unlikely that the service will be free.

Understating and equivocating

Lawyers hate to stick their necks out. It seems ironic that a profession that is in the business of giving advice is so reluctant to take a firm view.

Of course, we would hate to be wrong about anything, and for our clients to suffer as a result. So we couch our advice in equivocal language. We say:

> It would appear that …
> It may be that …
> It seems that …
> The court may very well hold that … on the other hand it may hold that …

and it is quite clear that we are trying to avoid taking a stand.

Admittedly, lawyers do have a problem. If we are advising on an uncertain area of law we cannot say:

> The law is that …

or

> It is a fact that …

but there is nothing to prevent us from saying:

> We think that you should …

or

> In our opinion …

or

> The better view is …

or

> We recommend that …

If we use that sort of language, it is still clear that it is only an opinion and not gospel. But at least we express an opinion, rather than an each-way bet. The client is entitled to that opinion because the client is paying for it. Couching the opinion in the language of understatement and equivocation only makes us look weak and incompetent.

As we saw in Chapter 5,[2] writing in a more direct manner can actually help our relationship with the reader. A story reported in the South African journal *De Rebus* in 1993 illustrates this.[3] A lawyer wrote to a government department, in a letter headed "without prejudice", to suggest that a case should be settled. His letter ended:

> Civil servants do not usually reply to letters, but please prove the exception to the rule by replying. If you are not prepared to say "yes" or "no", at least say something, even if it is only "goodbye".

The government department replied, also "without prejudice":

> We are not prepared to say "yes" or "no" and accept the alternative of saying "goodbye".

The lawyer responded:

> You amaze me! Since when has a civil servant had a sense of humour? Instead of marking your letter "without prejudice" you should have marked it "without precedent".

Choosing the right words

It is not always easy to choose the right words, especially when you have all the constraints on you that lawyers have. So much is riding

---

2   Pages 87-88.
3   Reported in "Outside View" (1993) 31(2) NSW *Law Society Journal* 96.

on our choice. And yet, as I've said several times in this book: it is our job to know the right words.

George Orwell, writing about the English language in 1946, described the problem this way:

> prose consists less and less of *words* chosen for the sake of their meaning, and more of phrases tacked together like sections of a pre-fabricated hen-house.[4]

Orwell's theory is that if you avoid the bad habits that he saw in modern written English, you can actually *think more clearly*. This is a view shared by Glanville Williams who wrote:

> Language is perhaps the greatest of all human inventions. Most people think of it merely as the chief means of communication, but it is much more than that: it is the chief medium of thought.[5]

Whether or not this is true as a technical matter, there is no doubt that the care we take in choosing our words and arranging our thoughts is obvious to the reader. Confused and tangled writing makes the reader suspect that it comes from a confused and tangled mind.

The next chapter focuses on some of the little words that have caused problems for lawyers over the years and offers a few suggestions on how to deal with them.

---

4   "Politics and the English Language", in 1985, *The Penguin Essays of George Orwell*, Penguin Books, London, p 356.
5   "Language and the Law" (1945) 61 *LQR* 71.

Chapter 11

Little words:
big problems

And and *or*

Though they are small words, *and* and *or* create many problems. Even very experienced drafters have problems with these words, and often have to think twice before deciding whether to use *and* or *or* in a particular case.

The last two sentences illustrate how *and* and *or* are used in the simplest cases. *And* usually shows we are talking about two things together: *both* apples *and* pears (together). *Or* usually shows we are talking about two things separately: *either* apples *or* pears (but not both). For example:

1. "Here is $2.00. Buy apples and pears"

means buy *both* apples *and* pears (together), but

2. "Here is $2.00. Buy apples or pears"

means buy *either* apples *or* pears (but not both).

Unfortunately, when *or* is used in legal drafting, it is not always clear what the writer meant. For example, in the sentence:

3. "You or your sister may buy the apples"

it looks like the writer intends to give *both* of you permission to buy, but probably only intends *one* of you to go to the shops. But it could also mean that *only one* of you (that is, *either* you *or* your sister) has permission to buy the apples. So there are four possible meanings: you may buy the apples, your sister may buy the apples, both of you may buy the apples, and only one of you may buy the apples.

But look what happens if we decide to use an *and*, since the *or* was so confusing in that sentence:

4. "You and your sister may buy the apples".

Is it any clearer? It seems to mean that both of you, *both* your sister *and* you, must go together. That is consistent with the simplest meaning of *and* that I described first. Apples and pears together. You and your sister together. But did the writer intend merely to give permission to both you and your sister, without intending to tell you who should act? It is not clear. The first possibility is the more likely, but can we rule out the other possibility?

Dick[1] points out that many of the cases on the interpretation of *and* and *or* concern wills. He cites cases in which courts have been forced to hold that *and* meant *or,* and *or* meant *and*.[2] The courts were forced to rewrite the provisions to give effect to the presumed intentions of the will makers. This does not show that *and* and *or* are uncertain or treacherous words: just that sometimes, on their own, they are not enough to make things clear.

Sometimes we need to add a few words to make it clear. We can rewrite all the examples just quoted with additional words to make their meanings clearer:

1. "Here is $2.00. Buy both apples and pears"
2. "Here is $2.00. Buy either apples or pears"
3. "Either you or your sister, or both of you, may buy the apples"
4. "You and your sister must both buy the apples together"

Examples 1 and 2 were both clear enough before the rewrite. And you can see that only a word or two was enough to make the meaning iron-clad. But examples 3 and 4 ended up needing a few extra words to make them clear.

In particular, example 4 needed a change from may to must to make it absolutely clear that both you and your sister are to act together. If we had left it at "You and your sister may both buy the apples together" we are still left wondering whether giving us permission to act together is the same thing as forbidding us to act alone. It is still ambiguous, and therefore we need to strengthen it by making the obligation clear by changing *may* to *must*. There is more about those words later in this chapter.

---

1   Dick QC, RC, 1995, *Legal Drafting in Plain Language*, 3rd edition, Carswell, Toronto, pp 104-107.
2   *Re Metcalfe* [1946] OR 882; [1947] 1 DLR 567 and *Re Ingram* (1918) 42 OLR 95.

Another way of illustrating that point about whether that *and* implied permission to act together and alone is this question: in the sentence "soldiers and scholars will be rewarded by their countries", do you qualify for reward if you are a soldier but not a scholar, or a scholar, but not a soldier? Or is it a requirement that you be both a scholar and a soldier?

The answer is that it is unclear. It is best to use additional words. Depending on what is intended, it would be better to write either "those who are both soldiers and scholars will be rewarded by their countries" or "soldiers, scholars and those who are both soldiers and scholars will be rewarded by their countries".

Some of the legal drafting textbooks analyse the different functions of *and* and *or* in detail and come up with various labels such as the "conjunctive" and "disjunctive" and "inclusive" and "exclusive" *ands* and *ors*. This is a useful analysis, but the rules are not easy to learn, and can be confusing to apply. When it comes to choosing the words to convey the appropriate meaning, in the interests of clarity and plain meaning, it is easier to add of few words of clarification.

Here are some of the useful ones:

> either A or B or both
> either A or B but not both
> any one of the following: A, B, C
> any one or more of the following: A, B, C
> each of the following, together or separately: A, B, C
> all of the following together but not individually: A, B, C

Notice that the last four examples are lists. Because the opening words are so clear, there is no need to use *and* or *or* in the list itself. The paragraphs do not need to be separated by either word.

Let's now look at the classic arrangement of a series of subparagraphs we see in legal documents, with an *and* or an *or* between the last two paragraphs. For example:

> The Seller warrants that:
> (a) the Seller has the power to enter into this agreement and transfer the property sold under this agreement to the Buyer;
> (b) as at the Completion Date the property agreed to be sold will be owned by it;
> (c) as at the Completion Date all the equipment and other assets described in Schedule A will be in good working order;

(d) all the liabilities of the Business have been disclosed to the Buyer; and

(e) the Seller has no knowledge of any claims against it that relate to the Business, which have not been disclosed to the Buyer.

Clearly, these warranties are meant to operate together: the Seller is making *all* the warranties, not just one or two of them. The word *and* is appropriate, but we have to wait until the end of the second-last paragraph before we find that out.

It is often even worse when the conjunction is *or*. For example:

The Cashier will not accept a cheque in payment without proof of identity. Identity may be proved by tendering:

(a) a passport;

(b) a certified copy of a birth certificate;

(c) a driver's licence;

(d) a bank passbook;

(e) a bank identity card; or

(f) two credit cards.

We are left in suspense until the end of the list as to whether the list is a list of alternatives or a cumulative list. It is much fairer on the reader to indicate your intentions up-front, by using the conjunction between each paragraph or item on the list. For example:

The Seller warrants that:

(a) the Seller has the power to enter into this agreement and transfer the property sold under this agreement to the Buyer; and

(b) as at the Completion Date the property agreed to be sold will be owned by it; and

(c) as at the Completion Date all the equipment and other assets described in Schedule A will be in good working order; and

(d) all the liabilities of the Business have been disclosed to the Buyer; and

(e) the Seller has no knowledge of any claims against it that relate to the Business, which have not been disclosed to the Buyer.

and:

The Cashier will not accept a cheque in payment without proof of identity. Identity may be proved by tendering:

(a) a passport; or

(b) a certified copy of a birth certificate; or

(c) a driver's licence; or

(d) a bank passbook; or

(e) a bank identity card; or

(f) two credit cards.

While some have criticised this practice as being repetitive or irritating, there is no doubt that it makes it abundantly clear whether the paragraphs are alternatives or cumulative. The Australian Parliamentary Counsel's Office agrees. It adopted the practice in 1989. Its *Plain English Manual* recommends:

127. If you need to show whether paragraphs are cumulative or alternative, put "and" or "or" at the end of each one (but don't mix "ands" and "ors" in the same string of paragraphs).

128. If there are a lot of short paragraphs, the "ands" or "ors" can look awkward. You can avoid using them altogether by dealing with the matter in the introductory words.

Example   say "each of the following:", "any one of the following:", or "any or all of the following:".

129. Sometimes it's unnecessary to show whether the paragraphs are alternative or cumulative. The sense makes it clear, or it doesn't matter which way they're read. However if there's any chance of confusion, make the meaning clear as described above.

130. Definitions are obviously independent, so there's no need to include "ands" or "ors" at the ends.[3]

I said that sometimes there is no need for any conjunction. If we have already used clear words to show whether our list is a list of alternatives or a list of items that accumulate together, then we don't always need to write *and* or *or* as well. For example:

The Buyer agrees not to carry on business in any of the following places for one year:

(a) Brisbane

(b) Sydney

(c) Melbourne

(d) Auckland

(e) Wellington

(f) Christchurch.

---

3   Paragraphs 127-130, p 28 online version as at 11 March 2003, <www.opc.gov.au>.

or

> "Insolvency" means the occurrence of any one of these things:
> (a) someone applies to a court for a winding up order
> (b) someone applies to a court for an order appointing a liquidator
> (c) a court makes a winding up order
> (d) a receiver is appointed
> (e) an official manager is appointed
> (f) a body corporate resolves to wind itself up
> (g) a body corporate enters a scheme of arrangement.

In cases like those, adding *and* or *or* doesn't add anything to the meaning, which is already clear.

Incidentally, in the last two examples, you'll notice that I removed the semi-colons as well. As we saw in Chapter 6, they do not add anything to the readability of the items in each list.[4] We could have done the same for the other lists with the *and*s and *or*s. But it is probably better to leave some punctuation before the *and* or *or*, just as you would pause before those words if you read the list aloud.

And/or

This expression has been reviled over the years as "unfortunate",[5] an "ugly device",[6] "verges on the inelegant",[7] "ugly and unnecessary"[8] and a "bastard".[9] It also has its supporters. And most obviously, it has its users.

The real problem with *and/or* is not its "ugliness", but its ambiguity. We know *and/or* means both *and* and *or*: but what does that mean? Mellinkoff catalogued five possible meanings for *and/or*.[10] Most often it is a sign that the writer has been unable to choose

---

4   See pp 110-111.
5   *In re Lewis* [1942] Ch 424 at 425.
6   Gowers (ed), 1965, *Fowler's Modern English Usage*, 2nd edition, Oxford University Press, Oxford, p 29.
7   Burchfield, RW, 1998, *The New Fowler's Modern English Usage*, revised 3rd edition, Oxford University Press, Oxford, p 53.
8   Gowers (Greenbaum and Whitcut eds), 1987, *The Complete Plain Words*, 3rd edition, Penguin Books, London, p 16.
9   *Bonitto v Fuerst Brothers & Co Ltd* [1944] AC 75 at 82 per Viscount Simon LC; Davis, JW in "An And/or Symposium" (1932) 18 *ABAJ* 574 at 575.
10   Mellinkoff, D, 1963, *The Language of the Law*, Little Brown, Boston, p 308.

between *and* and *or,* and takes the easy option. In that sense, writing *and/or* is a bit like writing *means and includes.* The writer wants to have it both ways but ends up by creating even more confusion.

If *and/or* can have at least five possible meanings, it is a most unwise and uncertain option to take. If what you mean is **both** *and* **and** *or,* as in apples *or* pears **as well as** apples *and* pears, then you should write:

> Apples or pears or both.

The New Fowler's Modern English Usage endorses this suggestion as "a more comfortable way of expressing the same idea", and notes that, in many contexts, just "or" would be sufficient.[11]

Shall and *must*

When I dealt with the future tense, I mentioned the way lawyers use the word *shall* for the "imperative".[12] I explained that lawyers like to use the word *shall* in a special sense – to express an obligation or to state a command. I said that when lawyers use the imperative *shall* and also draft in the future tense, things can become confusing. I said that to avoid this confusion, we should draft in the present tense – which gets rid of all the "future" *shalls* – and I said that it is also possible to avoid the imperative *shall* altogether. One way we can do that is simply by using *must,* instead of *shall,* to impose an obligation.

Must fits everywhere that *shall* does when it is used to impose an obligation. And no one can get *must* confused with the future. Therefore, our prime plain language principle – consider your reader – requires that we adopt *must* to prevent our reader becoming confused.

Compare the merits of *shall* and *must. Must* is a clear and definite word that imposes an obligation with certainty. It cannot be confused with the future. *Must* is also a commonly used word. We all know what it means. It is the word most people use when they speak about obligations.

Shall, on the other hand, is used less and less these days. It is not surprising. It is difficult enough to work out when to use *shall.*

---

11   Burchfield, RW, 1998, *The New Fowler's Modern English Usage,* p 53 (cited at note 7).
12   Page 140.

There is a set of rules for *shall*, which applied traditionally in England (but not, according to Gowers,[13] in Scotland, Ireland or America). The rules told the English when to use shall for the "plain future" (in the first person: *I shall go, we shall go*) and when to use it for volition, permission or obligation – the "imperative" *shall* (in the second and third person: *you shall go, he, she, it, they shall go*). In all the other cases the rule was to use *will*. But, according to the leading commentators and dictionaries,[14] those rules have been on the way out, even in England, for quite some time.

Still, lawyers tend to use *shall* to show a legal obligation. And they often forget the English rules, using the "imperative" *shall* for first, second *and* third persons. This, combined with their tendency to draft in the future tense, produces a repository of *shalls* un-rivalled elsewhere in the language!

Dr Robert Eagleson, who is a linguist, said this about the tendency of lawyers to misuse *shall:*

> Authorities on drafting ... bemoan the failure of lawyers to use *shall* correctly. Strangely, they never seem to consider that it might be *shall* itself that is the root of the problem. Its use to express obligation is archaic.[15]

In 1992 the US federal government's Style Subcommittee decided to abandon *shall*. The Style Subcommittee is part of the Standing Committee on Rules and Procedure, which works on all amendments to all the US federal court rules. The Subcommittee believes that this move led to the rules becoming sharper, because the drafters now have to think more specifically about the meaning of each rule.[16] As we saw in Chapter 4, the Federal Rules of Appellate Procedure, and of Criminal Procedure, have now been restyled. There is no *shall* left in any of the restyled rules.[17]

---

13 Gowers, 1987, *The Complete Plain Words*, pp 141-142 (cited at note 8).

14 Quirk, Greenbaum, Leech and Svartvik 1985, *A Comprehensive Grammar of the English Language*, London, Longman, pp 229-230; Gowers, 1987, *The Complete Plain Words*, pp 141-142 (cited at note 8); *Oxford English Dictionary, Macquarie Dictionary; Merriam Webster Third International Dictionary* and *Random House Dictionary of the English Language.*

15 *Clarity*, No 11, December 1988, p 6.

16 Garner, BA, 1995, *A Dictionary of Modern Legal Usage*, 2nd edition, Oxford University Press, New York and Oxford, p 940.

17 See p 72.

In the new South African Constitution, there is not a single *shall*. Wherever *shall* appeared in the earlier, interim Constitution, it has been replaced by *must* or the present tense, as in:

Interim Constitution

The executive authority of the Republic shall vest in the President, who shall exercise and perform his or her powers subject to and in accordance with the Constitution ...[18]

New Constitution

The executive authority of the Republic is vested in the President.[19]
The President must uphold, defend and respect the Constitution ...[20]

And in:

Interim Constitution

Every person shall have the right to life.[21]

New Constitution

Everyone has the right to life.[22]

The clarity here is almost poetic.

In the United Kingdom, the legislation that has emerged as part of the Tax Law Rewrite Project has generally used *must* in place of *shall* for the imperative. However, *shall* does appear from time to time in other recent legislation, as does *must*. There seems to be no hard-and-fast rule on this question, and to date there is no formal stylebook for either the UK Tax Law Rewrite Project or the Office of Parliamentary Counsel.[23]

British Columbia, which had been using *must* (to impose obligations) in its statutes for some years, formally adopted *must* in April 1997 as part of its 1996 statute consolidation and revision. To make their intentions absolutely clear, they added a statement to their Interpretation Act that "must is to be construed as impera-

---

18   Interim (1993) Constitution, section 75.
19   Constitution of the Republic of South Africa 1996, section 85(1).
20   Section 83(b).
21   Interim (1993) Constitution, section 9.
22   Constitution of the Republic of South Africa 1996, section 11. For more information, see Viljoen, F, "Baring the nation's soul through plain language", *Clarity* No 46, July 2001, p 15.
23   The UK OPC is the main source of UK primary legislation. But there are separate drafting offices for Scotland, Northern Ireland and Wales.

tive", mirroring the existing provision "shall is to be construed as imperative".[24]

But there is no doubt that *must* is an appropriate equivalent for the imperative *shall*. Gowers says so.[25] The Attorney-General of Victoria said so in 1985,[26] and instructed all parliamentary counsel in Victoria to use *must* instead of *shall* to impose an obligation. The Law Reform Commission of Victoria tells us to use *must*, rather than *shall*, to describe obligations.[27] The Australian government tells us that *must*, not *shall*, is the word for writers to use to express an obligation.[28] Both the Australian and the New South Wales Parliamentary Counsel's Offices also use *must* (or occasionally other expressions like *is required to* or *is to*) rather than *shall*, to impose an obligation or express a duty. The eminent legislative drafting expert GC Thornton has advised:

> It is preferable to use 'must' instead of 'shall' to impose an obligation. This is more in line with ordinary speech and avoids the confusion that the use of 'shall' may introduce.[29]

In the United States of America, the Practising Law Institute warned its members way back in 1981 not to use *shall*, and advised that *must* should be used to indicate a requirement.[30] And in Canada, in 1979, the Ontario High Court, Divisional Court, said this:

> The question of the interpretation of the word 'must' in a collective agreement has come before the Courts on only two occasions known to counsel ... In both of these cases it was held that 'must' was

---

24 Interpretation Act [RSBC 1996] chapter 238, section 29. Strangely, after the 1996 revision, Spencer J in *Lovick v Brough* ((1998-03-10) BCSC F970404, para [7], <http://www.courts.gov.bc.ca/jdb%2Dtxt/sc/98/03/s98%2D0356.txt>), thought that the purpose of the change from *must* to *shall* was to "strengthen" the imperative quality of *shall*, and he did not seem to recognise that the BC Interpretation Act says both *must* and *shall* are to be construed as imperative, without drawing a distinction between them.

25 Gowers, 1987, *The Complete Plain Words*, p 142 (cited at note 8).

26 Ministerial Statement of Mr JH Kennan MLC to Victorian Legislative Council on 7 May 1985.

27 1987, Law Reform Commission of Victoria, Report No 9, *Plain English and the Law*, p 61.

28 Eagleson, R, 1990, *Writing in Plain English*, AGPS Press, Commonwealth of Australia, Canberra, p 118.

29 Thornton, GC, 1996, *Legislative Drafting*, 4th edition, Butterworths, London, p 104.

30 Practising Law Institute Course Handbook, 1981, *Drafting Documents in Plain Language*, p 253.

mandatory. No case has been cited to us in which 'must' has been otherwise interpreted. The word "must" is a common imperative. It is hard to think of a commoner.[31]

Many lawyers in private practice have now adopted *must*. In 1990 the English Law Society published a text on legal writing, which recommends using *must* for the imperative *shall*.[32] Mellinkoff, in his *Dictionary of American Legal Usage says* "unless the context can be made crystal clear, prefer *must* or *required* to *shall*".[33] And it is now standard practice in many of the large Australian law firms to use *must* to impose an obligation.

We know that *must* is sufficient to create a covenant. Halsbury tells us that:

> no particular technical words are necessary for the making of a covenant. Any words which, when properly construed with the aid of all that is legitimately admissible to aid in the construction of a written document, indicate an agreement constitute, when under seal, a covenant.[34]

In fact, the statutes of some Australian states have for years told us that *shall* means *must*. For example, section 9(2) of the Interpretation Act 1987 of New South Wales says:

> In any Act or instrument, the word "shall", if used to impose a duty, indicates that that duty *must* be performed.[35]

This is not new – a corresponding section appeared in the predecessor of the 1987 Act: the Interpretation Act 1897.[36] The same sort of provision is in the Victorian Interpretation of Legislation Act 1984. Section 45(2) says:

> Where in this Act or in any Act passed or subordinate instrument made on or after the commencement of this Act the word "shall" is used in conferring a power, that word shall be construed as meaning that the power so conferred *must* be exercised.[37]

---

31 Judgment delivered by Reid J: *Re UAW and Massey-Ferguson Industries* (1979) 94 DLR (3d) 743 at 745.
32 Adler, M, 1990, *Clarity for Lawyers*, The Law Society, London, p 43.
33 1992, West Publishing Co, St Paul, Minn, p 403.
34 *Halsbury's Laws of England* (4th edition Reissue) Vol 13, para 248.
35 Emphasis mine.
36 Section 23.
37 Emphasis mine.

Despite all this, there is still some reluctance by lawyers to abandon *shall* in favour of *must*.[38] One of the most common arguments against the use of *must* is that it is "too harsh" – which implies that *shall* is somehow softer. If that is true, what are these "soft" obligations we lawyers have been writing about all these years, and how they are different from the new harsh ones? It is an argument that is impossible to answer, because it is based on taste, not logic. It really must be translated as: "we are not used to it", which of course is not an argument at all, but a complaint.

The Australian Office of Parliamentary Counsel has taken a robust approach to the problem. In its *Plain English Manual* it advises:

> We shouldn't feel any compunction in using "must" and "must not" when imposing obligations on the Governor-General or Ministers, because "shall" and "shall not" were acceptable in the past.[39]

Moreover, if we eliminate all of the "mistaken future" occurrences of *shall* and draft in the present tense, there will be fewer *musts* in the average document than there were *shalls*.

Some commentators believe that *shall* is still appropriate for "commercial" contracts, and that *must* is more appropriate for "consumer" contracts.[40] But that argument assumes that "consumers" are the only ones confused by *shall*, when there is plenty of evidence that even lawyers are confused. It also assumes that "consumers" are an identifiable sub-group, when in fact *every* client is a consumer of a lawyer's legal services. And it does not acknowledge the argument of the plain language movement that every document must take into account the needs of its readers, no matter what its purpose.

Other commentators still see a modest place for *shall* in legal writing. Some point to the origin of the command, noting that traditionally, *must* was used to describe a command that had its

---

38   See, for example, the exchange of views in the *Australian Law Journal*, at (1989) 63 *ALJ* 75, (1989) 63 *ALJ* 522, (1989) 63 *ALJ* 726 and (1990) 64 *ALJ* 168.

39   Paragraph 83, p 19 online version as at 11 March 2003, <www.opc.gov.au>.

40   See, for example, Aitken, JK, 1995, Piesse: *The Elements of Drafting*, 9th edition, Law Book Company Limited, Sydney, p 71 (although Piesse now allows that either "shall" or "must" may be used in private legal documents to express obligation) and Doonan, E and Foster, C, 2001, *Drafting*, 2nd edition, Cavendish Publishing Limited, London, p 181.

origin elsewhere, and that *shall* was used to express the command. So a sign might say, "Dogs *must* be on leashes in the park" (*describing* the command) but the Dog Regulations themselves would say, "Dogs *shall* be on leashes in the park" (*expressing* the command).[41] But the distinction is evident to the drafter, and not to the reader, who sees only the obligation.

Professor Joseph Kimble has argued that *shall* is the most mis-used word in the legal vocabulary, but agrees that if the choice is between *shall* and *must*, drafters should use *must*. In a 1992 article[42] he suggested that there might still be some virtue in retaining *shall*, but defining it in certain documents and legislation, along with *must* and other words of permission or authority. This, he felt, would enable us to retain some of the finer shades of meaning, such as whether an obligation is "mandatory" or "directory". But I countered by saying that retaining the shades of meaning is not the important thing. It is better to have a simple obligation, and *state the consequences of not obeying that obligation*, than to rely on definitions to tell you what degree of obligation there is.[43]

The fundamental objections to the word *shall* are that it is confusing, and out-of-step with current language usage. *Shall* is difficult to use correctly. We know that lawyers make mistakes when they use *shall*. It is difficult to teach them the correct usage. Legal drafting experts, including judges, have been complaining about its misuse for years. Commentators have also complained that it is imprecise and ambiguous. Professor Kimble identified hundreds of cases showing that *shall* can be strong or weak, as the court decides[44]. Dr Robert Eagleson and I listed six different legal uses of *shall*.[45] Bryan Garner listed eight shades of meaning – most from a single set of court rules.[46] Peter Butt and Richard Castle

---

41   For example, see the note from Nick Horn in "And yet more on the Thorny Busi-ness of Auxiliary verbs ...", *Clarity* No 48, Dec 2002, p 35, and "A Dainty Dish to set before the King: Plain Language and Legislation", *Plain Language Association International (PLAIN) Fourth Biennial Conference Proceedings Toronto, Canada, 26 – 29 Sept 2002,* <http://www.plainlanguagenetwork.org/conferences/2002/dish/1.htm>.

42   "The Many Misuses of *Shall*" (1992) 3 *Scribes Journal of Legal Writing* 61.

43   "*Shall* Must Go" (1992) 3 *Scribes Journal of Legal Writing* 79. See also "Must we Continue with *Shall*?" (1989) 63 *ALJ* 75.

44   "The Many Misuses of *Shall*" (1992) 3 *Scribes Journal of Legal Writing* 61.

45   "Must we Continue with *Shall*?" (1989) 63 *ALJ* 75 at 77.

46   Garner, BA, 1995, *A Dictionary of Modern Legal Usage,* p 940 (cited at note 16).

identified at least 10 separate uses of *shall* in private legal documents, including:

- to impose a duty
- in granting a right
- to give a direction
- in stating circumstances
- in a condition precedent
- to express the future
- to negate a duty or discretion
- to negate a right
- to express intention
- in a condition subsequent.[47]

The potential for confusion on the part of both reader and writer is obvious. It is safer to avoid *shall* altogether.

Must is one word that can do the same work as the *imperative shall*. There are other words and phrases that might do in some circumstances. But those of us who have been working with *must* for nearly 20 years find that it works. The obligations in our contracts have held firm. Since we banished *shall*, we have had no difficulty in expressing obligations, (whether directory, mandatory, declaratory or in any other sense) and our documents are better for it. Clients have noticed the change, and they like it. It is far too late to resuscitate *shall*.

One last word of warning on *shall* and *must*. *Must* replaces *shall* in *shall's* imperative sense. But you cannot simply replace every *shall* with *must*. Remember that the other reason you find *shall*s in documents is that lawyers have mistakenly drafted in the future tense. The way to correct that is to draft in the present tense. So:

> This agreement *shall be* governed by the law in force in New South Wales

is a mistaken future, and we should rewrite it in the present tense, like this:

> This agreement *is* governed by the law in force in New South Wales

---

47 Butt, P and Castle, R, 2001, *Modern Legal Drafting*, Cambridge University Press, Cambridge, p 99.

and *not* as:

> This agreement *must be* governed by the law in force in New South Wales.

But, by contrast:

> The borrower *shall* pay interest at a rate of 10% per year

is imperative – states an obligation – so it becomes:

> The borrower *must* pay interest at a rate of 10% per year.

Will

I must refer again to *will*, because even though we should be able to eliminate almost all instances of the word *will* (in its sense as the future auxiliary) from our documents by drafting in the present tense, some people argue that it is a word of promise and therefore should be used in legal drafting to express a promise. Holders of this view would write:

> The Lender will lend $100,000 to the Borrower and the Borrower will repay it within 30 days

in order to create mutual promises.

I can find no authority for this proposition as a matter of law. It may stem from a misreading of the advice of FH Callaway, QC, who wrote in 1975 on his view of the correct use of *shall* in these terms:

> Where it is necessary to use the future tense, "will" and not "shall" should be used, except in the rare case where a document speaks in the first person.
> The correct use is illustrated by contrasting the following clauses:
>> The goods shall be manufactured in accordance with the specifications set out in the Schedule.
>> The goods will be manufactured in accordance with the specifications set out in the Schedule.
> Strictly speaking the former is suitable for a covenant to manufacture the goods and the latter to express a warranty that they will comply with a certain description.[48]

Callaway was clearly referring to a warranty in these terms:

---

48   Callaway, FH, 1975, *Drafting Notes*, Law Institute of Victoria, p 9.

> The Seller warrants that the goods will be manufactured in accordance with the specifications set out in the Schedule.

The warranty is expressed in the present tense: *The Seller warrants that* and then describes the future manufacture of the goods in the future tense: *The goods will be manufactured*.

But a warranty need not always refer to the future. If it relates to a present state of affairs it is expressed in the present tense. For example:

> I warrant that I am the owner of the Land.

The problem with *will* is that it has the same problem as *shall*: in fact it looks even more like a mere prediction of the future. We must be careful to use it only when we write in the future tense. And we must remember to write in the future tense only when the present is inappropriate.

May

If *shall* traditionally implied obligation or command, then *may* is the language of permission. *May* states what is allowed. This is consistent with normal language use and is not liable to be confused with the future.

Unfortunately, the courts sometimes say that *shall* means *may* and *may* means *shall*. This is not due to any defect or ambiguity in either word: it is only done to correct poor drafting. *Black's Law Dictionary* notes that:

> In dozens of cases, courts have held *may* to be synonymous with *shall* or *must*, usu. in an effort to effectuate legislative intent.[49]

GC Thornton also recognised this point, when he wrote:

> Not infrequently, courts have been obliged to construe "may" as obligatory but these instances amount rather to judicial amelioration of drafting errors than to a licence to drafters to say one thing and mean another.[50]

So if justice must bend the rules of grammar occasionally to correct the poor drafting of lawyers, we should be all the more

---

49   Under *May*, 7th edition, 1999, West Group, p 993.
50   Thornton, GC, 1996, *Legislative Drafting*, 4th edition, Butterworths, London, p 104.

careful in our choice of words. We should also be careful to use *must* only when we wish to impose an obligation. When we want to give permission we should use *may*. If there is no obligation, but only a discretion, *may* is the word to use. So, for example:

> The Secretary may call a meeting of shareholders if the Directors propose to create a new class of shares

is permissive and gives the Secretary a discretion. The Secretary does not *have* to call the meeting, but if the Secretary wishes, the Secretary may do so. On the other hand,

> The Secretary must call a meeting of shareholders if the Directors propose to create a new class of shares

is mandatory. The Secretary is obliged to call a meeting. The Secretary has no discretion, no choice. Again, it illustrates the beauty of *must* in conveying the sense of obligation. But the main point to be made here relates to *may*: use *may* when you give permission – not when you impose an obligation, unless you add the word *only*.[51]

Shall not, may not and must not

If we should not be using *shall*, we should certainly not be using *shall not*. It causes even more difficulties than *shall* does alone. So we have only to make a choice between *must not* and *may not*. We could write either;

> The employee must not participate in a similar business.

or

> The employee may not participate in a similar business.

depending on whether it is a matter of command or permission. But what is the point of drawing a distinction between command (or obligation) and permission (or authority)? For all practical purposes, these two expressions mean the same thing. As Bryan Garner says, "these two are nearly synonymous".[52] In fact, as Garner points out, there is one other possible meaning for *may not* and that is *might not*, as in:

---

51   See pp 143-145 for a discussion of the meaning of *may only*.
52   1995, *A Dictionary of Modern Legal Usage*, p 942 (cited at note 16).

> The employee may not have time to participate in a similar business.

To avoid that potential ambiguity, and to continue the clear and definite meaning of the positive *must* into the negative, the plain language writer would usually choose *must not* over *may not*.

We have not yet finished with problem words and phrases, but we are learning what to avoid. In the next chapter, we look at the way the courts read and interpret our words. We focus on some of the rules the courts can use to help them interpret what we write, and ask the question: do those rules prevent us from drafting in plain language?

Chapter 12

What about the rules of legal interpretation?

How will our writing be read?

Lawyers are only too aware that our legal writing may be subject to interpretation by the courts and others, and they may use the various laws, rules and maxims of interpretation to help them interpret it.

We've already touched on some aspects of legal interpretation in this book. I've mentioned some of the common law rules of interpretation – *ejusdem generis* and *expressio unius* for example. Interestingly, the possible application of those two rules is an argument *for* using plain language rather than against it, because plain language advises lawyers to avoid "word strings" – the needless enumeration of particular instances when a general description will do.[1]

I've also mentioned the relationship between the recitals and the other introductory words of an agreement, and the operative part: the courts may restrict general words in the operative part by reference to more specific words in the recitals or elsewhere in the "non-operative" part of the agreement.[2] If the operative part of the agreement is clear and the recitals are ambiguous, the courts will apply the operative part over the recitals, and they will also prefer the operative part if both the recitals and the operative part are clear but inconsistent.[3] Again, this rule of interpretation favours a

---

1   See pp 120-121. The New South Wales Court of Appeal has recently held that using the *ejusdem generis* rule in statutory construction is rarely justified: *Deputy Commissioner of Taxation v Clark* [2003] NSWCA 91 at [127].

2   *Danby v Coutts* (1885) 29 ChD 500 and *Ex parte Dawes; re Moon* (1886) 17 QBD 275.

3   *Ex parte Dawes; re Moon* (1886) 17 QBD 275 in the judgment of Lord Esher at 286 (applied recently in Australia in *Western Power Corp v Normandy Power Pty Ltd* [2001] WASC 202).

plain language approach, which is to avoid recitals if you possibly can, and concentrate on getting the operative part right.

Laws governing interpretation

Most jurisdictions have laws that set out principles governing how laws must be interpreted. In Australia, each jurisdiction has an interpretation Act. These Acts lay down various presumptions of interpretation, set out some definitions of words that are commonly found in statutes, and elaborate on concepts such as time and distance and how to measure them. They govern the interpretation of the Acts of the relevant jurisdiction, and most of them also apply to subordinate legislation (like regulations and statutory rules) and executive instruments (issued under the legislation of the jurisdiction). Lawyers need to bear these interpretation Acts in mind when they are looking at the words of a law to work out what it means, and when they are choosing words, if they are drafting a law.

Those interpretation Acts do not apply to private documents, but there *are* interpretive provisions in other laws that we should also be aware of. For example, in the Conveyancing Act 1919 of New South Wales, section 181(1) provides:

> In all deeds, contracts, wills, orders, and other instruments (whether relating to property or not), and in any rules or regulations under this Act executed or made after the commencement of the Conveyancing (Amendment) Act 1930, unless the contrary intention appears, –
> (a) The masculine includes the feminine and vice versa.
> (b) The singular includes the plural and vice versa.
> (c) "Person" includes a corporation.
> (d) "Month" means a calendar month.

This section of the Conveyancing Act is prefaced by the words "unless the contrary intention appears" and so it lets legal writers in New South Wales substitute their own definitions. But if they do not, the Conveyancing Act definitions are implied in all instruments. There are similar provisions in the laws of other jurisdictions, and legal writers need to be aware of them.

As long as we are aware that interpretive (and other) laws may have a bearing on the meaning of our words and the way we put them together, the existence of interpretive laws is no bar to plain language. The mere fact that the law may have something to say about the words we choose should not prevent us from simplifying and clarifying our writing. It is our business to know what our words mean and what laws may affect our documents. That applies whether they are written in legalese, gobbledegook or plain language.

Other rules and maxims of interpretation

Apart from these interpretive laws, there are other rules of interpretation that can apply both to laws and to private documents. We have to bear these in mind while we are drafting. How many of them will interfere with our choice of plain words over "traditional" words or legalese?

Certainly there are no rules which require us to write in long sentences or long paragraphs. There are no rules which prohibit us from planning our writing, choosing a structure carefully, or arranging the information so the reader can find it. We know that the myth that punctuation should be disregarded in interpreting a document *is* a myth. There are no rules about paragraph numbers or numbering systems. We are free to put in headings, and we can provide that they are to be disregarded in interpreting the document – although it is hard to understand why anyone who has drafted their document with care would want to do that.

Let's look at some of the more common rules of interpretation, and consider how they might affect a plain language document.

1. **The literal meaning rule** says that words will be given their "literal", "ordinary" or "natural" meaning. Under this rule, if the meaning of the provisions of the document is clear, the courts will not look any further. The courts say that the "literal", "ordinary" or "natural" meaning is their "popular" meaning – as opposed to their "philosophical" or "scientific" meaning (whatever that may be). The two exceptions to words being given this "popular" meaning are "legal" and "technical" terms which are given their legal or technical meaning respectively, rather then their popular meaning (if there is one).

We have already discussed difficulties with the concept that words have a "natural" meaning.[4] We have also seen that the courts cannot get any real assistance from looking at what words meant in the past, in other circumstances.[5] So the court must look elsewhere for the popular meaning.

Courts applying this rule often resort to something that ordinary people use to find the "commonly accepted" meaning of a word: a dictionary.

2. **The golden rule**, which flows from the literal rule, has been stated by Lord Wensleydale as follows:

> The grammatical and ordinary sense of the words is to be adhered to, unless that would lead to some absurdity, or some repugnance or inconsistency with the rest of the instrument, in which case the grammatical and ordinary sense of the words may be modified, so as to avoid the absurdity and inconsistency, but no further.[6]

This rule, of course, does not even come into play unless there is a repugnance, inconsistency or absurdity when the words being considered are looked at in the light of the rest of the document. That involves the proposition that the words of a document are read in the light of the rest of the document, which brings us to the next rule.

3. **The document is to be read as a whole**. The Latin name for this rule is *noscitur a sociis* (something is known by its associates). The rule says that we must read any individual part of a document in the context of the whole document.

4. **The intention of the parties must be respected**. If the parties express a common intention in the document, the court will give effect to it. This rule only operates if the intention is there on the face of the document, although a court may construe words that indicate the intention of the parties in the light of surrounding circumstances. But if the words in a document are clear, a court will not speculate as to the intention of the parties.

---

4   See Chapter 2.
5   See p 24.
6   *Grey v Pearson* (1857) 6 HL Cas 61 at 106.

Those are the four main principles of construction, but there are several other principles that are more specific. Apart from *ejusdem generis, expressio unius,* and the principles governing the relationship between the "operative" and "non-operative" parts of an agreement, there are other principles, or "maxims", as they are often called. Here are some of the better known ones.

- *Contra proferentem* – in full, the maxim *verba chartarum fortius accipiuntur contra proferentem* – which says that the party responsible for choosing the language will have the document construed against them. Obviously that rule does not apply automatically. It is subject to the overriding principle that clear words prevail, which is inherent in the four main rules I've outlined.

- The "reasonable construction" rule says that in any case of ambiguity, if words are capable of two constructions, the reasonable construction is to be preferred on the basis that the court will the presume that would be intention of the parties. This is really just an extension of the court's efforts to ascertain the intentions of the parties if the words are not clear.

- A related rule is the rule that words are to be construed so that the object is carried out, and does not fail – *verba ita sunt intelligenda ut re magis valeat quam pereat.* Again, this rule looks at the intention behind the drafting.

- Words must be interpreted so as to give them some effect – *verba cum effectu accipienda sunt.* In other words, the court presumes if the writer of a document used a word, it was intended to mean something. Of course, this rule should encourage us to use fewer words, but choose them more carefully. Any unnecessary words – any padding – could alter the effect of the necessary or precise words. So we must avoid "elegant variation".

- Words are interpreted subject to the intention of the parties, not the other way around – *verba intentioni, non e contra, debent inservire.*

- Words are to be interpreted in keeping with the subject matter – *verba accipienda sunt secundum subjectam materiam*. This is similar to the *noscitur a sociis* rule – that we must read the individual parts of a document in the context of the whole.

- Another similar rule is *verba generalia restringuntur ad habilitatem rei vel aptitudinem personae* – general words are to be limited to the nature of the subject-matter or the aptitude of the persons affected by them.

- Words that are referred to in a document have the same meaning in that document as if they appeared there – *verba relata hoc maxime operantur per referantiam ut in eis inesse videntur*. This maxim applies to words that are referred to in a document, no matter whether they are outside the document, or elsewhere in the document. This of course means that the courts presume that the writer uses words consistently, so words used more than once in a document are assumed to bear the same meaning each time they are used. This is more incentive to choose words carefully and stick to them. This rule, combined with another rule I've mentioned – *verba cum effectu accipienda sunt* (words are presumed to have a meaning) means that inconsistency or elegant variation might be fatal.

Some of these principles are basically the same as or similar to each other, and some are quite inconsistent with each other. Trying to apply more than one rule can lead to contradictions. For example, it is difficult to see how to apply both the "literal" rule, which tells us to look *only* at the literal meanings of the words, and also apply the rule that words are to be construed so that the object of the document is carried out.

These pitfalls are not new. Commentators have complained for many years about the possible inconsistencies, and the fact that they are written in "dog Latin". In a book review of the 11th edition of *Maxwell on the Interpretation of Statutes* (1962),[7] CP Harvey commented:

> Take, for instance, the following: *Incivile est nisi tota lege perspecta una aliqua particula ejus proposita vel respondere,* cited by the authors at p 27. By all means try this over in your bath to the tune of Annie

---

7   Wilson QC, R, and Galpin, B, Sweet and Maxwell Ltd, London.

Laurie, but do not try to persuade me that it helps anyone to interpret anything.[8]

The position seems to be much the same in the United States. Mellinkoff, in his *Dictionary of American Legal Usage,* describes the rules of interpretation as:

> a loose assortment of ways to discover the sense, if any, in a piece of legal writing. The label *rule* gives an aura of general standard to what are usually very personal conclusions of interpretation, eg favouring intent … avoiding absurdity … The rules are not uniform and cannot be relied upon as guides to precise writing.[9]

In the same book, under the topic "maxims", Mellinkoff gives us a "maxim for maxims":

> A maxim is to law as a fortune cookie is to philosophy.[10]

And noting the existence of exceptions to "rules" of statutory construction, the Chief Justice of New South Wales recently observed that:

> In the field of statutory interpretation it may be best to never say "never".[11]

So while it might be sometimes difficult to apply these rules and maxims, or to reconcile them one with another, it is clear that the rules of interpretation do *not* create a context in which plain language drafting is dangerous.

None of these rules says "words will be construed according to what they meant the last time they were used" or "traditional or technical words are to be preferred over new or simple words". On the contrary, all the rules are designed to operate only if what the parties have written is confused, contradictory, unclear or does not reflect what they must have intended to write. If what is written is clear, the rules and maxims of interpretation simply do not apply.

---

8   (1963) 26 *Mod LR* 104.

9   1992, West Publishing Co, St Paul, Minn, p 578.

10   Same work, at p 402, quoting from Mellinkoff, D, "The Myth of Precision and the Law Dictionary" (1983) 31 *UCLA Law Review* 423 at 434.

11   *Deputy Commissioner of Taxation v Clark* [2003] NSWCA 91 at [126], Spigelman CJ.

What is the attitude of the courts?

The courts say again and again that they will not interfere if what is said in a contract is clear on the face of the contract. They will not put an artificial or strained meaning on words. Words mean what they say unless that wasn't intended *and* it is clear from the document, or the document and the surrounding circumstances together, what *was* intended.

A 1990 case on the Credit Act 1984 in the New South Wales Court of Appeal shows that no principle of interpretation can alter the meaning of words that are clear in their own right. In *Turner v Morlend Finance Corp (Vic) Pty Ltd*[12] there was argument about how the court should read a section of the Act, which, if it applied, would prevent another section from being relied on.

Justice Meagher refused to rewrite the clear words of the section. He said:

> [Counsel] conceded, quite correctly, that if sec 13(4) applied in the present case according to its terms sec 13(2) could not be relied on. But, he suggested, sec 13(4) should be read as if the words "(other than commercial vehicles or farm machinery)" were added after the words "a contract for the hiring of goods". Even under modern principles of statutory construction, this cannot be done. When statutory words are clear, even if the purpose informing them is not immediately apparent, the courts are not at liberty to mangle them to the point where they no longer mean what they say.

But how do the courts decide what a word means if it is not immediately apparent from the document itself? A 1991 case in the Court of Appeal of the Supreme Court of New South Wales illustrates a straightforward approach.

In *Provincial Insurance Australia Pty Ltd v Consolidated Wood Products Pty Ltd*,[13] the court had to consider the question "what is a canal?" It was an insurance case: the insured was a cabinet maker who had insured his factory against all sorts of risks, including water damage. There was a flood, and the factory and its contents were badly damaged.

The insured claimed on his insurance policy, but the insurers would not pay, because they said that in the policy there was an

---

12   (1990) ASC ¶56-006 at 59,127, Meagher JA.
13   (1991) 25 NSWLR 541.

exclusion clause, which excluded insurance cover for flood caused by water which had escaped from, among other things, a "canal".

There was no dispute about where the water had come from: the court found that the water had come from the nearby storm-water channel, which was blocked and had overflowed. The question was: is a stormwater channel a "canal"?

Now remember that this case involved an exclusion clause in an insurance policy – the very sort of contract and clause that lawyers are nervous about changing because, they say, there are years of legal argument and precedent about the technical meaning of the words. But look at the way the court dealt with the problem in this case.

The court found that the stormwater channel *was* the same thing as a "canal" as that word is understood in Australia. So the exclusion clause applied and the insurers did not have to pay. The court found this even though they recognised that if the words of the policy were ambiguous they would have to be interpreted *contra proferentem*,[14] because it was a contract of insurance.

The President of the Court of Appeal, Justice Kirby, said that "canal" should not be given a meaning that is disembodied and removed from its context. It should be looked at in its geographical context as well as in the surrounding text of the contract. He rejected various foreign sources that had been quoted to show that the word "canal" implies a navigable waterway. He accepted the Macquarie Dictionary definition (which did not require that a canal be "navigable") because the Macquarie Dictionary has been pre-pared specifically for use in Australia and gives meaning to words used in the Australian context.

Justice Mahoney agreed that the word "canal" had to be construed in its Australian context, where it was common to use the word to refer to a stormwater channel.

Justice Kirby went on to say that we should not take an artificial approach to construing documents, even if they are policies of insurance. He said:

> More fundamentally, there is no reason why policies of insurance should be construed in an artificial and microscopic way. The tendency of the modern approach to the construction of language is

---

14   In favour of the person who did not draft the contract (the insured).

to avoid the assignment of meaning of words taken in isolation. Instead, it is to seek to provide meaning to words in the context in which the words appear and for the purpose of achieving the imputed purpose of the user. Courts today, even more than in the past, insist on this purposive approach to the construction of statutory language.[15]

So *Provincial Insurance* shows us that when judges want to know the meaning of an ordinary word, even in an insurance contract, they will look it up an ordinary local dictionary and find the ordinary everyday meaning.

The High Court of Australia, too, has made it quite clear that it will not interfere with ordinary words, even if they are in an exclusion clause. In *Darlington Futures Pty Ltd v Delco*,[16] the judges of the High Court, in a joint judgment, summarised their view of how exclusion clauses should be interpreted:

> The interpretation of an exclusion clause is to be determined by construing the clause according to its natural and ordinary meaning, read in the light of the contract as a whole, thereby giving due weight to the context in which the clause appears, including the nature and object of the contract, and where appropriate, construing the clause *contra proferentum*, in case of ambiguity.

They went on to say that the same principle of interpretation applies to limitation clauses, and:

> the principle, in the form in which we have expressed it, does no more than express *the general approach to the interpretation of contracts* and is of sufficient generality to accommodate the different considerations that may arise in the interpretation of a wide variety of exclusion and limitation clauses in formal commercial contracts between business people where no question of reasonableness or fairness of the clause arises.[17]

Darlington Futures confirms that we are on perfectly safe ground in giving the words of a clause their ordinary meanings, in the context of the contract as a whole. Only if there is ambiguity do we look for other principles of interpretation that might apply, like *contra proferentem* in case of exclusion or limitation clauses.

---

15 *Provincial Insurance Australia Pty Ltd v Consolidated Wood Products Pty Ltd* (1991) 25 NSWLR 541 at 553.

16 (1986) 161 CLR 500 at 510.

17 (1986) 161 CLR 500 at 510 (my emphasis).

That sort of analysis is no different from the way we work out what words mean outside the legal framework. Up to the *contra proferentem* stage, it is the same way we would find out what any words means.

True, as lawyers we have to know about the doctrine of *contra proferentem*, and how it can affect what we write. But we should also know that it will only come into play if there is an ambiguity that can't be worked out by reference to the words themselves, the context of the contract or the presumed intention of the parties as to how the contract was to work. In a clear and unambiguous document, the technical rules of interpretation like *contra proferentem* are simply not needed. Recently, Justice Kirby of the High Court gave this warning to those who are distracted from simply looking at the language in question:

> In statutory construction, there is a tendency, noted in several recent cases, for judges and others to look first to a number of external sources for guidance, including judicial generalities or legal history. It is as if some who have the responsibility of interpretation of legal words find the reading and analysis of the texts themselves distasteful, like dentists happy to talk about the problem but loath to pull a tooth. In statutory construction this error of approach must be rooted out. The proper place to start is the statute … The same point of principle is applicable where the function in hand is to construe the terms of a written contract. The starting point must be the contract. Only later, if need be, may the decision-maker have resort to contextual materials and supplementary or extrinsic evidence in elaboration of the written text. This approach is equally applicable to a statute and a written contract because it is based on a principle informed by strong considerations of practicality. The text may be unarguably clear. In such a case, it will not be necessary, or ordinarily permissible, for the decision-maker to go beyond the written language from which the answer to the question in issue is to be found. If the text is so clear, that will normally be the end of the matter.[18]

---

18   *Royal Botanic Gardens and Domain Trust v South Sydney City Council* (2002) 186 ALR 289 at 307; See also *Hancock Prospecting Pty Limited v BHP Minerals Pty Limited* [2002] WASC 224 at [61] and Mason J in *Codelfa Construction Pty Limited v State Rail Authority (NSW)* (1982) 149 CLR 337 at 352. Contrast, however, the position in the United Kingdom where the approach to interpretation is not limited in the first instance to "internal linguistic considerations", but allows evidence to be admitted of all surrounding circumstances, without the need for ambiguity: *Prenn v Simmonds* [1971] 1 WLR 1361 at 1383-1384; *Investors Compensation Scheme Ltd v West Bromwich Building Society* [1998] 1 WLR 896.

How do the courts interpret plain language?

Although some judges have been sceptical of plain language, there are also many who support it. It seems that for every judge who refers disparagingly to "so-called plain English",[19] there are others who favour it.[20]

But the fear that courts will seize on plain language changes in statutes and documents to alter "well settled" meanings has not come true. In *Boehm v Director of Public Prosecutions*,[21] archaic language used in the Supreme Court Act 1958 of Victoria had been rewritten in plain language. The question was whether this resulted in removing a right of appeal that existed under the old legislation. The Supreme Court of Victoria ruled that it did not:

> Provisions rewritten in plain English, like mere amending provisions, should not be treated as altering the character and operation of the previous provisions unless that intention is clearly indicated[22]

The same court took the same approach in *R v SA*.[23] And even if the courts are tempted to do otherwise, in some jurisdictions

---

19 For example, Tadgell J of the Supreme Court of Victoria in *R v Roach* [1988] VR 665 at 670; Olney J of the Federal Court of Australia in *Secretary, Department of Social Security v Pellone* (1993) 47 FCR 130 at [18]; and Burchett J of the Federal Court of Australia in *Simon Graduate School of Business Administration Inc v Minister Administering the National Parks and Wildlife Act 1974 (NSW)* (1994) 51 FCR 243 at [9].

20 For example, Kirby P in *Dousi v Colgate Palmolive Pty Ltd (No 2)* (unreported, NSWCA, 12 May 1989) where he called for a "plain English" redraft of the Limitation Act 1969 (NSW). Justice Kirby, now of the High Court of Australia, is a patron of the plain language organisation "Clarity". See also Mahoney JA of the NSW Court of Appeal in *Government Cleaning Services v Ellul* (unreported, NSWCA, 12 August 1996) and Wilcox J of the Federal Court of Australia in *McMullin v ICI Australia Operations Pty Ltd* (1998) 156 ALR 257, where he required a class action notice to be written in "plain English". Joseph Kimble and Barbara Child have done research in the US that indicates that judges prefer documents written in plain language (Kimble, J, "Plain English Wins Every Which Way" (1987) 66 *Michigan Bar Journal* 1024; Kimble, J and Prokop, J, "Strike Three for Legalese" (1990) 69 *Michigan Bar Journal* 418 and Child, B, "Language Preferences of Judges and Lawyers: A Florida Survey" (1990) 64 *Florida Bar Journal* 32. And, as we saw in Chapter 4, judges are now attending courses on judgment writing that teach plain language principles. See also Palyga, S, "Is it Safer to Use Legalese or Plain English? What the Judges Say", *Clarity* No 43, May 1999, p 46.

21 [1990] VR 494.

22 [1990] VR 494 at 498.

23 [2001] VSCA 117.

there is legislation to reinforce the position. For example, the Acts Interpretation Act of Queensland 1954 says this:

14C Changes of drafting practice not to affect meaning
If-
    (a) a provision of an Act expresses an idea in particular words; and
    (b) a provision enacted later appears to express the same idea in different words for the purpose of implementing a different legislative drafting practice, including, for example-
        (i) the use of a clearer or simpler style; or
        (ii) the use of gender-neutral language;
the ideas must not be taken to be different merely because different words are used.[24]

Can black mean white?[25]

One last thing on interpretation: some people make the mistake of assuming that, because the courts sometimes say that *black* means *white*, or *shall* means *may*, or *may* means *shall*, or other ordinary words have extraordinary meanings, we cannot use ordinary words in drafting. They say we cannot be sure that words will always mean what they seem to mean, and therefore plain language is dangerous.

That is a mistaken analysis. It makes the exception govern the rule.

As we have seen, the courts interfere only if they must, in order to give effect to the intention of the parties or the legislature. They give ordinary words extraordinary meanings only if they must.

This happened in the High Court of Australia some years ago, when the court held that the word *entry* means *entry by means of*

---

24 The identical provision appears in other Acts, both in Queensland and in other jurisdictions: eg the Consumer Credit Code schedule 2, and Co-operative Housing and Starr-Bowkett Societies Act 1998 (NSW) schedule 1. However, on p 196 at note 24, I mentioned that Spencer J of the British Columbia Supreme Court found in *Lovick v Brough* ((1998-03-10) BCSC F970404) that the replacement word *must* was "more mandatory" than the original *shall* in a revised statute, despite the Interpretation Act stating that both *shall* and *must* are to be construed as imperative.

25 In *Mitchell v Henry* (1880) 15 Ch D 181 the English Court of Appeal ruled that black might be white among cloth manufacturers, depending on expert evidence. See also *Jones v Evans* [1944] 1 KB 582 in which it was held that a married woman was within the definition of "single woman".

which the offender takes possession or intends to take possession of the premises.[26] But the court did that only in the context of section 207(1) of the Crimes Act 1958 (Vic) to give the intended effect to that section. The court did not prevent the rest of us from using the word *enter* in its simple sense in our writing.

The real problem in that case was that the drafter of the section used the word *entry* without explaining the special sense in which it was used. The very fact that the case came to court indicates that more words were needed to make the meaning of the section clear.

In summary, the rules of interpretation are perfectly compatible with a practice of plain language drafting. And the case histories of those who have adopted a policy of plain language drafting bear this out.[27] They have consistently reported less, not more, time spent in court interpreting documents.

Now we can be confident that the courts are prepared to give ordinary words their ordinary meanings. So let's list some of the words we want to avoid in our drafting, and look at the alternatives.

---

26   *Prideaux v Director of Public Prosecutions (Vic)* (1987) 163 CLR 483.
27   See Chapters 3 and 4.

Chapter 13

A plain language vocabulary

Plain language drafting is more than just a matter of using simple words. Less than half this book is devoted to words. The rest looks at writing for your audience, choosing the appropriate tone, planning, structure, design and layout, readability, devices to help your reader find things, the new electronic writing media, testing documents, and some "philosophical" matters.

But throughout this book I have singled out some particular words and phrases for criticism. Sometimes it is because they are imprecise or inaccurate. Other times it is because they are archaic, not English, or not used by anyone but lawyers. Sometimes they're just plain difficult.

What follows is an alphabetical list of problem words and phrases, with a corresponding list of words you could use as alternatives. The alternative words might not mean exactly the same thing as the problem words in all cases. Sometimes it is because the word we're trying to avoid is unsatisfactory, and sometimes it is because it is difficult to anticipate the meanings of a word in every set of circumstances. Sometimes the word in the "Avoid" list is perfectly fine in some circumstances (like *any*, or *all*, for instance) but should be avoided in others.

It is difficult to be dogmatic when we are talking about a list of words without a context. That's why I've suggested the words as *alternatives* rather then *equivalents.*

But in *every* case the alternative is an alternative you should consider. The alternative is easier to understand and often it means exactly the same thing as the word I recommend you avoid. You may find that you consider both words and still choose the word I recommend you avoid. The point is that if you do that you must know *why* you've chosen it and *why* the alternative is not appropriate in your case. And tradition is not a good enough reason.

One last lawyerly disclaimer: it isn't a complete list. No doubt you'll be able to add to it. I encourage you to do so.

Avoid	Alternative
ab initio	*from the start*
above (as in *see above*)	be specific instead
abovementioned	be specific instead
accordingly	*so, therefore*
afforded	*given*
aforementioned	be specific instead
aforesaid	omit
aggregate	*total, sum*
agreeance	*agreement*
all	*the*
all and singular	*all*
and/or	*and, or, either ... or ... or both*[1]
any	*the*
a priori	*from assumed principles*
as a result of	*because of*
assist	*help*
at any time	omit
at this point in time	*now*
beforementioned	be specific instead
below (as in *see below*)	be specific instead
bequeath	*give*
bona fide	*good faith, genuine, honest*
by virtue of	*because of, under*
cease	*stop*
chattels	*goods*
commence	*begin/ start*
consequently	*so*
considers expedient	*thinks fit*
contained in	*in*
covenant and agree	*agree*

---

1   See p 187.

Avoid	Alternative
the day and year first hereinbefore written	*on the date of this agreement,* (or state the date)
deem to be	*treat as, consider to be, take to be*
determine (as in *terminate*)	end, finish
devise	*give*
each	*the*
effected	*made, done*
employ	*use*
enclosed please find	*we enclose, here is*
endeavour	*try*
estop	*stop, prevent*
et al	*and the others, the rest*
et seq	*and those following*
every	*the*
exceeding, in excess of	*more than, over*
expeditiously	*quickly, as soon as possible* (or state a time limit)
expend	*spend*
expiration	*end*
extinguish	*end*
facilitate	*help, assist*
fails to	*does not*
for and on behalf of	*for*
foregoing	be specific instead
for the duration of	*during*
forward	*send, give*
forthwith	*immediately, as soon as possible, now* (or state a time limit)
from time to time	omit
furnish	*give*
gift (verb)	*give*
give consideration to	*consider*
give devise and bequeath	*give*
grant	*give*
hence	*therefore*

Avoid	Alternative
henceforth	*from now on*
hereafter	*after* (and state date or time)
hereby	omit
herein	*in this agreement* (or other document)
hereinafter	*after* (and state date or time), *from the date of this agreement*
hereinafter called	omit, or use *called*
hereinbefore	*before* (and state date or time), *before the date of this agreement*
hereof	*of it*
hereon	*on it*
hereto	*to it*
heretofore	*before* (and state date or time), *before the date of this agreement* (or other document)
hereunto	*on it* (or omit)
herewith	omit, or use *with it* or *with this* (and specify)
hitherto	*before* (and state date or time), *before the date of this agreement* (or other document)
howsoever	omit, or use *however, no matter how*
implement	*carry out, fulfil*
indemnify, keep indemnified and save harmless	*indemnify* (plus a clause stating that there is no need for the indemnified party to suffer loss before requiring payment)
indicate	*show, tell, say*
initiate	*begin, start*
in personam	*personal, personally*
in pursuance of	*because of*
in regard to	*about*
in relation to	*about, for, as to*
in respect of	*about, for, as to*
institute proceedings	*begin* or *start proceedings, sue*
instrument	*document*

Avoid	**Alternative**
inter alia	*among other things*
in the event of	*if*
in the event that	*if*
in the future	*after the date of this agreement* (or state date or time)
in the past	*before the date of this agreement* (or state date or time)
in witness whereof the parties have hereunto set their hands and affixed their seals	*executed as a deed*
irrespective of	*whether or not, even if*
is authorised to	*may, can*[2]
is entitled to	*may, can*[2]
is not entitled to, has no power to	*cannot,*[3] *must not*
is not permitted to	*may not*
is not required to	*need not*
is required to	*must*
is permitted to	*may*
issue	*give*
it is important to note that	omit
it is lawful for	*may, can*
it may necessitate	*you may have to*
last will and testament	*will*
loss occasioned thereby	*resulting loss*
make an application	*apply*
make a statement	*state*
make payment	*pay*
make provision	*provide*
means and includes	*means, includes*
mens rea	*state of mind*
moneys	*money*
monies	*money*

---

2   But use *may* with care: see pp 202-203.

3   This usage is recommended by the Australian Parliamentary Counsel's Office (*Plain English Manual* p 39 online version as at 11 March 2003, <www.opc.gov.au>).

Avoid	**Alternative**
mutatis mutandis	*with the necessary changes*[4]
mutually agree	*agree*
nothing in this clause (document)	*this clause (document) does not*
not less than	*at least*
not more than	*at most*
notwithstanding	*despite, even if*
now	*on the date of this agreement,* or state date
now therefore this agreement witnesseth	omit, or use *the parties agree*
null void and of no effect	*has no effect*
obiter dictum	*part of the judgment not essential to the decision in the case*
on behalf of	*for*
on each occasion when	*whenever*
otherwise than	*except*
per stirpes	*the share of a deceased parent is divided equally among their children, with descendants of a deceased child dividing the deceased child's share between them*
the premises (in the sense of "the matters")	*this agreement, this deed*
prima facie	*at first glance*
prior to	*before*
provide	*give*
provided that	*but, if*
punctually	*on time*
purchaser	*buyer*
pursuant to	*under, according to*
quantum	*amount*
re	omit, or use *about*
relating to	*about*

---

4   In *R v Z(DA)* [1992] 2 SCR 1025, the Supreme Court of Canada held that the expression *where the context requires* was a plain language equivalent of *mutatis mutandis*.

Avoid	Alternative
release remise and forever quitclaim unto	release
request	ask
res ipsa loquitur	it speaks for itself
rest residue and remainder	rest, balance
retain	keep
said	the, that, those
the same	use a pronoun
save	except
save and except	except
shall (present)	draft in the present tense
shall (future)	will
shall (imperative)	must
subsequently	then, after, later
subsequent to	after
such	the, that, those (or use a pronoun)
sui generis	the only one of its kind
sui juris	of full legal capacity
terminate	end, finish
terms and conditions	terms
testament	will
testamentary disposition	will
thence	afterwards, then
thenceforth	afterwards, from then on
thereby	by it
therefor	for
therein	in it
thereinafter	afterwards, from then on, later
thereof	of it
thereon	on it
thereto	to it
therewith	with it
these presents	this agreement, this deed
to the effect that	so
to wit	namely

Avoid	Alternative
uberrimae fidei	*utmost good faith*
undermentioned	omit, or use *as mentioned later*, or be specific
until such time as	*until*
unto	*to*
upon	*on*
upon the expiration	*at the end*
upon the {occurrence of X {happening	*when X happens*
utilise	*use*
vendor	*seller*
we should point out that	omit
whatsoever	omit, or use *whatever, no matter what*
where	*when, if*
WHEREAS	*RECITALS, BACKGROUND*
whereby	*by it, by which*
whereof	*of it*
whereon	*on it*
wheresoever	omit, or use *wherever, no matter where*
whosoever	omit, or use *whoever, or no matter who*
with a view to	*to*
with regard to	*about*
with respect to	*about*
with the result that	*so that*
will and testament	*will*

Chapter 14

Email and the internet

Is the internet the single biggest revolution in communication in the past century? Certainly in 1991, when the first edition of this book was published, it was possible to write a book on legal writing without mentioning the internet and electronic mail (email). It is not possible to do that now.

Email

Email is ubiquitous. It is the most used aspect of the internet. An estimated 10 billion email messages were sent *per day* in the year 2000, and that figure is expected to rise to 35 billion per day in 2005.[1]

Lawyers today routinely write to their clients and to each other by email. Email messages are even replacing telephone conversations: it is often easier to contact someone by email than to play "telephone tag" with them. Letters written on paper are becoming less common, and are reserved for the more formal pieces of communication: letters of advice, opinion and instruction, letters of agreement that have contractual effect, letters that threaten litigation or other dire consequences, briefs for barristers and so on.

Email and the internet do not, of themselves, require a different kind of writing. They are simply different media for the writer to work in. But lawyers writing today – whether in plain language or not – often write in the form of email, or use the internet to publish written material on web sites or electronic bulletin boards. Different conventions are emerging in email writing. Email and the internet have special features that have implications for the way we write. That is why I have devoted this chapter to writing email and

---

1   Collins, Dr M, 2001, *The Law of Defamation and the Internet*, Oxford University Press, Oxford, p 19; see also <www.idc.com/software/press/PR/SW101000 pr.stm>.

for the internet, and another one (Chapter 16) to designing documents for the computer screen.

Immediacy

Email is just about immediate. In fact, with "instant messaging" it *is* immediate. (Instant messaging allows you to find out if the intended recipient of your message is logged onto the internet and, if so, you send a message that can be received instantaneously.)

Perhaps because of the immediacy of delivery, people tend to respond to email more quickly than they would to a letter. That immediacy can have undesirable consequences, which I deal with later in this chapter.[2] But it has major advantages for efficiency in communication. It is even possible to refer readers directly to information on the internet by means of a "hyperlink".[3] This saves them the trouble and time of having to locate the reference themselves. By using a hyperlink (written as "http://www.hyperlink.com", for example) we can allow the reader to refer instantly to the additional information we want them to see.

Internationality

Email is international. It is just as quick and easy to exchange messages with a friend or colleague in another country and another time zone, as it is to do so with the person in the next room. We can post a message on a web site and we have no idea who may stumble across it. They could live anywhere. This in itself raises issues of communication: will the reader of the email or web site understand the way we use the language, even if it is a language we have in common? It is not just a question of slang. Some words that belong to the formal lexicon could also be misunderstood by an audience unfamiliar with them. What is a hire car? A thong? A flat? We can even cause confusion with things such as dates (is 4/5/03 the 4th of May or the 5th of April 2003?), or measurements

---

2   See p 236 (Defamation).
3   A hyperlink is a set of characters or a symbol or image in a "hypertext" document which links (by means of a mouse click) to another place in the same or another document. A hypertext document is one that is designed to allow those links.

(how many kilometres – or kilometers – in a mile?). Conventions of spelling and notation may vary. Communicating with an international audience reminds us yet again to focus on the prime directive of plain language – consider your reader.

The international nature of email and the internet can have undesirable consequences too. Again, I deal with them later in this chapter.[4]

Informality

Email sits somewhere on the formality scale between the phone call and the letter. Writers tend to use a conversational manner in email – sometimes using contractions like "yr" for "your" and "pls" for "please". They may begin with "Hi" rather than "Dear" and they can make up their own "letterhead" and "signoff".

Some lawyers have rejected this level of informality. A number of law firms do not allow their employee (or junior) lawyers to send email – just as they do not allow their employee (or junior) lawyers to sign mail. In many firms, only the partners can sign letters. This is to ensure that the partners retain control over all of the significant communication that takes place in the firm's name.

They have a point: communicating by email and the internet means that everyone is now a potential international publisher. Type up an email, press the send button, and in a flash your message can be broadcast worldwide. There's no "cooling-off" period. There's no secretary to type up a draft for careful checking. There's no time lag in which errors and intemperate words can be picked up and altered. Email delivery is not only almost instantaneous, it is practically irrevocable. As author William Zinsser put it in his book *On Writing Well*:

> It's a spontaneous medium, not conducive to slowing down or looking back.[5]

What is the significance of this for the way we write?

Earlier in this book[6] I discussed "tone" in legal writing, and observed that when lawyers write letters in the course of their

---

4 See p 236 (Defamation).
5 2001, 6th (25th anniversary) edition, HarperResource Quill, New York, Introduction, p xi.
6 Pages 12 and 85-88.

work, they tend to adopt only one, quite formal, tone. This does not necessarily apply to email – email style tends to be less formal. And email, by its nature, is more immediate. So the writing style of email tends to be shorthand, even abrupt, and sometimes breathless.

Symbols, emoticons and abbreviations

There is another emerging difference between email writing and other writing. Email writers have found new uses for certain symbols to enhance communication. They may use asterisks for *emphasis*, angled brackets to convey a <different> shade of meaning, or underscoring_to_make_a_point.

Email writers have also developed new symbols that they use to convey emotions. These symbols are known as "emoticons" (from the words "emotion" and "icon"). A writer arranges standard keyboard characters – often sideways – to form pictures. For example, a smile is arranged like this:

:-)

Emoticons can give clues to the subtext of the writing and the intention behind it. This brings the writing closer to verbal communication, where we have the advantage of facial expression and body language to help us make our intentions clear.

The web site "Emoticon.com" describes the role of the emoticon this way:

> The very nature of communicating on the Internet allows people to express thoughts and feelings with an openess [sic] and frankness unusual in face to face or phone conversations. The trouble is that on-line *conversations* are really a cross between a letter and a phone call. The potential for misunderstandings, without the tone and expression of a voice, or signals given out by body language, are considerable. Email, newsgroups, the 'Net' – all rely on the written word – and the written word is so easy to misinterpret (ask lawyer$!).
>
> As a result of this, a shorthand version of expressing moods has emerged on the Net and together with certain behavioral rules form *nettiquette* [sic].[7]

---

7   <www.emoticon.com/serious.htm>. For more on linguistic "netiquette" and style , see Hale, C and Scanlon, J, 1999, *Wired Style: Principles of English Usage in the Digital Age,* Broadway Books, New York and Walker, JR and Taylor, T, 1998, *The Columbia Guide to Online Style*, Columbia University Press, New York.

Other emoticons include:

:-(	Sad
:,(	Crying
:-0	Yelling
:-@	Screaming
:-X	A kiss (or my lips are sealed)
:-y	Said with a smile
:-|	Frowning, or grim
;-)	Winking, just kidding
|-o	Bored
:-r	Sticking tongue out
:-&	Tongue-tied
# -)	Oh, what a night!

Some might say that emoticons are completely inappropriate to use in legal correspondence. However, because of the effect they can have on the tone of our writing, they can be an important element in the communication mix. For example, as Dr Matthew Collins points out in his book *The Law of Defamation and the Internet*:

> Tone of voice and facial expression will sometimes neutralize words which would, if read in print, convey a defamatory meaning … emoticons can be used to neutralize words which would otherwise be defamatory.[8]

Some of the abbreviations used in email are known as "TLAs" (three-letter acronyms). This label is misleading though, because most TLAs are not acronyms, strictly speaking. (Acronyms are *words* formed from the initials or parts of several words.) And some of the TLAs have more than three letters.

For example:

AAMOF	As a matter of fact
BTW	By the way
CMIIW	Correct me if I'm wrong
EOL	End of lecture
FAQ	Frequently asked question(s)
FITB	Fill in the blank
FWIW	For what it's worth

---

8   Collins, Dr M, 2001, *The Law of Defamation and the Internet*, p 89 (cited at note 1).
     See also the section on defamation later in this chapter (p 236).

FYI	For your information
HTH	Hope this helps
IAC	In any case
IAE	In any event
IMHO	In my humble opinion
IMO	In my opinion
IOW	In other words
NRN	No reply necessary
OIC	Oh, I see
OTOH	On the other hand
TIA	Thanks in advance
TIC	Tongue in cheek
TTYL	Talk to you later
TYVM	Thank you very much
WYSIWYG	What you see is what you get.[9]

The informality of email can also lead to other breaks with convention, such as using upper case for emphasis, or even for the whole message. The latter can have a serious effect on readability. I discuss this in Chapter 16 in the context of electronic document design.[10]

Spelling and typing errors

Another result of both the informality and the immediacy of email is the fact that spelling and typing errors are rife. The trend seems to be to tolerate this to a degree, in the interests of quick and efficient communication. "No one reads email with red pen in hand", say the authors of "Wired Style", an English usage guide for the digital age.[11] That's a sensible approach – but only if it is appropriate to the relationship between the parties. If the parties have an informal relationship, minor errors may not be a problem. If the relationship is more formal, or if accuracy and attention to detail is an issue (as it often is), spelling errors should not slip through. As lawyers, it reflects badly on the skill and care we bring to the affairs of our clients if we ignore this.

---

9   These emoticons and "TLAs" were collected from urls: <www.emoticon.com>, <www.windweaver.com/emoticon.htm> and <www.pb.org/emoticon.html>.
10   See p 281.
11   Page 3 (cited at note 7).

A related issue, while we are considering the new writing technology, is the spell checker. This handy time-saver can lull the writer into a false sense of security, as this poem illustrates:

CANDIDATE FOR A PULLET SURPRISE

I have a spelling checker,
It came with my PC.
It plane lee marks four my revue
Miss steaks aye can knot sea.
Eye ran this poem threw it,
Your sure reel glad two no.
Its vary polished in it's weigh.
My checker tolled me sew.
A checker is a bless sing,
It freeze yew lodes of thyme.
It helps me right awl stiles two reed,
And aides me when eye rime.
Each frays come posed up on my screen
Eye trussed too bee a joule.
The checker pours o'er every word
To cheque sum spelling rule.
Bee fore a veiling checker's
Hour spelling mite decline,
And if we're lacks oar have a laps,
We wood bee maid too wine.
Butt now bee cause my spelling
Is checked with such grate flare,
Their are know fault's with in my cite,
Of nun eye am a wear.
Now spelling does knot phase me,
It does knot bring a tier.
My pay purrs awl due glad den
With wrapped word's fare as hear.
To rite with care is quite a feet
Of witch won should bee proud,
And wee mussed dew the best wee can,
Sew flaw's are knot aloud.
Sow ewe can sea why aye dew prays
Such soft wear four pea seas,

And why eye brake in two averse
Buy righting want too pleas.[12]

There's no avoiding proofreading, unfortunately, no matter what form our writing takes.

Does informal = plain?

If email writing is less formal and more flexible in tone than other forms of legal writing, and if it uses symbols, emoticons and abbreviations to help get the message across, does that make it plain? Not necessarily.

As we have seen, plain language involves more than questions of tone and formality. Plain language must be clear, straightforward and unambiguous. It must take into account the needs and abilities of its audience. There are questions of vocabulary, structure, sentence length and punctuation. But there are no hard-and-fast rules. What is clear to one reader may not be clear to another. The medium of email may suggest that a less formal style is appropriate, but the information itself still needs to be conveyed in the clearest way possible. If informal language, contractions, abbreviations and even emoticons help to get the message across effectively, then they are useful aids to communication.

But the informal, one-to-one nature of email can also be misleading: will the recipient of your email be its only reader? Forwarding email is only a matter of a click of the mouse. Will there be more than one audience for the email? Will the email have to be looked at later, after some time, when the context and surrounding circumstances are not as clear as they are at the time of writing? Could a shorthand means of writing become a hindrance to communication? Could the reader misunderstand you?

And what about mistakes? If email and the internet make everyone a potential international publisher, they also make everyone potentially internationally negligent – and, as we'll see later in

---

12 Poem by Emeritus Professor Jerrold H Zar, the Graduate School, Northern Illinois University, DeKalb, Illinois, USA. Title suggested by Pamela Brown. Based on opening lines suggested by Mark Eckman. Originally published in *Journal of Irreproducible Results*, January/February 1994, p 13. Reprinted ("by popular demand") *Journal of Irreproducible Results*, Vol 45, No 5/6, 2000, p 20. Reproduced with the kind permission of the author, and *Journal of Irreproducible Results*.

this chapter, potentially internationally defamatory. So it is important to plan, draft, scrutinise, check and double-check email, just as you would a letter. In fact, it is probably *more* important, since it is possible to retrieve a letter that has not yet been posted. Email is posted with the touch of a finger, and it is virtually impossible to get it back.

It is also important to be sure where your email is going. It is very easy to send email to the wrong person by misaddressing it, or pressing "send" or "reply" by mistake. The results could be disastrous. In addition, the recipients of email can easily forward your email messages on to others. As Dr Matthew Collins has pointed out, an email message intended for one reader can easily be republished to a different, unintended, worldwide audience.[13]

The immediate and universal nature of email is a blessing for clear communication, but it can also be a curse.

The myth of the paperless office

A subsidiary point about email and the internet is the one about the paperless office. It used to be said that computers would mean that paper and filing would become a thing of the past. But most of us have discovered (sometimes painfully) that it is wise to keep emails for later reference, or even as evidence, and that you cannot assume that they will stay on your computer. They can be deleted in error, or at the end of a set period after which the system administrators automatically delete them. Even back-up tapes are regularly destroyed. Prudent lawyers always print out and file important emails for the record.

Web sites

So far in this chapter we have been considering the special features of email, but that is not the only writing lawyers do for publication on the world wide web. Law firms, barristers' chambers, courts, law societies, legal aid organisations, community legal centres and other law-related groups now have web sites and "home pages". There they project their image, publish newsletters, give commentary on legal issues and otherwise communicate with clients,

---

13   Collins, Dr M, 2001, *The Law of Defamation and the Internet*, p 21 (cited at note 1).

potential clients and the world at large. They write the documents to be published on those web sites. And they publish them to the world at large.

As with email, the special feature of publishing material on web sites – the factor that sets it apart from other forms of writing – is the immediate and international nature of the internet. "This is the only media context in which your audience is sitting at a keyboard, ready and able to respond now", says Scott Rosenberg, of *Salon.com*.[14] And if you post a document to a web site, or send an email, you have no control over who might read it, or where. An intemperate thought hastily written and sent, or an ill-judged assertion could be read by anyone with access to the internet. Even an email directed specifically to one person can be copied or forwarded on to countless recipients in many jurisdictions in an instant, with one click.

Defamation

I've suggested that email and the internet makes everyone potentially liable for international defamation. The issue has recently come before the courts in Australia and in various other countries. Although these cases have concerned publications on the world wide web of electronic versions of magazines, and messages posted on electronic bulletin boards, the same general principles apply to publishing email, since that is also published via the internet, passing from server to server. The sender of defamatory email can be sued for the email sent to the intended (direct) recipient, *and* for the republishing the email to others, if it was reasonably in contemplation that the email could be republished – sent on – to others.[15]

The High Court of Australia recently ruled on this issue in *Dow Jones & Company Inc v Gutnick*.[16] That case was the first time a court of ultimate appeal had decided on jurisdiction in a case of alleged defamation published on the internet.

---

14 Quoted in Hale, C and Scanlon, J, 1999, *Wired Style: Principles of English Usage in the Digital Age*, p 5 (cited at note 7).

15 It would be "reasonably in contemplation" that someone would republish, or send on, an email if it contained information that might be interesting to others.

16 (2002) 194 ALR 433.

Australian law

In the *Gutnick* case an Australian businessman sued Dow Jones & Company Inc, the publisher of the *Wall Street Journal, Barron's* magazine and *Barron's Online,* for defamation in the Australian State of Victoria. In October 2000, *Barron's* magazine published an article that was critical of Mr Gutnick. He denied the allegations made in the article. The article was also published in the electronic version of *Barron's* magazine, *Barron's Online.* Mr Gutnick resides in Victoria, and that is where he alleged his reputation was damaged by the *Barron's* article. He undertook to the court that he would sue only in Victoria for the damage to his reputation there.

Dow Jones & Company Inc argued that "publication" on the internet takes place once only – in the place where the item is first "published" on computer servers. In this case the relevant servers were maintained by Dow Jones in New Jersey, USA. Dow Jones argued that the internet article was published only in New Jersey.

The High Court held that the law of defamation in Australia applied to the internet just as it applies to all other media of publication. The defamation occurs where the damage to the reputation occurs. Normally that is where the defamatory material is available in comprehensible form. Material from the internet is not available in comprehensible form until a person downloads it to a computer. That had happened in Victoria, even though there were only 300 Victorian subscribers to *Barron's Online,* and just 14 print copies had been sold there. The High Court ruled that publication had taken place in Victoria and Mr Gutnick was entitled to sue Dow Jones & Company Inc there.

The judges of the High Court were well aware of the potential logistical problems this creates for anyone publishing anything on the internet. It did not daunt them. In the majority judgment, they said:

> the spectre which Dow Jones sought to conjure up in the present appeal, of a publisher forced to consider every article it publishes on the World Wide Web against the defamation laws of every country from Afghanistan to Zimbabwe is seen to be unreal when it is recalled that in all except the most unusual of cases, identifying the person about whom material is to be published will readily identify the defamation law to which that person may resort.[17]

---

17   (2002) 194 ALR 433 at 447.

After the *Gutnick* case, according to Australian law, internet publishers publish at their own peril. So, potentially, do senders of email. They publish not in a single place, but potentially in every place where, and at every time when, the published material is comprehended by the reader, listener or observer, and causes harm to someone's reputation.

But the story continues. With jurisdiction established, the matter has been set to be heard in the Victorian Supreme Court later in 2003. Meanwhile, Dow Jones' lawyer is representing the American reporter for Barron's in an appeal to the United Nations Human Rights Committee on the issue of violation of free speech.

English and Canadian law

The High Court of Australia's decision in the *Gutnick* case is not as astonishing as media commentators made out at the time. Defamation law in Australia remained essentially unchanged. Dr Matthew Collins has pointed out that the case is:

> part of a growing body of international jurisprudence. It is consistent with the approach adopted so far by courts in England and Canada.[18]

He notes that courts in England and Canada had previously applied the same principles to both print and internet publications.[19]

The English law on this point was recently summarised by The Law Commission in its paper *Defamation and the Internet*:

> each communication to a third party constitutes a separate tort which takes place in the country in which the statement is heard, read or seen.[20]

---

18 Collins, Dr M, 2003, *Defamation and the Internet after Dow Jones v Gutnick* (paper delivered at a Centre for Media and Communications Law (University of Melbourne) seminar, 31 March 2003, Sydney) p 17.

19 Same paper, pp 7-10, noting *Berezovsky v Michaels* [2000] 2 All ER 986; *Scapira v Ahronson* [1999] EMLR 735; *Chadha v Dow Jones & Company Inc* [1999] EMLR 724; and *Kitakufe v Oloya* (unreported, Ontario Court of Justice, Himel J, 2 June 1998).

20 *Defamation and the Internet, A Preliminary Investigation:* Scoping Study No 2, December 2002, para 4.4, <www.lawcom.gov.uk/files/defamation2/pdf>.

United States law

However, the position in most of the United States is quite different. Just three days after judgment in the *Gutnick* case was delivered, the US Fourth Circuit Court of Appeals decided a case that illustrates just how far apart US law stands from Australian, English and Canadian law on this issue.

In *Young v New Haven Advocate et al*,[21] the court held that a Virginia prison warden could not sue the publishers of two Connecticut newspapers for defamation in his home State of Virginia. Two small Connecticut newspapers had published articles on the internet that allegedly defamed the prison warden. The court applied its "traditional standard for establishing specific jurisdiction" as adapted for the internet by the court in *ALS Scan, Inc v Digital Service Consultants, Inc*.[22] That standard involves more than simply allowing publication in a particular place. In order to establish specific personal jurisdiction over a "foreign" defendant, the plaintiff must show that the defendant:

(1) directs electronic activity into the State,
(2) with the manifested intent of engaging in business or other interactions within the State, and
(3) that activity creates, in a person within the State, a potential cause of action cognisable in the State's courts.[23]

None of these connections was established: one of the publications had no subscribers in Virginia, and the other had only eight. The publishers did not target Virginia readers and they didn't even send a reporter to Virginia to cover the story – they got their story by phone interviews.

Another decision of the US Court of Appeals only a couple of weeks after the *New Haven Advocate* case followed the same reasoning. In *Revell v Lidov*,[24] an item that was allegedly defamatory had been published on a bulletin board on the web site of the School of Journalism of New York's Columbia University. The plaintiff, who lived in Texas, claimed to have been defamed, and sued in Texas. The court held that the publisher must be shown to

---

21   315 F 3d 256 (4th Cir, 2002).
22   293 F 3d 707 (4th Cir, 2002).
23   293 F 3d 707 at 714 (quoted in 315 F 3d 256 at 263).
24   317 F 3d 467 (5th Cir, 2002).

have conducted business in Texas or otherwise have sufficient connection with Texas, so that it would reasonably anticipate being sued in Texas. The court held that the publisher did not have that kind of connection with Texas and so jurisdiction was denied: the plaintiff could not sue for defamation in Texas.

Given the global nature of the internet, the gradual development of case law in each jurisdiction is not going to settle the issue quickly. As the UK Law Commission concluded:

> Although we have some sympathy with the concerns expressed about "unacceptable levels of global risks", any solution would require an international treaty, accompanied by greater harmonisation of the substantive law of defamation. We do not think that the problem can be solved within the short to medium term. We do not therefore recommend reform in this area at the present time.[25]

Justice Kirby acknowledged the global nature of the problem in his judgment in the *Gutnick* case:

> In default of local legislation and international agreement, there are limits on the extent to which national courts can provide radical solutions that would oblige a major overhaul of longstanding legal doctrine in the field of defamation law. Where large changes to settled law are involved, in an area as sensitive as the law of defamation, it should cause no surprise when the courts decline the invitation to solve problems that others, in a much better position to devise solutions, have neglected to repair.[26]

As I write, lawyers and publishers are struggling to reach some kind of consensus on the issues raised by these cases. A group of media lawyers, meeting in Durban, South Africa, in October 2002 produced a draft set of principles (the "Durban Principles") which deal with forum and jurisdiction issues applying to material posted on the internet. And the "preliminary" Draft Hague Convention on Jurisdiction and Foreign Judgments in Civil and Commercial Matters[27] proposed a scheme for deciding jurisdiction in cases of international defamation among the Contracting States to that Convention.

---

25 *Defamation and the Internet, A Preliminary Investigation:* Scoping Study No 2, December 2002 para 1.16, <www.lawcom.gov.uk/files/defamation2/pdf>.
26 (2002) 194 ALR 433 at 475.
27 Adopted by the Special Commission on 30 October 1999, <http://www.hcch.net/e/conventions/draft36e.html>.

Summary

Email is now a common method of communication used by lawyers. The immediacy and informality of email require special attention. What we think may be clear at the time of writing, and in the context available to the writer, may not be at all clear to the recipient or to other, subsequent readers. Informality does not necessarily produce plain language communication.

Our ability to communicate immediately and internationally by email and the internet poses special problems, such as:

- the potential for mistakes that cannot be undone
- the inability to limit or control who may receive our emails
- international defamation.

But while the internet and email communications revolution has brought us problems we had not dreamed of a few decades ago, it is also important to keep things in perspective. As William Zinsser reminds us:

> The new information age, for all its high-tech gadgetry, is, finally, writing-based. E-mail, the Internet and the fax are all forms of writing and writing is, finally, a craft, with its own set of tools, which are words. Like all tools, they have to be used right.[28]

One of the other "tools" of writing is document design. We'll look at the basic principles of document design in Chapter 15. After that, in Chapter 16, we'll focus on the special way those principles apply to documents designed to be read on the computer screen.

---

28   2001, *On Writing Well*, 6th (25th anniversary) edition, HarperResource Quill, New York, Introduction, p xi.

Chapter 15

Document design basics

Why worry about document design?

In the past, very few lawyers thought much about the design or look of their documents. Apart from giving a little thought to a numbering system, they often left all matters of style and layout to the typist. And of course, there were some documents that had to be in a prescribed format, or typed on a set form. But communications experts have long known that document design has an important effect on the reader's ability to read, find, understand and use the information in a document. That makes good design an essential element of plain language writing. In the words of Canadian plain language advocate and editor Diane Macgregor:

> A plain language document, by definition, is words and design working together to create clear communication.[1]

Even the most wonderfully thought-out and structured document can be difficult to read if it is poorly designed. For example, large blocks of print discourage readers. So does small print. So does an inappropriate typeface.

But good document design can encourage readers, and make them more efficient in extracting information from a document. Legal writing is hard enough to understand as it is. Legal writers who want to give their writing its best chance of being read and understood will pay attention to document design.

For the average lawyer, it is not too difficult to dabble in document design. Wordprocessing software gives you plenty of options. With laser printers and desktop publishing we can now produce a professional product with a minimum of effort.

---

1   Email to PLAIN's discussion group (plainlanguage@yahoogroups.com) 13 May 2003. Thanks to Diane Macgregor for permission to quote her.

And yet, putting all those choices and opportunities in the hands of amateurs can result in documents which are so packed full of features that they are just as difficult to read as the old "undesigned" documents. It is very easy (and tempting) to produce a document that is too busy, or contains a design feature which actually *hinders* comprehension. So we need to make sure that we either consult an expert, or at least learn the basics of document design, before we start to dabble in publishing.

The starting point in document design is the same as it is in writing: consider your reader. In designing a document we need to make the information clear, relevant and usable, and select techniques and design elements that support those aims and that are appropriate for the purpose.

Here are some of the basic things the experts will tell you about documents designed for printing on paper.[2]

Legibility and readability

First, we must distinguish between two specific qualities in the context of typography: legibility and readability.

Legibility is the characteristic of letters, numbers and other symbols that enables us to tell them apart by shape. This depends on several factors, including the form of the characters, the width of their strokes, and the spaces between the characters. If it is easy to tell the shapes of different characters apart, their typeface is said to be highly legible. If the text is not very legible, readers will be slower to read it and reading will be more fatiguing.

Readability is an attribute that enables us to extract meaningful information from characters and groups of characters (words, sentences, tables, footnotes and other forms of text). Material is said to be highly readable when the composition of the text allows a reader to extract information from it easily. Readability also depends on factors like vocabulary, sentence structure and many of the other topics covered in this book.

Thus, a random grouping of letters like jwrtidf may be legible, but it is not readable.

---

2   Chapter 16 covers design for documents to be read on a computer screen.

It is the quality of legibility that we look for as we consider some of the mysteries of typography. For readability, we need to look at other aspects of document design.[3]

Typeface

There's a bewildering array of typefaces, or fonts,[4] available to anyone with a computer and wordprocessing software. And they come in all sizes and styles. Do you just choose the one that you like best? No. Typography is a technical area, and there is now a small body of research about the effects of different typefaces on legibility and comprehension. An Australian, Colin Wheildon, has been influential in this field. This is what he says about typography:

> Typography must be clear. At its best, it is virtually invisible.[5]

Serif or sans serif?

Although there are various ways to classify typefaces, one of the distinctions that is easiest for the novice to understand is the one between "serif" or "sans serif" typefaces. Serifs are the little extensions at the end of each letter. They originated in Roman times. The other defining characteristic of serif letters is that each letter is usually made up of both thick and thin strokes. The body text in this book is printed in serif typeface.

Sans serif typefaces are, literally, "without" the serifs, and the letters usually have uniform strokes. The chapter numbers and titles in this book are printed in sans serif type.

The experts have long thought that, in large amounts of text, serif typeface is easier to read than sans serif text. This is either because the serif lines "lead" the eye across the page, or because

---

3   For more about legibility and readability, see Beaufort Wijnholds, A de, 1996, "Using Type: The Typographer's Craftsmanship and the Ergonomist's Research", <http://www.plainlanguagenetwork.org.type/type.htm>.

4   "Font" is the word for the individual members of a typeface family. For example, in the Bodoni family there are various fonts, including Bodoni condensed, Bodoni bold, Bodoni italic bold, etc. Boldness and italics are "type styles".

5   Wheildon, C, 1995, *Type & Layout: How typography and design can get your message across – or get in the way*, Strathmore Press, Inc, Berkeley, California, p 19.

the serifs, together with the thick and thin strokes, make serif letters easier to recognise. Colin Wheildon's research supports this theory as far as it applies to blocks of text. In his tests, five times as many readers showed "good" comprehension of text when it was printed in serif type, as opposed to sans serif.

However, much of the research about the legibility of serif typefaces was done in the 1920s and 1930s, and often involved comparing only a limited number of typefaces, so that research is not necessarily conclusive for today. Readers in the 1920s and 1930s were not as familiar with sans serif typefaces as we are today. One theory is that we read most easily that which we are most used to. Research by the Communications Research Institute of Australia in the 1990s suggests that readers in Australia are familiar with sans serif fonts and have no problem reading them efficiently.[6]

Then again, according to the Australian government *Style Manual*:

> Serif typefaces are still the predominant choice for prolonged reading because most readability tests confirm that most people prefer them.[7]

In his revision of the UK Timeshare Act 1992, plain language expert and typographer Martin Cutts noted that the typeface used in the original Act (and most UK government Bills, Acts, White Papers and Regulations) is the "ubiquitous" Times. Times is a serif typeface. It has a narrow character width, described by Cutts as "perhaps more suited to the narrow columns of newspapers (for which it was designed)".[8]

Cutts used another serif typeface, Plantin, for his revision. Like Times Roman, Plantin was designed to conserve paper. It is considered a fine typeface for books, journals, and textbooks. Cutts describes it as "clearer and more elegant". He notes that it has slightly wider characters, superior and more legible italics, bold and small capitals, and looks better in large sizes. It is important to

6 MacKenzie, M, 1994, "Our changing visual environment: Questions and challenges", *Communication News*, 7, No 4, Communications Research Institute of Australia, Hackett, Australia, pp 11-14.

7 2002, *Style Manual for Authors, Editors and Printers*, 6th edition, John Wiley & Sons Australia Ltd, p 331.

8 Cutts, M, 2000, *Lucid Law*, 2nd edition, The Plain Language Commission, High Peak, England, p 39.

consider all these variations in font and size when choosing a typeface.

This book is set in Book Antiqua, yet another serif typeface, quite similar to Plantin. Its generous width makes it legible at small sizes.

Sans serif typefaces are often used for headings or headlines because they provide a good contrast to serif body text. Because headings are shorter and more prominent, it is not as necessary to print them in the *most* readable typeface. But you should still choose a readable typeface, and one which is compatible with your body text.

Sans serif typefaces are not as subtle as serif typefaces, and they are drawn proportionally larger. So they are also easier to read when the type is very small, and their "clean" look can be useful for material that may have to be reduced, or photocopied many times,[9] or that will be shown on a computer screen.[10] They are also more legible against moving or complex backgrounds.

Today it seems the choice between serif and sans serif fonts is not as significant as it was once thought. Designers are free to choose between any number of highly legible typefaces, and there are other factors that are just as important to legibility.

Type size

Type size is usually measured in points. A point is approximately 1/72 of an inch. The older research on type size suggests that a type size of between 9-12 points is best for reading.

Colin Wheildon found that from a sample of 4,000 people, around 75% found it easy to read type from 10-12 points.[11] Felsenfeld and Siegel recommended a 10 point type, with a moderate "x" height.[12] But Dr Janice Redish has pointed out that much of the older research is based on measurement for old type

---

9   See Felsenfeld, C and Siegel, A, 1981, *Writing Contracts in Plain English*, West Publishing Co, St Paul, Minn, p 192.

10   See Chapter 16.

11   Wheildon, C, 1995, *Type & Layout: How typography and design can get your message across – or get in the way*, pp 140-146 (cited at note 5).

12   Felsenfeld, C and Siegel, A, 1981, *Writing Contracts in Plain English*, p 193 (cited at note 9); "x-height" is another measure of the height of letters, based on the height of the letter x – indicating the height on most lower case letters.

set in cold metal. Reproduction on a laser printer is not as good. She states that the modern thought on type size for desktop publishing is from 12-14 points.[13]

The Australian government *Style Manual* recommends using type with a size between 9-12 points for continuous reading, and larger type (between 14-20 points) for older or visually impaired readers.[14] Martin Cutts chose a main body text type size of 11.5 point (Plantin) for his revised Clearer Timeshare Act 1993. This book is set in 10 point (Book Antiqua) for the main body text.

Here is the same typeface in some different type sizes:

This line is in Book Antiqua 9pt.

This line is in Book Antiqua 10pt.

This line is in Book Antiqua 11pt.

This line is in Book Antiqua 12pt.

This line is in Book Antiqua 13pt.

This line is in Book Antiqua 14pt.

There is at least one other complication in choosing a type size: not all typefaces *look* the same size, even if they have the same point rating. This is because of variations in letter shapes, and because point doesn't measure letter *width*, only height. Readability also depends on the amount of space around the letter, which is another thing that can easily be manipulated in word-processing systems. But now we are beginning to get down to a level of detail at which lawyers might begin to feel uncomfortable. At this point in a decision about typography, it is probably time to call in an expert document designer.

Here are some different typefaces, all in 10pt. You can see how each looks a different size:

This line is in Book Antiqua 10pt.

This line is in Palatino 10pt.

This line is in TimesRoman 10pt.

---

13 See Krongold, S, "Writing Laws: Making them Easier to Understand" (1992) 24 *Ottawa L Rev* 495 at 539. Dr Redish wrote the section of the article which deals with document design.

14 2002, *Style Manual for Authors, Editors and Printers*, p 330 (cited at note 7). For more information about designing text for older readers, see Hartley, J, 1994, *Designing Instructional Text*, 3rd edition, Kogan Page, London, Chapter 12.

This line is in NewCenturySchoolbook 10pt.
This line is in Bookman 10pt.
This line is in Helvetica 10pt.
This line is in AvantGarde 10pt.
This line is in Courier 10pt.

Line length

Lines of type that range too far – or not far enough – across a page are hard to read. That is why so much reading material is presented in columns. Lawyers don't often use columns in their writing, and columns don't suit numbered paragraphs too well – the eye can't always range down one side of a page to get an idea of the total of the listed items. But double columns can make text more readable. For example, if you need to fit more words on a page, and are forced to reduce type size to achieve the result you want, the smaller print will be more readable in columns.

For text presented in one single column, the experts recommend a line that is anything from 40 – 72 characters of type.[15] Wheildon found that 38% of readers found text hard to read if it was set wider than 60 characters.[16] This also means that the smaller the typeface you use, the shorter the line should be.

In the previous two paragraphs of this book, which are printed in Book Antiqua 10pt type, the full lines of type range between 52 and 61 characters in length.

Justified or ragged?

Text can be set "justified" (with a straight margin) to the left, or the right, or the left *and* right margins (fully justified). Or it can be left ragged.

---

15   Dr Redish recommends 50-70 characters: see Krongold, S, "Writing Laws: Making them Easier to Understand" (1992) 24 *Ottawa L Rev* 495 at 530. So does Martin Cutts: Cutts, M, 2000, *Lucid Law*, 2nd edition, The Plain Language Commission, High Peak, England, p 42. So do Felsenfeld and Siegel: Felsenfeld, C and Siegel, A, 1981, *Writing Contracts in Plain English*, p 197 (cited at note 9). The Australian government *Style Manual* recommends 40-80 characters, or 6-12 words per line for readability (varying according to font and size): 2002, *Style Manual for Authors, Editors and Printers*, p 332 (cited at note 7).

16   Wheildon, C, 1995, *Type & Layout: How typography and design can get your message across – or get in the way*, p 125 (cited at note 5).

For most purposes, body text is justified on the left, so that there is a straight line of text down the left margin. The only remaining question is whether to do the same on the right margin. This book is justified on the left and right, as are most books with a lot of text.

The experts are divided on which is easier to read: fully justified or left justified with ragged right margin. Wheildon's research comes down heavily in favour of left and right (or "fully") justified text for better comprehension. But that research involved text set in three columns.[17] Redish prefers left justified text with ragged right margins, because, she says, the different shapes of the lines help the reader to move from line to line of text. It also avoids too many hyphens, which can result from the spreading out of text to fill a line of justified text. And it avoids the extra spaces between words that you sometimes see in poorly justified text, particularly in newspaper columns.[18]

On the other hand, fully justified text looks "neat" and professional. And if it is well done, for most documents, the problems are not great. I have tended to use fully justified text in more formal legal documents, and left justified with ragged right margins in letters. The team working on the redesign of New South Wales legislation reviewed the literature on this issue and decided to stay with fully justified text for main body text.[19] More recently, in 1999 when the Connecticut General Assembly adopted a new style and format for Bills and amendments, they carefully considered the recommendation of their document design consultant to use ragged right margins. However, some legislators and staff were not comfortable with it, and the Assembly went with fully justified text instead.[20]

Typographers are still arguing about whether ragged right margin or fully justified text is "better", and there does not appear to be conclusive proof either way. It is more a matter of personal

---

17   Same work, p 110.
18   Krongold, S, "Writing Laws: Making them Easier to Understand" (1992) 24 *Ottawa L Rev* 495 at 542.
19   Parliamentary Counsel's Office & Centre for Plain Legal Language, 1994, *Review and Redesign of NSW Legislation*, New South Wales Government, Sydney, pp 21-22.
20   Shapiro, L, "Legislative document design in Connecticut", *Clarity* No 45, December 2000, p 18.

preference, and whether you want a more relaxed (left justified and ragged right margin) or formal (fully justified) look to your document. There seems to be no significant difference in readability, except for poor readers. Studies have shown poor readers are faster readers of text that has ragged right margins.[21]

One thing we do know is that it is not easy to read fully justified text in narrow columns. That arrangement produces too few words per line and odd spacing. Justification cannot be considered without also considering line length.

Here are examples of justified and ragged text:

Justified left and right ("fully" justified)

The experts are divided on which is easier to read: justified or ragged right margin. The experts are divided on which is easier to read: justified or ragged right margin. The experts are divided on which is easier to read: justified or ragged right margin.

Justified left and ragged right

The experts are divided on which is easier to read: justified or ragged right margin. The experts are divided on which is easier to read: justified or ragged right margin. The experts are divided on which is easier to read: justified or ragged right margin.

Ragged left and justified right

The experts are divided on which is easier to read: justified or ragged right margin. The experts are divided on which is easier to read: justified or ragged right margin. The experts are divided on which is easier to read: justified or ragged right margin.

Ragged left and right (centred)

The experts are divided on which is easier to read: justified or ragged right margin. The experts are divided on which is easier to read: justified or ragged right margin. The experts are divided on which is easier to read: justified or ragged right margin.

---

21 Beaufort Wijnholds, A de, 1996, "Using Type: The Typographer's Craftsmanship and the Ergonomist's Research" at 3.3.2 (cited at note 3).

White space

All the experts emphasise the importance of having plenty of white space around your text. It takes up space, it makes your documents longer, but it makes them easier to read and more inviting. One typographer recommends using wide margins on a page to allow the page to "breathe".[22]

You can draw attention to items (like the quotes in this book, for example, or the numbers in a margin) by surrounding them with white space. You can also indicate the structure of your material with white space. For example, you can signal to your reader that a particular section of text has ended, by leaving more white space at the end of that section than elsewhere. And you can tie a heading more effectively to the text it relates to, by leaving more space above the heading than below. The headings in this book follow that rule.

White space does one other important thing: it refreshes your reader. We all have personal experience of this from our reading. How often have you finished a chapter of a novel, seen the end of the page, turned over just to see what's next, or to mark your place, and then some time later realised that you *just kept reading?* Your interest is renewed by the new page and the white space.

One expert suggests you need to leave about 15-20% white space in page layouts – more on the outside to force items together rather than pushing them apart.[23] Other experts have suggested leaving up to 50% of a page for margins or other white space.[24] Whatever the proportions, one thing is certain: white space is not usually wasted space. Even if it makes your documents longer, it will make them more likely to be read, and better understood.

Do not forget the space "between the lines". Typographers call this "leading" (pronounced "ledding"). It is also called "line

---

22 Tarbet, M, 1996, "Regarding text fonts for readability", *UTEST electronic subscription list*, quoted in Beaufort Wijnholds, A de, 1996, "Using Type: The Typographer's Craftsmanship and the Ergonomist's Research" at 3.3 (cited at note 3).

23 "Producing Successful Publications: Layout and Design Points", *B & C Business and Communication Papers*, excerpts reprinted in *Rapport* No 11, Spring 1994, p 14.

24 See Parliamentary Counsel's Office & Centre for Plain Legal Language, 1994, *Review and Redesign of NSW Legislation*, New South Wales Government, Sydney, p 17, quoting separate works by Rubenstein (1988) and Conover (1990).

spacing". Most wordprocessing software allows you to choose line spacing at standard measurements, or to specify your exact requirements. Setting the optimum line spacing involves a compromise that depends on the typeface and type size you are using, the line length, and whether or not your text is fully justified.[25]

Having plenty of space between the lines is handy for text that might have to be annotated by hand, but again there's a trade-off. The greater the space between the lines, the more probable it is that, after reading to the end of a line, the reader skips to the wrong following line. On the other hand, there is evidence that in the case of text with more "leading", or wider line spacing, readers judge type size to be larger, and reading comfort may increase.[26]

And if you increase the space *between paragraphs*, and decrease the space *between lines*, you can help the readers "skim" more easily. This technique was used for the new, reader-friendly style for Bills and amendments that the Connecticut General Assembly adopted in 1999. They increased paragraph spacing from 1.5 to 2.0 and decreased line spacing from 1.5 to 1.2,[27] and found it "dramatically" improved the readability of their documents.[28]

One final thought on white space: using more white space means using more paper. That not only costs more – and paper is *very* expensive, but there is also the environmental effect to consider. If we are too extravagant with white space, not only are we likely to use more trees, but we also risk alienating an environmentally conscious audience.

Diagrams, tables, charts and other graphics

Lawyers have traditionally dealt in words, and until recently have been reluctant to describe concepts in any other way. But things are changing. Now we can see not only tables and formulas in

---

25 Martin Cutts has suggested setting leading at about a fifth of the type size (so 12 point type might have leading at 2.5 or 3 points): Cutts, M, "Lucid Layout", *Clarity* No 45, Dec 2000, p 6.

26 Beaufort Wijnholds, A de, 1996, "Using Type: The Typographer's Craftsmanship and the Ergonomist's Research" at 3.5 (cited at note 3).

27 These measurements are in terms of line spacing rather than in points (1 line = 12 points).

28 Shapiro, L, "Legislative document design in Connecticut", p 17 (cited at note 20).

legislation,[29] but also flow charts, logic trees and boxes with yes and no or ticks and crosses in them.[30]

It happens in private documents too: some years ago, one of my legal colleagues decided that what her client needed was not a standard-form contract, but a contract in the form of a checklist. Lawyers are becoming more adventurous about presenting complex concepts in different formats.

But most of us are design amateurs, and most of us will need some help if we want to go beyond the absolute basics. You only need to go to seminars given by lawyers and look at the pictorial or graphic material they present in their handouts, slides and PowerPoint presentations, to see that most lawyers know next-to-nothing about how to present material visually. They fill their presentations with so much material that it becomes even more confusing for the audience. Sometimes, it is wiser to get help.

Finding things

We must remember that not all our readers will read our document from cover to cover. They may (or may not) do that the first time, but the *next* time they look at the document they will almost certainly dip into it to find the parts that they are interested in. So it will help them to use the document efficiently if we give them directions.

Some of the things we can use in our documents to give directions are:

- headings
- numbering
- symbols like asterisks, or the "bullets" (•) I'm using now
- signals

---

29 For various examples of financial formulas, see the (Qld) Consumer Credit Amendment Regulation (No 1) 2003.

30 For example, Local Government Act 1993 (NSW), Income Tax Assessment Act 1997 (Cth). See also the Australian Office of Parliamentary Counsel's *Plain English Manual*, pp 31-37 and *Working with the Office of Parliamentary Counsel: A guide for clients*, 2nd ed, July 2002, pp 30-32 and 51-66, <http://www.opc.gov. au/about/documents.htm>, and Penfold, H, QC, 2001, "When words aren't enough: Graphics and other innovations in legislative drafting", a paper given at the *Language and the Law* conference, University of Texas at Austin, 6-8 December 2001.

- highlighting
- indenting
- indexes and tables of contents.

Let me deal with each of those individually (using headings, of course).

Headings

It is obvious enough that headings can help readers find what they are looking for. It can also help them understand what they are about to read. But headings can only do that if they are *meaningful* headings. For example, how helpful is the heading **Introduction**? It tells you that something is being introduced, but it doesn't tell you what. The reader knows that it is likely that the writer will introduce the topic in some way, but has no idea what the writer has in mind.

In this book, when I wrote my plan, I had as the first heading **Introduction**. After that came Chapter 1. Then I thought again. I decided what I wanted to say by way of introduction. I devised a heading that explained it better than **Introduction**. That was how the first chapter in this book came to *be* Chapter 1 – rather than an Introduction, and that is why Chapter 1 is called **What is this book about?**

You'll notice that Chapter 1's title is in the form of a question. I find that questions are often very useful as headings. They seem to make you focus your mind on the real issue, rather than describing things in the abstract. For example, I think a heading which reads **What stamp duty is payable?** is more descriptive and more precise than simply the words **Stamp Duty**. Other times, a short label is all that is required. Whatever best helps the reader to decide whether this is the section they are interested in.

Another approach to headings is to give the answer in the heading. For example, **Stamp Duty is not payable**, **The case should be settled**, or **The facts do not establish negligence**. The heading then acts as a summary of what follows, so that readers not only know at a glance *where* the information they want is, but also, in brief, *what* it is.

Headings can be very helpful to readers, but it is possible to overdo things. Not every paragraph needs a heading. Only use a heading when a new topic is introduced. And every heading need not be in the form of a question. Some readers say they find too many questions annoying.

Be careful, too, when you use headings to summarise the text. There is no need to do this if the text itself is very short, or if it results in a heading almost as long as the text itself. You have probably seen the kind of thing I have in mind. You often see it in the articles of association of companies, where writers have felt compelled to put a heading on every clause in the memorandum and every paragraph in the articles, however short they may be. If you adopt that policy, then when it comes to very short clauses or paragraphs, the heading gives the whole show away. For example, I have seen articles of association and headings like this:

Calls paid in advance may be entitled to dividend
Dividends in proportion to the amount paid up may be paid on each share in respect of which any moneys have been paid in advance of calls.

Calls paid in advance give no participation in profits
Any moneys paid on shares in advance of calls shall not confer a right to participate in the profits of the company.

The headings say as much as, if not more than, the articles themselves. The text becomes repetitive, almost superfluous.

If you are using numbering in your document, it helps the reader to find the information they are looking for if you include the number in the heading, hard over to the left margin, like this:

1. What is this document for?

There is more on this technique later, under **Indenting**.[31]

Finally, for more complex documents, or for documents in which you have a multi-level structure, you may wish to have more than one level of heading – both headings and sub-headings. That can be a very effective way to show to your reader the logic underpinning your document. But if you do this, you must be consistent in the way you signify headings and sub-headings, so that the reader always knows which level of the structure they are in. Make sure that sections with comparable degrees of importance

---

31   See p 267.

have the same style of heading, and that that style indicates the heading's level of importance.

In this book I have headings, like **Numbering** (immediately below) and occasionally sub-headings, like *Securities and Exchange Commission* (under the heading **Government departments and agencies**, in Chapter 4). The heading has more "weight" than the sub-heading, so it is easy to see the pecking order.

Numbering

Numbering is another thing that can help people find their way around a document. Like a heading, it acts as a sign post. The writer can use it to refer the reader to different parts of the document, both in the document itself, and later, if it is being discussed. It can also show the order in which things should be done, considered, and so on.

Numbering is good for lists, because it indicates how many things there are in a list. For that reason, it is essential to use numbering when you are listing in a document the things that need to be done or the items that are enclosed. Numbers are better for that purpose than other symbols, such as dots or asterisks. With numbers, the reader can mentally (or even physically) check off the items as they are done or received.

When we write letters, we only need a simple numbering system. I think Arabic numbers (1, 2, 3 etc) are better than roman upper case (I, II, III) or lower case (i, ii, iii), because they are more common in non-legal drafting. Arabic numbers are also better for lists than alphabet characters because using letters of the alphabet makes it harder to work out how many things are in the list. What item number in a list is item (g)?

In other documents we might need a system with several "levels" of numbering. Like headings, numbering can show the reader the logic underpinning the document. There are plenty of numbering systems to choose from. But choosing a system of numbering is more than just a matter of taste. There are advantages and disadvantages to most systems.

Numbering systems for legislation

The old statutory system of numbering commonly used in the British Commonwealth is this:

- Sections have whole Arabic numbers (eg 801).
- Subsections have bracketed whole Arabic numbers (eg (1)).
- Paragraphs have bracketed lower case letters (eg (a)).
- Sub-paragraphs have bracketed lower case roman numerals (eg (i)).
- Sub-sub-paragraphs have bracketed upper case letters (A) (these days most legislative drafters try not to use sub-paragraphs and sub-sub paragraphs).
- If the legislators need to squeeze another section in between two sections that already have numbers they use an unbracketed small upper case letter (eg section 801A).
- The whole number sequence does not appear for each sub-section or paragraph (eg section 801(2) would be numbered as (2)).

But there are several disadvantages to this system:

- You have to memorise the order of the levels because they don't follow a "natural" sequence, as decimal numbers do.
- You can end up having to refer to sub-sub-paragraph (a)(i)(A) of section 801(1) or section 801(1)(a)(i)(A) for short.
- If you have a series of long subsections that go for several pages, you can lose track of what section you're in.

The Law Reform Commission of Victoria recognised these difficulties and recommended a new numbering system for our laws.[32] Its basic features are:

- Decimal numbering, but modified so that the main idea is given a whole number (eg 805, 806 etc) and the subsidiary provisions – exceptions, qualifications and the like – are given a decimal point (eg 805.1, 805.2 etc).
- A new number series (eg 100, 200 etc) is adopted for each new part to allow room for amendments and to help readers find different sections.
- It only allows for three levels of numbering (eg 801, 801.1, 801.1.1). After that it uses dots (·) or dashes, to be used sparingly, perhaps for items in a list.

---

32   Law Reform Commission of Victoria, Report No 33, May 1990, *Access to the Law: the structure and format of legislation*, p 16.

Two disadvantages I can see with that system are:

- It is difficult to refer to the dots and dashes: the Law Reform Commission's Report recommended[33] the citation for a dot in a section be in this form: "first dot-point in section 41".

- The fact that numbering is not always sequential (because a new number series is used for each part) means that we could jump from, say, section 725 to section 800, and this might lead to confusion as to whether anything is left out.

These criticisms are minor, though, and I don't know of any numbering system that is perfect for all types of document.

Redesigning legislative numbering systems

The redesigned format of NSW legislation[34] did not adopt a decimal numbering system, although it was considered. It was decided not to change from the traditional system, for several reasons. One reason was that full decimal systems do not work well for legislation that will be amended: what section number goes between sections 1.1 and 1.2? (1.1.1 is reserved for subsections). Another reason was that it can add clutter when the decimal numbers begin to add up. (They are working with a smaller B5 sized page). Another reason was the practical one that changing all legislation over to a new system would be very costly. In the end, the decision was that the other design improvements would mean the existing numbering system would work better. But occasionally decimal numbering crops up in subordinate legislation,[35] particularly if the "client"[36] asks for it.

In Canada, the legislative counsel considered and rejected full decimal numbering 20 years ago. But decimal numbers are used in

---

33   Same work, p 21.

34   The Centre for Plain Legal Language worked with the New South Wales Parliamentary Counsel's Office to develop an improved design for NSW legislation. Almost all NSW Acts passed from 1995 are in the new format.

35   For example, the Northern Territory's Work Health Rules.

36   The government department, instrumentality or other body that needs the drafting done for them.

existing legislation in most Canadian jurisdictions for adding new sections and subsections.[37]

In Australia, the old Income Tax Assessment Act 1936 presented a special challenge to any numbering system. It is over 5000 pages long and has been amended many times. Its numbering system didn't handle those amendments well, so it ended up with strange section numbers like 159ZZZZA.

The Tax Law Improvement Project (known as TLIP)[38] experimented with several numbering systems in its rewrite of Australian tax laws. It has come up with a new system with several of the features of the Victorian Law Reform Commission's system, and with other variations. The Project had a number of key objectives which the new system had to meet. They were:

1. Each unit of law should have a unique number to identify it.
2. For any two conceivable numbers within the system, it should be immediately apparent which one is higher.
3. Numbers should be easy to read.
4. Numbers should be able to be said aloud without being ambiguous.
5. The system should flow "naturally", and be predictable.
6. The system should follow existing drafting conventions unless there is a reason to abandon them, but allow change if they are causing problems.
7. Each number should identify the "building block" to which it belongs.
8. The system should cope well if a large amount new material is inserted later.[39]

The Project Team thought the new system they devised met all those objectives. They admitted that was not perfect, but they were confident that the system would work well in practice, especially for a law which is amended extensively and often. The new,

---

37 Elliott, DC, 1994, *Writing Rules: structure and style*, paper given at the conference "Linguists and Lawyers – Issues we Confront", Århus, Denmark, 24-27 August 1994, p 19.

38 See p 68.

39 Adapted, with minor changes, from Tax Law Improvement Project, 1995, Information Paper No 2, *Building the New Tax Law*, Commonwealth of Australia, Canberra, p 23.

rewritten Income Tax Assessment Act 1997 has chapters, parts, divisions, subdivisions, sections and smaller units, all numbered.[40]

One of the major innovations was inspired by objective no 7 – that numbers identify the "building block" to which they belong. This means that some numbers – section and part numbers – are "double-barrelled". For example, section 5-15 tells you it is section 15 in division 5. Part 5-6 tells you that it is Part 6 of Chapter 5. There are also gaps in numbering the divisions at the end of parts, and gaps in the part numbers at the end of chapters. This is to leave room to insert material without disturbing the number sequence.

These numbers are quite a change, and produce some of their own problems. For example, the gaps in the numbering of divisions and parts in the new tax laws are disconcerting to some. Others are more appreciative:

> while it may be difficult for some of the "old lags" to adapt to the new numbering scheme, the basic approach of the TLIP legislation does appear to offer a period of logic and order and a significant improvement over the old Act.[41]

Interestingly, despite the suspension of TLIP[42], new tax legislation generally continues to use the innovative numbering scheme (and other contemporary design and drafting principles) developed by the TLIP, even for laws that stand alone from the Income Tax Assessment Act 1997.[43]

The rewrite of the New Zealand Income Tax Act[44] retains the alphabetical Part numbers of the existing Act (for example, Parts CE and CF), but it also employs a gap in the middle of the alphabet. Here, too, the aim is to allow leeway for the future so that drafters

---

40   There are some lists in the form of bullet points.

41   Woellner, Prof R and Zetler, J, 2000, "Tiptoe through the TULIPs: an Evaluation of the Tax Law Improvement Project", *Current Commercial Law eZine*, Vol 7, No 1, May 2000, p 16, <http://www.lawbookco.com.au/academic/ccl-ezine/html-files/archive.asp>.

42   The TLIP may yet be resuscitated. The federal government's tax advisory body, the Board of Taxation, has called for a major restructuring of income tax law. It is considering a project to rewrite the tax law again, or to consolidate the two separate tax Acts ("Push to simplify income tax rules", *Australian Financial Review*, 3 June 2003, p 1).

43   See, for example, A New Tax System (Goods and Services Tax) Act 1999 and A New Tax System (Australian Business Number) Act 1999 (both Cth).

44   See p 68.

can avoid using subparts with three-letter identifiers (such as CEA between CE and CF).

I believe there is no one "right" answer on numbering. The system you choose should depend on the type of document and how it is used. I do see the advantages of a decimal system – but I usually work with a hybrid system that is decimal at least at the section or clause level. For me, it emphasises the difference between the section and subsection, clause and subclause.

A few hints

Here are a few other practical hints to bear in mind when deciding on what numbering system best suits your document:

- keep it as simple as possible – so it is easy to remember
- don't mix too many styles
- if sequence or counting is important, numbers are better
- check what automatic numbering systems your wordprocessing software has; if one is suitable it will save time
- bear in mind the effect the system you choose will have on the margins and tabs in your document.
- it is also important *where* you place your numbers. I have already referred to this earlier under **Headings**,[45] and I deal with it again later under **Indenting**.[46]

Symbols

If it is not important to keep your list sequential, or if the document is less formal, or unlikely to be discussed at great length or dissected, you might prefer not to number your list, and instead use other symbols like asterisks, dashes, arrows or the "bullets" (·) I've been using over the last few pages. They are a bit more "graphic" than numbers, and less formal, so in some circumstances they might be better for attracting attention.

---

45   Page 254.
46   Page 267.

Signals

There's another thing you can do to help the reader find their way around the document. Give them signals that point the way to additional information that might help them understand the material better.

For example, many legal documents use definitions for special words and phrases. The traditional way of indicating that a word or phrase is defined is to use an initial capital for the defined expression each time in appears, and the first time it appears it has inverted commas around it. But, as we saw in Chapter 7, this system has some disadvantages.[47] One alternative to the initial capital is to use a numbered footnote, asterisk, icon (representative picture) or some other marker in the text, which cross-refers either to a note at the foot of the page or to a marginal note.

This method works well to draw the reader's attention to all sorts of subsidiary information. But it has its disadvantages, especially if there are too many signals on each page. One commentator has remarked that too many asterisks can look like "fly spots".[48]

Highlighting

I like to use **bold type** for my headings because it is dramatic. That is my choice. But I don't use underlining or upper case in my text unless I am quoting something that is underlined or in upper case. There is a reason for that.

Words that are underlined are more difficult to read because the eye is distracted from the letters by the line. Words written in upper case are more difficult to read than words in lower case. When we read a line of type, we recognise letters by the shapes of the top half of the letters. In lower case, the top half of letters are more distinctive, and surrounded by more white space. The vertical extensions on lower case letters ("ascenders", as in b and d, and "descenders", as in y and p) help us to recognize them. In upper case, the letters are squarer, and we need more effort to

---

[47] Page 133.
[48] Bennett, J, 1993, "Slaying Small Print: The St George Mortgage", in *Plain Language in Commercial Documents*, BLEC Books, Melbourne, p 50.

distinguish them.[49] Upper case also takes up as much as 30% more room. Compare these examples.

DEAR MR SMITH,

I AM SORRY TO INFORM YOU THAT YOUR APPLICATION FOR THE POSITION HAS BEEN UNSUCCESSFUL. HOWEVER, IF YOU AGREE, WE WILL KEEP YOUR CURRICULUM VITAE ON FILE AND CONTACT YOU SHOULD ANY SIMILAR POSITIONS BECOME AVAILABLE IN THE FUTURE. THANK YOU FOR YOUR APPLICATION AND YOUR INTEREST IN OUR COMPANY.

<u>Dear Mr Smith,</u>

<u>I am sorry to inform you that your application for the position has been unsuccessful. However, if you agree, we will keep your curriculum vitae on file and contact you should any similar positions become available in the future. Thank you for your application and your interest in our company.</u>

Dear Mr Smith

I am sorry to inform you that your application for the position has been unsuccessful. However, if you agree, we will keep your curriculum vitae on file and contact you should any similar positions become available in the future. Thank you for your application and your interest in our company.

Dear Mr Smith

I am sorry to inform you that your application for the position has been unsuccessful. However, if you agree, we will keep your curriculum vitae on file and contact you should any similar positions become available in the future. Thank you for your application and your interest in our company.

The first two examples are much harder to read than the last two. The last example also shows how the emphatic effect of bold type diminishes with overuse.

I sometimes use bold type for highlighting text because it draws the eye to the highlighted text, but there are alternatives. In fact, a 1992 study showed that bold type tends to draw *too much*

---

49   Wheildon, C, 1995, *Type & Layout: How typography and design can get your message across – or get in the way*, pp 63-64 (cited at note 5); Felsenfeld, C and Siegel, A, 1981, *Writing Contracts in Plain English*, p 194 (cited at note 9).

attention to itself.[50] That is why typographers generally keep bold for headings and labels, and use italics and upper case for emphasis. Another alternative is using a different font or typeface.

In this book I have used italics for emphasis rather than bold type. That is because there is plenty of text, and there are quite a few headings in bold type for the reader to cope with. If I had used bold type for emphasis throughout the book, it might have become tiresome. Italics are a good alternative because they are easier to read than underlined words and they traditionally convey emphasis to the reader. But again, if they are overused their effect diminishes.[51]

With wordprocessing software it is just as easy to use bold type or italics as it is to use underlining. And both italics and bold type are much easier on the reader's eyes.

Another option is to use a different typeface to highlight something. But again, you need to choose carefully, depending on what you want to use the typeface for. For example, we know that if you use a serif typeface for your body text, headings in sans serif typeface make a good and effective contrast.[52] But if you want to highlight something in the body text itself, some typefaces won't give enough contrast, and some will be annoying. That is why people mostly choose the same typeface, but in italics or bold, to highlight body text.

Other reading and navigational aids

You could also consider putting some of your text in boxes. This was done in New South Wales in the Local Government Act 1993. Unfortunately, the drafters used boxes both for the "Introduction" information for each chapter, and for the "Notes" which give subsidiary information. That tends to give the impression that both these items are the most important information – and that both are equally important. It is probably wiser to use boxes for only one

---

50 McAteer, E, 1992, "Typeface emphasis and information focus in written language", *Applied Cognitive Psychology* 6(4), pp 345-359.

51 Dr Janice C Redish has written that italics may be the best choice · for highlighting definitions. She thinks that italics are less obtrusive than capitals or bold type. See Krongold, S, "Writing Laws: Making them Easier to Understand" (1992) 24 *Ottawa L Rev* 495 at 540. See also Chapter 7, pp 119-121.

52 See p 246.

kind of information – the information you think your reader should read first. And for the record: that experiment was not repeated in the current format of New South Wales legislation.

Boxes and other innovative design techniques were also extensively used in the Income Tax Assessment Act 1997, which was the result of the Australian government's Tax Law Improvement Project. In that Act there are boxes at the beginning of various Divisions and Subdivisions of the Act that contain text explaining what the Division or Subdivision is about. There are also boxes that contain "Method Statements" which give working examples of how to do the calculations required by the law. And there are boxes for text set out in tables.

The Income Tax Assessment Act 1997 also has diagrams, including a picture of a pyramid explaining the underlying structure of the Act, and a diagram which gives a map of Subdivision 20-B of the Act. There are checklists, flow charts, and other reader aids too. There are cross-references and explanatory notes sprinkled throughout the text.

While there has been some criticism of the redrafted Act, there seems to be much appreciation for the improved layout, innovative design features and navigation aids. As two commentators put it:

> While immense effort was and will be required to "retool", at least one "old lag" finds the use of diagrams, flow-charts, cross-referencing, notes and checklists often generally useful and helpful as are the flow charts, diagrams, "Method Statements", the Map, Tables and the vastly improved Explanatory Memoranda.[53]

And:

> Combining tables, examples and notes in synergistic ways, embedded in a fundamentally restructured and more logical framework have, anecdotally, proven much simpler to teach and for students to understand, than their predecessors.[54]

Other Australian Commonwealth legislation features a wide variety of new reading and navigational aids. The redesign of New South Wales legislation also included some new navigational aids. There are now running headings on each page, which give the

---

53 Woellner, Prof R and Zetler, J, 2000, "Tiptoe through the TULIPs: an Evaluation of the Tax Law Improvement Project", pp 22-23 (cited at note 41).
54 Same work, p 23.

name of the Act and part, and the clause and part numbers. The page number is now in a running footer.[55]

Colour

Computers and photocopiers now allow us to consider the luxury of colour in our documents. But for amateurs in printing, it may be a luxury we don't need. Studies show[56] that for text, as for the Model T Ford, you can choose any colour you like, as long as it is black. Even text printed in very dark colours is nowhere near as readable as black type. If you want to print black text onto a coloured background, it had better be a background in a very light tint. Tests have shown that comprehension levels drop 7% if the background is not white. The darker the background tint, the lower the comprehension level. Readers do *say* that they find a lightly tinted background more attractive. But that preference seems to give no boost to their comprehension levels.[57]

Colour works best when it is used for a purpose, not just to be decorative. For example, colour can be used to structure material: a block of colour behind text can indicate that it belongs together – that the material is related. On the other hand, randomly placed blocks of colour can confuse the reader or distract attention from the text. If the colour is poorly chosen it can make the text less readable. And don't forget that some of your readers may be colour blind.

There is yet another factor to consider in terms of colour: cultural differences. For example, certain colours can be very significant for certain readers, and the meaning of colours can vary greatly from country to country. White may mean purity in many western cultures, but in some eastern cultures it signifies death. Green can be the colour of environmental sensitivity, but it is also the colour of Islam.

---

55 See, for example, Retirement Villages Act 1999 and Callan Park (Special Provisions) Act 2002 (both NSW).

56 Wheildon, C, 1995, *Type & Layout: How typography and design can get your message across – or get in the way,* Chapter 6 (cited at note 5).

57 Same work, pp 87-96.

Indenting

You can get a good idea of the difference that indenting can make by comparing the current and the old design of New South Wales legislation. In the current format, numbered sections are positioned to the left of the page, and subsections appear at the next indent. Text does not wrap around under the section numbers, as it did in the old format. The current format looks like this:

2. **Commencement**
> (1) This section commences on the date of assent to this Act.
> (2) Section 3 commences on a date to be proclaimed. Section 4 commences on 1 March 1996.

The old format had text wrapping right round, like this:

Commencement
> 2. (1) This section commences on the date of assent to this Act.
> (2) Section 3 commences on a date to be proclaimed. Section
4 commences on 1 March 1996.

Notice how, in the second (old) version, the heading is aligned to the left margin, so that the section and subsection numbers are hidden by the heading on top of the numbers and the text below them. The system of indenting in the first (current) format allows you to scan down the left margin for section and subsection numbers to find the ones you want.

Indexes and tables of contents

Indexing is a very specialised field, and good indexing is quite an art.

Except for more "permanent" documents, such as laws, books and more "public" documents like articles of association, public trusts, charters and constitutions, we have to face the fact that there is not enough time to index most legal documents. But our readers still need to be able to find their way around our documents. It should be possible to provide at least a table of contents or a list of headings for documents that are longer than just a few pages. And that is all the more reason to use meaningful headings.

A table of contents isn't much use unless it gives page or paragraph numbers, but remember that if you insert the page numbers and then later amend the document, the page numbers may need to be altered. Wordprocessing software can do tables of contents automatically and update them as the document changes. In fact, many allow you to build a table of contents at the same time as you build your document, using it as a kind of framework to hang your words from. This is a useful feature for plain language writers, who like to begin their documents with an outline or plan.[58]

Summary

- As lawyers we have always been concerned first and foremost with text. But we must also think about document design if we want our writing to be readable, and to give it its best chance of being understood.
- If you understand some of the basic design principles, you can make quite a difference to the readability of your document.
- Plain language lawyers will consider carefully the typeface, font and size, line length, justification and white space they use in their documents. They will use diagrams, tables, charts and other graphics, as well as text, to explain the concepts they write about.
- Plain language lawyers will use meaningful headings, sensible numbering, symbols, signals, well-chosen high-lighting, perhaps colour, and indenting, indexes and tables of contents to help their readers find things in their documents.

And one final word on document design: lawyers who pay no attention to the way documents look have not completed the task of communication. Although they may have produced a document that works as a matter of law, they have not done their duty. They have not made sure that their documents can be easily read. In this respect, they have even been compared to the Roman tyrant Caligula, who cruelly inscribed his laws on top of pillars too high for the people to read.[59]

---

58 See pp 92-94.
59 Felsenfeld, C and Siegel, A, 1981, *Writing Contracts in Plain English*, p 176 (cited at note 9).

In the next chapter we'll see that the principles of document design that apply to documents printed on paper do not necessarily apply in the same way to documents designed for viewing on a computer screen. When you read something on paper you are looking a flat fixed surface that reflects light. When you read something on a computer screen you see a dynamic surface that emits light. Each surface has a different effect on your eyes. That has implications for document design, as we'll see in Chapter 16.

Chapter 16

Designing documents for the computer screen

Chapter 14 looked at the effect of the internet and email on our writing. Chapter 15 discussed the principles of traditional document design. This chapter brings the two topics together to deal with the special features of designing documents that will be viewed on a computer screen.

Web sites

The internet has not only brought us email; it has also brought us web sites. As we saw in Chapter 14, law firms, barristers' chambers, courts, law societies, legal aid organisations, community legal centres and other law-related organisations now have web sites and "home pages" to communicate with clients, and the world at large. These web sites are not just written, they are also "designed", often by professional web site designers.

Also, web based legal research is now the preferred method of many lawyers, especially those with computer skills and familiarity with the internet. So courts, judges and law reporters need to have regard to the issue of electronic document design when publishing judgments and other material on the internet.

The development of the internet, and in particular web sites, has prompted document designers and others to look again at the design principles that were developed for material printed on paper.

Understanding design principles

I observed in Chapter 15 that the average computer gives the average lawyer plenty of design options. But I pointed out the pitfalls of "dabbling in publishing", without having a firm grasp of the basic principles of document design. The same warning applies with even more force in designing documents to be read on web sites and on the computer screen. However, it helps to understand some of the issues that make designing for the computer screen a growing area of expertise.

Recent research suggests that established document design guidelines might not apply in the same way to material displayed electronically. And new research questions the validity of some of the old guidelines – even in the print context.[1] Much of the print-based research was done in the 1960s, and there is evidence that reading habits have changed since then, and more evidence to suggest that our reading habits can govern what we consider to be "readable".

The general principles of information design that we noted in Chapter 15 remain the same: consider your reader, make the information clear, relevant and usable, and select techniques and design elements that support those aims and are appropriate for the purpose. But the computer screen brings into play new technical factors (such as the reflection of light and the phenomenon of pixels[2]) and human factors too. So the new medium has refocused attention on the basic assumptions of document design.

Skimming or scanning

The first thing to question is the most basic assumption of all: that people *read* web sites. According to several of the experts, they don't.[3] Web guru Jakob Nielson says:

> People rarely read Web pages word by word; instead, they scan the page, picking out individual words and sentences. In a recent study[4] John Morkes and I found that 79 percent of our test users always

---

1 See p 245.

2 The dots of light that make up the images on a computer or TV screen. See pp 275-279.

3 Spool, JM, Schroeder, W, Scanlon, T, Snyder, C, 1998, "Web sites that work: Designing with your eyes open", *Proceedings of CHI '98, Human factors in computing systems*, Los Angeles, California, ACM 18-23, <http://portal. acm.org/citation.cfm?doid=286498.286626>.

4 Morkes, J and Nielsen, J, *Applying Writing Guidelines to Web Pages*, 6 January 1998, <www.useit.com/papers/webwriting/rewriting.html>.

scanned any new page they came across; only 16 percent read word-by-word.[5]

On that basis, Nielson has this advice:

> Web pages have to employ **scannable text**, using
> - highlighted **keywords** (hypertext links serve as one form of highlighting; typeface variations and color are others)
> - meaningful **sub-headings** (not "clever" ones)
> - bulleted **lists**
> - **one idea** per paragraph (users will skip over any additional ideas if they are not caught by the first few words in the paragraph)
> - the **inverted pyramid** style, starting with the conclusion.
> - **half the word count** (or less) than conventional writing.[6]

This is actually good advice for plain language writing in general.

A new kind of document structure?

If people are scanning rather than reading, they are probably not following a linear method of absorbing material. They are not reading from beginning to end, but are selecting chunks of information from different parts of the material available on the computer screen. They are darting around from document to document, from web page to web page via hyperlinks, sometimes starting in the middle or end and working backwards. This suggests that on-screen documents might require a *completely different structure* from print documents.

To work out what structure will work best, the key, as always in plain language writing, is to think like the user. If you can work out how the user is going to come to your material and what they are going to want from it, then you are on the way to developing a usable structure for an on-screen document.

Organising material for the computer screen

The Australian government's *Style Manual* recommends authors and editors work closely with electronic publishing specialists to find the best structure for on-screen publications. The *Style Manual*

---

5   Nielsen, J, "How Users Read on the Web", *Alertbox*, 1 October 1997, <www.useit.com/alertbox/9710a.html>.
6   Same work.

also gives some hints for organising material for use on the computer screen. In summary, it recommends that authors:

- Break content down into smaller logical units (to avoid forcing readers to scroll too much).
- Keep to a maximum of 5 A4 pages for any one section meant to be read independently.
- Use one heading per screen (or "window").
- Consider using a web-type structure rather than the sequential or hierarchical structures more common in print-based documents. Web-type structures arrange content in "associative" patterns, which allow readers to move from place to place within a document or between web sites. This is a flexible structure, but it can also confuse, as the reader takes in information in a potentially random order.
- Use the various "signposting" techniques recommended for printed documents, as adapted for screen-based documents. For example, visually highlighting material on the screen, such as headings, lists, key words, text in boxes or margins, and captions.
- Use bridging words, cross-references and hyperlinks to link associated material.[7]

Structure to help your reader

In Chapter 15, we saw how headings can be a very effective way to show the reader the logic underpinning the document. This is especially important for documents designed to be read on a computer screen. The reader can get physically lost if they lose track of the structure of the document. The hierarchy of information in the document is the way the reader will navigate through it and select information to read. A tight, well-organised and clearly labelled structure is vital.

Remember that the reader is coming in to the document "cold". Categories, titles and other names used as headings and labels and options might mean something to you, but they can completely mystify the reader. Writing for the web means you must cater for those who are completely unfamiliar with your world.

---

7   See 2002, *Style Manual for Authors, Editors and Printers*, 6th edition, John Wiley & Sons Australia Ltd, p 42 and following pages for more detail.

Another technique already mentioned can help here. Summarising material at the beginning of each section, rather than at the end, helps two types of "skimming" reader. First, the summary may be enough for the person who needs only the minimum detail and does not want to have to read the full text. Second, it can help direct those who *are* looking for detail to the exact detail they want.

Variable factors on the computer screen

According to Jim Byrne from the Making Connections Unit in the School of Law and Social Sciences at Glasgow Caledonian University, it is vital to maximise the readability of your documents onscreen, since reading speed and comprehension are 10–20% slower for web documents than those printed on paper. He points out that when you prepare a document for display on a computer screen, there are additional practical and technical factors to take into account, including:

- The same fonts are not available on all operating systems.
- Some typefaces are designed to look good on screen, some [are] designed to look good on paper. Those designed to look good on paper (particularly serif fonts) tend to look 'messy' on screen.
- Text size is dependent on screen resolution and operating system being used.
- The type of browser used can affect how the text looks.
- Users have their computers set up with different defaults and can change the preferences on their browsers.[8]

So now that we've looked at the more general factors, let's consider some specific design features.

Typeface

Not only does the typeface (or font)[9] you choose look different on the screen from the way it looks on paper, you cannot even be sure that the reader will see the same typeface you have chosen. There

---

8   2003, *Understanding web typography – an introduction* <www.ispn.gcal.ac.uk:81/ MakingConnections/articles/accessibletext>.

9   As noted in Chapter 15, "font" is the word for the individual members of a typeface family. For example, in the Bodoni family there are various fonts, including Bodoni condensed, Bodoni bold, Bodoni italic bold, etc. Boldness and italics are "type styles".

are technical ways to get around that problem, but the safest and simplest course of action is to pick a typeface that is likely to be available on most operating systems.

As long as you choose a typeface that is reasonably readable (for example, not too fanciful, exaggerated or florid), typeface choice does not make a significant difference in legibility or readability.[10] As mentioned in Chapter 15, legibility is the characteristic of letters, numbers and other symbols that enables us to tell them apart by shape. Readability is the ability to extract meaningful information from characters and groups of characters. Thus, a random grouping of letters like jwrtidf may be legible, but it is not readable.

But don't use too many different fonts. If you use a few fonts, use them consistently. Then you can use the same fonts as an organisational tool – to group together similar information. This can help your reader to grasp the structure and logic of your document. You are using design to help the reader, not just to decorate the screen.

Typefaces designed for the screen

Some typefaces have been designed specifically for screen use. Pioneer web font designers saw that the relatively low resolution of the computer monitor was not suitable for print-based typefaces. There were simply not enough pixels to display the subtlety and style of those typefaces. So the designers developed the technique of "bit-mapping" to increase the readability of on-screen text.[11] In bit-mapping, pixels are arranged by the designer to maximise the clarity and legibility of each character. Bit-mapped typefaces include **Geneva** (taken from **Helvetica**), New York (taken from Times) and Monaco (taken from Courier). The disadvantage of bit-mapped typefaces is that they do not always keep their clarity when the type size is increased, and you can get rough and jagged edges.

---

10   Bernard, Mills, Peterson and Storrer, 2001, "A Comparison of Popular Online Fonts: Which is Best and When?" *Usability News 3.2*, <http://psychology. wichita.edu/surl/usabilitynews/3S/font.htm>.
11   Same work.

Certain typefaces were specifically designed from scratch for the computer screen: for example Verdana and Georgia. Verdana is a sans serif typeface and Georgia has serifs.[12] Both look as good on low-resolution screens and both are relatively readable and clear in smaller type sizes. Other typefaces recommended by web-based typographers include Arial (sans serif) and Times New Roman (serif). Arial seems to be the most popular font used on the web, but typographers recommend Verdana, especially for small-sized type on low-resolution screens. Web design expert Jim Byrne prefers Times New Roman for documents that will be printed to be read later.[13] That is likely to be an important consideration for lawyers writing for the web.

Serif or sans serif?

It seems there is no strong evidence either way on whether serif or sans serif typefaces are better for on-screen reading. Some say that the "clean" lines or "clarity" of sans serif typefaces make them a good choice for type on the screen.[14] Others have found no significant difference in legibility, and very little difference in the reading time between serif and sans serif typefaces. However, it does seem that at smaller sizes sans serif typefaces are easier to read.[15]

Space between characters

One other important factor is the amount of space between the characters of a typeface. In some typefaces, the individual characters can touch, which reduces legibility. Both Georgia and Verdana (created for screen use) have been designed to ensure the individual characters never touch.[16]

---

12 See p 244 for a description of serif and sans serif typeface.

13 2003, *Understanding web typography – an introduction*, <www.ispn.gcal.ac.uk:81/ MakingConnections/articles/accessibletext> (under the heading "A selection of 'safe to use fonts'").

14 2002, *Style Manual for Authors, Editors and Printers*, p 331 (cited at note 7).

15 Bernard, Mills, Peterson and Storrer, 2001, "A Comparison of Popular Online Fonts: Which is Best and When?" (cited at note 10); Will-Harris, D, 2002, *Typofile Magazine*, <http://www.will-harris.com/typoscrn.htm>.

16 For more information, see Will-Harris, D, 2002, *Typofile Magazine* (cited at note 15).

Perception and preference

Several commentators point out that reader perception and preference can be important in web design, even though that preference may not be based on logic or fact. Jim Byrne puts it this way:

> The typeface used on a Web page, or indeed any document, affects the way we feel about the content ... one page looks formal and serious, another informal and friendly, yet another may be modern and cool. Clearly the typography of a page designed to support a children's TV program (http://www.bbc.co.uk/cbbc/) should be different for one designed for a politics course in a university (http://www.ksg.harvard.edu/prg/) ...
>
> So typography, whether on the Web or otherwise has a job to do; to support and re-enforce the message being presented by the content, or tell you something about the writer or publication that the page is part of. It should give the reader clues about the nature of an article or content they are about to read.[17]

Type size

The evidence about type size on-screen suggests that there is no difference in the legibility of the most commonly used fonts in 10pt, 12pt and 14pt. One 2002 study[18] showed no difference in accuracy and reading speed between four serif fonts and four sans serif fonts. Another study a year earlier supported this finding.[19] The Australian government *Style Manual*[20] recommends using a larger type size than you would use for documents printed on paper, usually 12pt or larger. And in an article called "The Best Faces for the Screen", web design expert Daniel Will-Harris writes:

> *The bigger the better.* You can use *any* typeface on-screen if you use it large enough.[21]

---

17   2003, *Understanding web typography – an introduction*, <www.ispn.gcal.ac.uk:81/ MakingConnections/articles/accessibletext> (under the heading "Why would you want to control the text on a Web page?").

18   Bernard, M, Lida, B, Riley, S, Hackler, T and Janzen, K, 2002, "A Comparison of Popular Online Fonts: Which Size and Type is Best?" *Usability News, 4.1*, <http://psychology.wichita.edu/surl/usabilitynews/41/onlinetext.htm>.

19   Bernard, M, Mills, M, Frank, T and McKown, J, 2001, "Which font do children prefer to read online?" *Usability News 3.1*, <http://psychology.wichita.edu/ surl/usabilitynews/3W/fontJR.htm>.

20   2002, *Style Manual for Authors, Editors and Printers*, pp 325 and 330 (cited at note 7).

21   2002, *Typofile Magazine*, <http://www.will-harris.com/typoscrn.htm>.

Of course, you can go too far. As information design expert Ron Scheer advises:

> You don't need super-sized fonts and graphics. Your message area is a small screen viewed at close range, not the side of a bus.[22]

Reader age is also a factor with type size. There is good evidence to show that older adults are more accurate with, and prefer, larger font sizes. Researchers have shown that 14pt font size is more legible for older adults, who also read faster, and prefer the 14pt to the 12pt fonts. Interestingly, the same study showed that older adults preferred sans serif fonts to serif fonts.[23] The US National Institute on Aging and the National Library of Medicine have produced a checklist called "Making Your Website Senior Friendly" which sets out useful guidelines well backed by research. That checklist recommends using sans serif typeface and 12 or 14 pt type size for body text. Much of the advice offered in the checklist applies to readers of all ages.[24]

However, because it is not possible to predict the specific print-size requirements of your reader, it is sensible to allow the reader to adjust your type size as it appears on *their* screen, to suit them.[25]

Colour and texture

The research into colour in web design confirms that background textures and colours do affect the readability of text. Text with a plain background is quicker for readers to search than text on a medium-textured background. But if the background is to be textured then the text will be more readable if there is a high contrast between the colour of the text and the background.

Most studies have shown that dark characters on a light background work better than light characters on a dark background.

---

22 Scheer, R, 2002, "Make your home page mean business", <http://saywhatyoumean.com/html/business.html> para 19.

23 Bernard, M, Liao, C and Mills, M, 2001 "Determining the best online font for older adults" *Usability News 3.1,* <http://psychology.wichita.edu/surl/usabilitynews/3W/fontSR.htm>.

24 2001, <http://www.nlm.nih.gov/pubs/checklist.pdf>.

25 For information on how to do this, see Byrne, J, 2003, *Accessible web text – sizing up the issues,* <http://www.ispn.gcal.ac.uk:81/MakingConnections/articles/textsize>.

Hill and Scharff showed in a 1997 paper[26] that web site users say that the colour combination most readable is the traditional black text on white background. That is consistent with research done for readers of print on paper.

However, web sites have other practical considerations that might militate against a pure white background: computer screens can flicker and there is the glare factor to contend with. So, as software usability researcher Michael Bernard points out, "it is common for web sites (such as this one) to have an off-white background in order to reduce the flicker and glare associated with white backgrounds".[27] In addition, certain patterns can clash with the patterns of the screen's pixels, and certain colours can "strobe" or flare on-screen. Colours and patterns can be manipulated on the computer to avoid these effects.

The Australian government *Style Manual* confirms that dark text on light background has been found more readable than the reverse. Black text on a white background rates the highest readability. White on blue, and red on yellow rank "fairly highly". Red on green, and magenta on blue are the least readable combinations. It is important to have a good level of contrast between background and foreground.[28]

I mentioned in Chapter 15 that colour works best in document design when it is used for a purpose, not just to be decorative. That is just as important when your document is designed for the computer screen. You can use colour to help the reader find what they are looking for, by using it to group related material together, and show logical connections. Also in Chapter 15 we saw that certain colours can be culturally significant for certain readers.[29]

White space

The commonly accepted rule is that to enhance the readability of a document printed on paper, you should have plenty of white space

26 Hill, A and Scharff, LF, 1997, "Readability Of Websites With Various Foreground/Background Color Combinations, Font Types And Word Styles", <http://hubel.sfasu.edu/research/AHNCUR.html>.

27 Bernard, M, 2002, *Criteria for optimal web design (designing for usability)*, <http://psychology.wichita.edu/optimalweb/print.htm> under the heading "Background textures and colors can affect the readability of text".

28 2002, *Style Manual for Authors, Editors and Printers*, pp 341-342 (cited at note 7).

29 See p 266.

around the text. But the limited research into the use of "white" space on web sites shows that this is not necessarily so. One study actually found that web sites with more white space "fared worse in terms of users' success in finding information" than web sites with more dense text.[30]

This may be stretching the point too far. Some researchers who were suspicious of those results conducted another study into white space on web sites.[31] Their study showed, interestingly, that there was no significant difference in the time participants took to complete certain set tasks: the amount of white space did not affect performance. However, the users reported that the participants found web sites with too little white space difficult to read, and they were annoyed by too much white space. They reported that too much space made the web site feel "empty", and requires too much scrolling.

It seems that readers of web sites prefer "medium" levels of white space. But it is difficult to specify the optimal amount of white space because there are many factors at work in a web site, and the content and layout can vary greatly.

Line length

Quite a few of the commentators recommend shorter over longer line lengths for material to be read on a computer screen. They suggest line lengths of between 40 and 60 characters, or 11 words per line. However, the studies so far show mixed results. Some studies show that readers tend to prefer, and be more accurate with, shorter line lengths. Other studies show that longer line lengths produce shorter reading times. With a longer line length there is less "scrolling" down the page – and studies have shown that readers resist excessive scrolling.[32]

---

30 Spool, JM, Schroeder, W, Scanlon, T, Snyder, C, 1998, "Web sites that work: Designing with your eyes open" (cited at note 3).

31 Bernard, M, Chaparro, B and Thomasson R, 2000, "Finding Information on the Web: Does the Amount of Whitespace Really Matter?" *Usability News 2.1*, <http://psychology.wichita.edu/surl/usabilitynews/2W/whitespace.htm>.

32 Bernard, M, 2002, *Criteria for optimal web design (designing for usability)* (cited at note 27) (under the heading "The optimal text line length is dependent upon several factors").

The Australian government's *Style Manual* makes the point that it is hard to scroll efficiently on a screen that displays text in two or more columns. Given that it also recommends using larger type size, it suggests using single column text for on-screen documents.[33]

Using upper case

In Chapter 15[34] I noted that words written in upper case are harder to read than words in lower case. However, the upper case seems to be having something of a resurgence in the age of email and the internet. This is probably because email requires us all to become typists, and the less competent typists are looking for shortcuts. Unfortunately, often the shortcuts help only the writer, and make life difficult for the reader.

The following advice for inexperienced typists comes from Meg Pickard:

> THERE IS ONE KEY ON YOUR KEYBOARD WHICH CAN IMPROVE YOUR COMMUNICATION SKILLS INSTANTLY WITH A SINGLE TAP. IT'S NOT THE SPACE BAR – THOUGH THAT IS A PRETTY USEFUL KEY IN ITSELF, AND CERTAINLY HELPS TO PREVENT ALLYOURWORDSRUNNINGTOGETHERINABIGMESSLIKETHIS. THE KEY THAT WILL HELP PEOPLE UNDERSTAND – AND LIKE – YOU BETTER IS THE HUMBLE CAPS LOCK KEY WHICH TURNS A SHOUTY NONSENSE MAGICALLY INTO an ocean of reasoned calm. Ahhhhhhh. However, take note – a single tap is all that is required, uNlEsS yOu WaNt tO sEeM liKE a tWeLve yEAr OLd.[35]

Underlining

It is best to avoid underlining on web sites, except to indicate a hyperlink.[36] Underlining is now a recognised web convention for that purpose.[37]

---

33   2002, *Style Manual for Authors, Editors and Printers*, p 332 (cited at note 7).

34   Page 266.

35   Originally posted at ickle.org: <www.ickle.org/archive/capslockkey.html>.

36   A hyperlink is a set of characters or A symbol or image in a "hypertext" document that links (by means of a mouse click) to another place in the same or another document. A hypertext document is one designed to allow those links.

37   See p 283 (heading **Web Conventions**).

Graphics etc

Amazingly, recent evidence indicates that users may actually *ignore* graphics (diagrams, illustrations, animated pictures etc) on a web site. Research done by the US Poynter Institute indicates that the first time users visit a web site, they are twice as likely to look at text, and tend to ignore the images on the site. The users in the study only looked at the images on their second or third visit to a site.[38] One reason for this could be that web site users are ignoring material that they expect to be advertisements. Some support for this theory comes from two studies, which found that users ignored advertisements placed at the top of a web page (where advertisement "banners" are usually found) and paid more attention to advertisements placed lower down the page.[39]

On the other hand, researchers have shown that graphics and other visual aids are better than text for getting across simple messages. Text was shown to be more persuasive for complex messages.[40]

This raises the interesting question of how effective as communication are the new, more complex, animated graphics and "interactive" design techniques. These techniques are often described as "youth oriented" or as aiming to reach members of the "MTV Generation" or "Generation X" and their younger siblings. The assumption is that:

> the "TV generation" are developing different ways of reading and processing visual information to preceding generations. Not restricted to reading sequentially and contiguously, the Post-modern and post-Post-modern generations appear to have developed what we might call "quick-grab literacy – the ability to absorb multiple hybrid visual codes and quick bytes of instant information."[41]

---

38 Poynter Institute, 1998, *The Stanford Poynter Project*, <http://www.poynterextra.org/et/index-col.htm>.

39 Benway, JP, 1998, "Banner blindness: The irony of attention grabbing on the world wide web", *Proceedings of the Human Factors and Ergonomics Society 42nd Annual Meeting, USA, 1,* 463-467 and WebReference.com, 1997 (quoted in Bernard, M, 2002, *Criteria for optimal web design (designing for usability)* (under the heading "Users may often 'instinctively' ...") (cited at note 27)).

40 King, WC, Dent, MM and Miles, EW, 1991, "The persuasive effect of graphics in computer-mediated communication", *Computers in Human Behavior, 7,* 269-279.

41 MacKenzie, M, 1994, "Our changing visual environment: Questions and challenges", *Communication News, 7,* No 4, Communications Research Institute of Australia, Hackett, Australia, pp 11-14 at p 12.

However, there is already some evidence to indicate that animated graphics can distract users from the text on the page and may cause them to miss the main points.[42] If the message of the text is important, experts suggest keeping animated graphics to a minimum.

Web conventions

Researchers have shown that users overwhelmingly prefer sites that follow the usual web conventions.[43] Although Michael Bernard points out that there are very few of them, he lists some:

- Follow the standard hyperlink[44] colors: blue for non-visited hyperlinks, purple for visited hyperlinks, and red for active hyperlinks (but if you have a site with a blue background – or any dark color – please choose a color that can clearly be contrasted from the background color. That is, if the choice is to either violate the standard or not be visible, choose visibility!).
- Place a navigational link to the homepage at the upper left corner and bottom of each page.
- Place the site's internal hyperlinks at the bottom of each page (in addition to other places).
- Images and text space should not cause horizontal scrolling on lower resolution screens.
- At the bottom of each page, place the date that the page was updated and the URL address.
- The text should facilitate the scanning of information.
- Use ALT-Tags[45] for graphics, especially for graphics that search as hyperlinks.

---

42   Benway, JP and Lane, DM, Dec 1998, "Banner blindness: Web searchers often miss 'obvious' links", *Internetworking*, 1.3 <http://www.internettg.org/newsletter/dec98/banner_blindness.html>; Wright, P, Milroy, R and Lickorish, A, 1999, "Static and animated graphics in learning from interactive texts", *European Journal of Psychology of Education*, XIV, 203-224.

43   Bernard, M, 2002, *Criteria for optimal web design (designing for usability)* (under the heading "How can I make sure my site follows general Web conventions?") (cited at note 27); Nielsen, J, *Alertbox*, 1997, <www.useit.com>.

44   See note 36.

45   An ALT-Tag is a short text description of (in this case) an image which is visible even if the image fails to load.

Bernard also suggests that web designers follow the convention of underlining hyperlinks when they are text based (for example, <http://psychology.wichita.edu/optimalweb>).[46]

Readers with special needs

We have already seen that older readers may be more comfortable reading a larger type size. We have seen that cultural differences can also be significant.[47] Much of the research into legibility and readability has taken place in the United States, so it may not apply to readers from other cultures. Readers with disabilities may also have special needs.

Guidelines to help web site developers have been published by a group called the World Wide Web Consortium (WC3). This group has member organisations all over the world working together to develop common protocols for the Web. Their Web Accessibility Initiative has developed guidelines, checklists and techniques to help web designers make web sites accessible for people with a variety of disabilities.[48] And in Australia, the Human Rights and Equal Opportunity Commission has produced advisory notes on accessibility of web pages.[49] They take into account the WC3 web accessibility guidelines.[50]

For the more general audience, the evidence suggests that most of us are most comfortable reading what we are most used to. For some, that might mean the Times or Times New Roman fonts we see in books and our daily newspapers. But that doesn't hold true for everyone. Australian research indicates that Australian readers are now familiar with sans serif text too.[51] This suggests that we

---

46 Bernard, M, 2002, *Criteria for optimal web design (designing for usability)* (under the heading "Make action-objects visible") (cited at note 27).

47 Page 278 under the heading **Colour and texture**.

48 See <http://www.w3.org/WAI/Resources/#gl> for the guidelines, checklists and techniques and <http://www.w3.org> for information about WC3. One of the guidelines requires the "clearest and simplest language appropriate for a site's content".

49 <http://www.hreoc.gov.au/disability_rights/standards/www_3/www_3.html>.

50 See also p 285 under the heading **Best practice guidelines**.

51 MacKenzie, M, 1994, "Our changing visual environment: Questions and challenges" (cited at note 41).

should ask the members of our target audience what they want. And we should seriously consider testing.[52]

Best practice guidelines

Some organisations have developed Best Practice Guidelines for web sites. In Australia, the National Office for the Information Economy has produced a guide to the minimum standards applying to Australian Commonwealth web sites.[53] The government of Canada has an Internet Guide web site, which gives tips on how to evaluate web sites and improve and test their usability.[54]

There are some guidelines particularly directed to lawyers and legal web sites. For Australian legal web sites the Legal Information Standards Council has developed "Best practice guidelines for Australian legal web sites".[55] And in February 2003 the Elawyering Task Force of the American Bar Association approved and published "Best Practice Guidelines for Legal Information Web Site Providers".[56]

The Legal Information Standards Council guidelines refer specifically to the need for information that does not exclude or disadvantage people with a disability (as required by the Australian Disability Discrimination Act 1992).

Summary

Lawyers, courts, judges and other law-related organisations are now commonly communicating with their audiences through the internet and via web sites. They need to be aware that web sites and documents displayed via the internet should not just be written; they should be designed according to recognised document design principles. Some of the principles to keep in mind are:

- Document design principles may apply differently to documents displayed on a computer screen. But the general principles remain the same.

---

52   See Chapter 17.

53   2001, *Guide to Minimum Website Standards*, <http://www.noie.gov.au/projects/egovernment/better%5Fpractice/mwsguide/introduction.htm>.

54   <http://www.coi-dpi.gc.ca/ig-gi/e/wse-esw/wse-esw_e.asp>.

55   <http://www.lawfoundation.net.au/lisc/recommend/bpguide.html>.

56   <http://www.elawyering.org/tools/practices.shtml>.

- Make sure your text is "scannable": use keywords, headings and sub-headings, lists, and one idea per paragraph.
- Start with your conclusion and halve your word count.
- Think like your reader to work out what structure will work best.
- Consider using an electronic publishing specialist to help structure your documents.
- Break down content into smaller units, with a maximum of 5 A4 pages for any one section.
- Use one heading per screen, "signposting " techniques, "bridging" words, cross-references and hyperlinks.
- Make sure your headings and labels are helpful to non-expert readers.
- Use summaries at the beginning of each section to help them select the detail they need.
- Reading speed and comprehension are considerably slower for web-based documents.
- Within limits, the exact choice of typeface does not make a significant difference to legibility, but some typefaces (such as **Verdana** and Georgia) have been designed specifically for the screen.
- Don't forget that screen-displayed documents may be printed out to read later.
- Choice of typography also reinforces the message and tells you something about the writer or publication.
- Most 10, 12 and 14pt fonts are probably equally legible on-screen, but some experts recommend using larger type size than you would for paper documents, especially if your readers are older.
- Don't use too many fonts, and do use them consistently, to show the structure and logic of your document.
- Colour choice is governed by technical considerations as well as cultural ones. Use colour to group related material together.
- It is important to give readers enough white space in on-screen documents, but it is equally important not to have too much, which requires excessive scrolling.

- Use line lengths of 40-60 characters, but again avoid forcing excessive scrolling.
- Don't over-use upper case.
- Keep animated graphics to a minimum if your text message is important. Text is more persuasive for complex messages.
- Follow web conventions and best-practice guidelines.
- Pay attention to any special needs of your readers.

That last point – paying attention to your reader's special needs – suggests not only that we might want to ask them what they want or expect, but also that we might want to find out how they handle what we've written and designed for them. Which brings us to the topic of the next chapter – Testing Your Writing.

In Chapter 17 we consider the idea of "testing" documents, to see if the intended readers *can* actually read them. To the lawyer in a busy private practice, the idea of "testing" his or her legal writing might not sound feasible. But there are various types of testing. Testing can be as simple as asking a colleague to read what you have written and make suggestions. Or it can be as extensive as the testing that has been done on legislation in major projects like the Australian Corporations Law Simplification Program and the Tax Law Improvement Project. So let's keep an open mind about testing, and see what it involves.

Chapter 17

Testing your writing

How can we tell if our readers understand?

If you've reached this chapter by reading the 16 chapters before it, you've been prepared to put in a great deal of effort for plain language writing. If you were a plain language lawyer before you read this book, you know that it takes care and effort to rewrite an old form or precedent in plain language. If you have ever produced complex legal documents (such as mortgages, guarantees, leases, trust deeds, prospectuses or legislation) in plain language, you know the investment of time, intellect and money it can involve.

Can we be sure that this actually makes things easier for our readers? There is evidence that plain language generally improves people's comprehension of legal documents, as we saw in Chapter 3. But how can we tell if that is happening in any specific case? The answer lies in testing.

Do lawyers really need to bother about testing?

In the first edition of this book, there was no information at all on the topic of testing. I had chosen to following my own advice and write for my audience, and I had decided that my audience would include a large percentage of lawyers who were unsure of plain language, or sceptical, or even hostile. I wasn't sure they'd be ready to think about testing documents on potential readers.

In the years since then we've come a long way. Lawyers have begun to see how testing documents can actually be relevant to them, and help them in their daily work.

Lawyers draft all sorts of documents. A great many are single page letters addressed to one person, who may well have no problems at all in understanding exactly what the writer means. I'm not suggesting that we always need to test those single purpose documents. But some of the documents we prepare are more complicated documents that people will consult regularly to check their rights and obligations. And some are public documents of great significance. Lawyers need to know that there are ways of checking whether their documents are likely to do the job they are supposed to do.

Testing plain language legislation

Testing has obvious advantages for legislation, for example. Several legislative drafting offices already test draft laws on readers.

At the end of Chapter 15, I mentioned that the Australian Corporations Law Simplification Program and the Tax Law Improvement Project used extensive testing. The team working on rewriting the Corporations Law used focus group testing to get feedback on structure of the laws, the texts themselves (some had two rounds of testing) and the new document design. They used testing more to diagnose problems with the structure or the text rather than to measure the text's effectiveness. In the tax law rewrite, some of the testing was in the form of "protocol reading". Individuals were carefully observed to see how they handled the text. Sometimes the text tested was not the finished product, but a "prototype". This enabled drafters to explore various drafting approaches to see if they should be pursued.[1]

Also in Australia, the Commonwealth Office of Parliamentary Counsel (OPC) had decided to test two documents a year with user groups.[2] However, events overtook that decision when the Corporations Law Simplification Program and the Tax Law Improvement Project began redrafting two of the most significant pieces of Commonwealth legislation, and systematically testing their drafts. OPC drafters worked on each project and took part in the testing processes.

Since then, legislation drafted by the OPC is tested whenever a client[3] requests it. Usually this is done by means of exposure drafts,

---

1   Robinson, V, 2001, *Rewriting Legislation – Australian Federal Experience*, paper presented to a conference in Ottawa, Canada in March 2001, pp 6-7, <www.opc.gov.au/plain/docs.htm>.

2   *Clearer Commonwealth Law: Report of the Inquiry into Legislative Drafting by the Commonwealth*, 1993, Commonwealth of Australia, Canberra, p 102.

3   The government department, instrumentality or other body that needs the drafting done for them.

either aimed at the general public or at a particular interest group. Exposure processes allow interested people to comment in writing, or at focus group meetings (often attended by the drafters). First Parliamentary Counsel Hilary Penfold says that feedback from exposure drafts relates more often to policy than to drafting matters, but even so the nature of the feedback can show how well people have grasped the subject matter of the drafting, and therefore how well the drafter has communicated the ideas.[4]

Recent examples of public exposures of draft Bills include:

- Various pieces of tax legislation
- Electronic Transactions Bill 1999
- Gene Technology Bill 1999
- Financial Services Reform Bill 2000
- Designs Bill 2001
- Corporations Amendment Bill 2002.

More public exposure and testing of Australian legislation is likely in the future. In 2002, the Board of Taxation[5] recommended the use of improved consultation processes to develop tax legislation, including "thorough road-testing of draft legislation and related products prior to their implementation".[6] The government accepted this recommendation.[7] Treasury is now in the process of developing guidelines to implement the Board's recommendations. At the beginning of the Executive Summary of its Report to the Treasurer the Board said:

> The Board believes that more effective community input to the development of tax legislation will result in better tax system outcomes. In particular, effective consultation with the community should improve the quality of tax legislation.[8]

---

4   Telephone interview with M Asprey, 6 May 2003.

5   A body that advises the Treasurer on (among other things) the quality and effectiveness of tax legislation and the processes for its development, including the processes of community consultation, and other aspects of tax design.

6   Board of Taxation Report *Government Consultation with the Community on the Development of Taxation Legislation*, March 2002, Recommendation 3(iii), p vi, <http://www.taxboard.gov.au/content/review.asp>.

7   Treasurer's Press Release, 2 May 2002.

8   Board of Taxation Report *Government Consultation with the Community on the Development of Taxation Legislation*, p iv (cited at note 6).

As mentioned in Chapter 4,[9] in 1995 the Canadian government chose a portion of the Explosives Regulations (the Consumer Fireworks Regulations) for a pilot project to rewrite government regulations in plain language. A Department of Justice team ran the project, which demonstrated not only that it was possible to write technical material in plain language, but also the value of extensive user consultation and usability testing.[10]

Then in 2000, as part of the plan to rewrite the Employment Insurance Act in plain language, the Canadian government decided to test different versions of some sections of the Act. The testing showed that reading a law and answering questions about it can be a challenging task both for the general public and informed legislation users alike. It also showed that the users did not like certain choices the drafters had made. As a result, the drafters changed their approach. But the researchers found that users appreciated many of the plain language drafting techniques: in particular, improvements in layout and navigational aids. Users reported that they felt less intimidated by the document as a result of these techniques: they inspired user confidence.[11]

In New Zealand in 1998, as part of the project to rewrite the Income Tax Act 1976,[12] researchers tested three versions of a portion of tax legislation (dealing with exempt income). One was the original provision from the 1976 Act, and the others were two (different) simplified versions prepared for the rewrite of that Act. The researchers found that both simplified versions showed higher comprehension rates than the original version, for both professional and non-professional users. Surprisingly, even the tax professionals found the plain language versions quicker to comprehend than the original versions, which they must have been more familiar with. However, professional users did report that they felt uncertain using the new versions. The study also showed that testing in the early stages of drafting a law can give the

---

9   Page 70.
10   The final report of the testing is at <http://canada.justice.gc.ca/en/ps/rs/ rep/wd95-4e.html>. See also the report *Consumer Fireworks Regulations Usability Testing*, Department of Justice, Canada, 1995.
11   GLPi and Schmolka, V, 2002, *Results of Usability Testing Research on Plain Language Draft Sections of the Employment Insurance Act*, <www.hrdc- drhc.gc.ca/ae-ei/loi-law/glpi-english.pdf>.
12   See p 68.

drafters valuable feedback and insights which they can use while they are still in the process of drafting.[13]

Before the introduction of a new format for New Zealand legislation on 1 January 2002, the Parliamentary Counsel Office undertook testing in the form of an extensive survey of users of legislation including Members of Parliament, judges, librarians, academics, lawyers, legal publishers and members of the public. Participants received a survey pack with sample formats (in particular, typeface) and were asked to rank the samples in order of preference. The participants' preferences as to typeface were adopted in the new format.

Testing other legal documents

If you are a private legal practitioner, testing documents can be relevant to your daily law practice too – perhaps more relevant than you think. For example, lawyers around Australia have been working to produce industry-standard plain language shopping centre (or "retail") leases. The process of getting a lease which all the interested parties agree on involves negotiation – and testing. Some of the lawyers who worked on those standard form documents decided to test draft clauses on the building owners, managers, tenants, valuers and others who would be involved in administrative processes like rent review and building maintenance. Input from all these people helped shape better leases which were easier to work with in practice. And what a great marketing exercise! Lawyers were going to their clients, and asking "how can we make this a better document for you?" The result can be a better partnership between lawyer and client.

If you are considering putting in the effort to build up your firm's forms and precedents, you might consider involving your regular clients in the process. That way, not only do you build better documents, but you can market your services as well.

---

13   McLaren, Prof M, Harrison, Dr J and McAra, E, 1999, *Report on accessibility of new income tax legislation* (unpublished). My thanks to Dr Harrison and Prof McLaren for drawing my attention to this report, and to the Policy Advice Division of the NZ Internal Revenue Department for allowing me to use it.

Testing makes a better product

Testing does not necessarily have to be formal or time consuming or expensive. At the most basic level, it is really just a part of the writing process: part of the research you need to do to produce a document that is fit for its purpose, and part of the editing you should do to produce the best document you possibly can.

Testing can tell you things about your writing that you would never see yourself. It can show up problems with a document that two lawyers negotiating and haggling would miss no matter how long they argued. It does this because it brings different points of view and different sensibilities to the same document. And it takes the document out of "theory" and into "practice".

Testing can also help you get to know your audience, and that can help your drafting. For example, the Australian Corporations Law Simplification Project team found it helpful to be able to picture their readers:

> A very valuable by-product of document testing sessions is that you get to know your audience personally as it were. The abstract reader becomes a real person across the table trying to make sense of your document. In the tea or coffee break, you discuss that person's professional interests, hobbies, grievances and enthusiasms. When you go back to the office to revise the draft you have a much more vivid and particularised image of the reader. This image is an amalgam of the individuals you have met and got to know in the testing sessions.[14]

Testing takes time, and sometimes money, but it may save time, money and embarrassment in the long run. Consider an important public document like a company's prospectus, for example. It is vital that prospectuses don't mislead or deceive the public. How can you tell whether a prospectus is likely to mislead or deceive? The client will be relying on you as a lawyer to guarantee that. What is your protection?

Testing can give you an indication of the kinds of problems that readers might have with the final version of the prospectus. If you test it on the same class of reader as the prospectus is aimed at, it can give you hard evidence of the reaction of members of that class. It will help you detect potential problems before they arise.

---

14   Robinson, V, 2001, *Rewriting Legislation – Australian Federal Experience*, p 7, para 23 (cited at note 1).

Lawyers are lagging behind the commercial realities on this issue. Manufacturers of all kinds of products, from cars and computers to toys, put them through tough testing programs before release. This ensures that the product does what it is supposed to, is durable and won't explode in the customer's hands. Why should our product – legal documents – be exempt from that kind of treatment?

There is a growing body of learning about what manufacturers call "Usability Testing". Much of that knowledge also applies to testing plain language documents for "usability". Two of the leaders in this field are Dr Janice C Redish and Dr Joseph S Dumas, who have particular expertise in testing legal documents. They have written this about the experience of testing:

> Watching users is both inspiring and humbling. Even after watching hundreds of people participate in usability tests, we are still amazed at the insights they give us about the assumptions we make.[15]

What to test

If there is time, you could test almost everything you write. This might sound like overdoing things, but consider this: one leading Australian law firm has a standing rule that if the secretary or wordprocessing operator who types a document cannot understand the language in it, that person can return that document to the author for revision. That is a first line of testing.

Some lawyers ask a few people around their office for help if they have a particularly difficult drafting problem. This has the advantage of giving you more than one viewpoint and more than one perspective. It is another kind of testing.

Sometimes we may have to fall back on testing our own material on ourselves. This is the most primitive form of testing, more properly called "revising". But even when you revise your own work, you can try to look at it with a different standpoint – a reader's standpoint. To do that requires retiring some distance from the document. Sometimes it is helpful to leave the document overnight to try to get a fresh perspective.

---

15 Dumas, JS and Redish, JC, 1999, *A Practical Guide to Usability Testing*, Revised edition, Intellect Books, Exeter, UK, p 32.

Many lawyers I know have another, informal test they apply to the documents they write or edit for someone else: they ask themselves if a particular relative or acquaintance could understand the document (Uncle Arthur, say, or a neighbour, or a young cousin – specially selected for this purpose because of they are not experienced in legal matters). Although it is unscientific, this method is at least an attempt to get another perspective.

More and more lawyers are moving to standardise these informal systems by developing checklists, or even formal style guides, for themselves or for their firms. This has been done in legislative drafting offices for many years. It gives standards to "measure" a document against, and so it helps keep documents consistent in style. It also saves the time that can be wasted in different people going over and over the same small points.

No document is in itself too small or too unimportant to test. You can use a small or informal test to match a small or informal document.

Communication is a complex process, and there is so much room for error. We must do what we can to verify the process.

When to test

There is no point in finding out all the things that are wrong with your document once you have dotted all the "i"s and crossed all the "t"s, organised the printing and signed the covering letter. You need to begin testing (or at least test once) fairly early in the drafting process, before your ideas have become fixed and you've gone too far to turn back. If you test early, you'll be more receptive to suggestions, more open to changing strategy, and have more time to incorporate changes. If you test early, you'll find out early if you have any fundamental misunderstandings about how the document works in practice.[16]

If time and money allow, you can test again once you've "fixed" the problems that the first test showed up. You might have fixed the wrong things, or made the problems worse. The only way to know for sure is to test again and compare results.

And if the circumstances are right, you might be able to test again *after* the document has begun to be used. For example, if you

---

16   See the reference on p 289 to "prototype" testing.

have produced a new form, you could test it after it has been introduced. Then you can see exactly how it is actually used in everyday situations, once it has been filled out and has been processed. Then if any problems emerge, you can make changes again.

How to test: informal methods

So what are our options for testing? I've already suggested 5 informal, but very basic methods that you might already be using. They are:

- Ask the person who types your work whether they understand it.
- Ask one or more of your other colleagues.
- Revise your own work, but do it after a break, to get a fresh perspective.
- Put yourself in someone else's shoes, and judge your own work as if you were that person.
- Develop a checklist or style guide to measure your documents against.

Remember, though, that in the writing process your primary aim is to *consider your reader*, and so you are writing primarily for that person. Setting your own criteria for a document, or imagining yourself in some other person's shoes is not the same thing as writing to meet the needs of your actual reader.

There are two other fairly simple methods you might consider using if more formal testing is not possible or appropriate for a particular document.

1. *Ask clients for comments*

Earlier I mentioned the efforts to produce standard form "retail" leases. Testing in that context can involve a more formal testing procedure,[17] or it can be as simple as matter of circulating a draft document or clause to as many of the interested parties as you wish, and asking for comments – especially comments which will help the document or clause to work *in practice*.

---

17   See following section **How to test: more formal methods** on p 299.

2. Use a computer program

There are several computer programs that check text for grammar and style, and even give you readability statistics.[18] Some come as part of wordprocessing software.[19] Some are available on the world wide web.[20] These programs can be helpful, because they can alert you to things that you hadn't realised about your writing. For example, they can tell you if your sentences are long, or you use too many passives. But there are problems, too. Because they are computer-run, they are inflexible. They apply the same standards (or range of standards) to every document. They don't take into account any special needs of your particular audience. And they won't pick up ambiguities or gaps in your logic. In some programs, it is necessary to eliminate full stops (periods) from abbreviations and the like, because the program will read a full stop as a sentence end and give a better score. So they are "blunt" instruments. But from time to time they can be useful to remind you of your bad writing habits.

Readability formulas

Readability formulas are reasonably easy to use, but the statistics they produce can have serious drawbacks. The Flesch Reading Ease Test, the Flesch-Kincaid Grade Level, the Gunning FOG index, the Coleman-Liau Grade Level or the Bormuth Grade Level are all examples of tests which use readability formulas. I referred to the Flesch Reading Ease Test in Chapter 4 in the context of the US Plain Language Statutes.[21] These formulas use things like the number of syllables or letters in a word and the number of words or letters in a sentence to determine readability. So a sentence with short, difficult words could receive a better score than a sentence with longer, easier words.

---

18 See next section, **Readability formulas**.

19 The Flesch-Kincaid formula comes with Microsoft Word. Note that (as at my press-time) Microsoft's version does not score above grade 12, although the formula was designed to score up to grade 16/17. Grammatik comes with WordPerfect.

20 For example, Readability Calculations (<www.micropowerandlight.com>), GrammarExpert Plus (<www.wintertree-software.com>) and Spellcatcher Plus (<www.spellcatcher.com>).

21 See p 63.

For example, Lewis Carroll's:

> Twas brillig, and the slithy toves did gyre and gimble in the wabe;
> all mimsy were the borogroves, and the mome raths outgrabe.[22]

receives good score of 70.10 on the Flesch Reading Ease Test –
which rates it as slightly easier to read than "standard" writing. It
also receives a good Flesch-Kincaid Grade Level – 6.34, which
means that that it could be read by a person with 6.34 years of
schooling. And so it probably could – but what does it mean?

The basis of these scores is also questionable for another
reason: the Flesch tests were first developed for the military in the
1940s in the United States. Critics of the Flesch-Kincaid reading
grades point out that the scale is geared to a fifth grade reading
level, since a fifth grade education was considered sufficient for
military recruits in the 1940s. They say the scale is increasingly
unreliable above sixth grade.

There's also the question of what the "grade level" actually
means. A text rated at grade six level means that average sixth
grade students would find the text a real challenge to their abilities.
Therefore a large proportion of sixth graders would not understand
much of the text. Some of the other readability formulas were
developed for, and tested on, children, so their application to adults
is doubtful.

There are other criticisms: Dr Mark Hochhauser lists several of
them in a 1999 article, and responds to each of the criticisms as
well. Here's a summary of his criticisms:[23]

- The grade levels of readability formulas are not equivalent across all formulas.
- They ignore text structure and organisation.
- They are limited: you can use short sentences and short words and still be obscure.
- They don't consider the reader as an individual with background, culture, motivation and so on.
- Readability formulas encourage dumbing down.

Hochhauser's response comprehensively dismisses the last
criticism. The other criticisms reveal the weakness of readability

---

22 *Through the Looking Glass*, Chapter 1.
23 "Some pros and cons of readability formulas", *Clarity* No 44, Dec 1999, p 27.

formulas. Nevertheless, readability formulas can have their uses. For example, quoting a poor readability score may convince its author that it needs rewriting.[24]

For many reasons, readability formulas are unlikely to be an accurate measure of the readability of legal documents by adults in, say, Australia in the 21st century. I once applied the Flesch Test to an extremely difficult section of the Australian Income Tax Assessment Act 1936.[25] Although it rated as "fairly difficult", that rating indicated that a high school student could read it.[26] But even experienced tax advisors have significant problems understanding that particular section. It received a reasonable score because it had many subsections, all separated by semi-colons (which the test counts as the end of a sentence). And it contained short words like "tax" and "cash" and "deem" and "income". But that didn't make it any easier to understand. So you can see that these formulas have their limits as measures of comprehension.

How to test: more formal methods

There are other more formal methods of testing. The one to choose depends on several things. What sort of a document is it? How often will it be used? Who will use it? How much time and money is involved in the document? How much time and money is available for testing? And what sort of access do you have to people who are prepared to read legal documents that just *may* be less-than-scintillating?

If you have a project that warrants more than just informal testing, you might need to consider getting expert help. Testing, like document design, is easy to do on a basic level, but to get a professional result you probably need to consult a communications expert.

---

24 This point is made in another excellent review of the value of readability formulas: the Plain Language Institute's *Plain Language Notes*, Feb 1993, Vol 1 No 3.
25 Section 21A, which deals at great length and in great detail with "non-cash business benefits" received by taxpayers and how they can be deemed to be income for tax purposes. A new Income Tax Assessment Act 1997 rewrote portions of the old 1936 Act, including section 21A. But the 1936 Act remains on the books (partly to cater for the affairs of taxpayers before the 1997 Act came into being, and partly because not all of the 1936 Act has been rewritten). See p 68.
26 Test applied using Microsoft Word 6.0.1 software, grammar check function.

Here is a brief description of nine testing techniques which the experts use. You might be able to adapt them to your own circumstances. Each method involves assembling a group of people who represent the likely users or reader of your document (a "user group").

The aim here is to try to get a group that represents as closely as possible the type of people who will be reading and using the document. You don't necessarily have to have a huge group – just a representative one. You may prefer to test several smaller groups rather than one large one, to give participants a better chance to contribute.

You may choose to conduct the tests within the environment of your own organisation, or you may prefer a "laboratory" situation. A laboratory can be anything from a room set up with no distractions and a good ability to observe the group at work, to a fully fledged usability lab, with test room and observation room.[27]

Once you have selected the group and the testing environment, you have several options.

1. Interview

Give your group sufficient time to read the document you are testing, and then interview them after they have read it. This will tell you if anything has worried or confused your readers. You can also ask them questions about what they might have expected to find in the document, or how they would use it themselves. In an interview, you can adjust the questions you ask, depending on the responses you get to previous questions. You could do the interview individually, or in a group, but if you interview the group you need to make sure that you get a view from the quieter members of the audience.

You can also do an interview in conjunction with the other tests I'm describing.

2. Set a multiple choice questionnaire

This option is probably easiest on the participants, because they don't have to explain in words their understanding of the

---

27   Dumas, JS and Redish, JC, 1999, *A Practical Guide to Usability Testing* (cited at note 15) has a whole chapter (Chapter 15) on the test environment.

document. It is also easy on the questioner, because it does not have to be done individually. But on the other hand, a questionnaire may well reflect the mind-set of the questioner, and it does not allow for discussion or elaboration. The questions might completely miss some aspects of the document that are confusing or ambiguous.

3. *Set some problems*

This option will give you a good idea of whether the document is *usable:* that is, whether people can use the document as they will need to in reality. You probably need to set a range of problems so that you cover as much of the document as you can. But again, the problems you set might miss some of the confusing or ambiguous aspects of the document.

4. *Set a comprehension test*

In a full comprehension test, you could include multiple choice questions and problems like those I've just described, with the idea of anticipating the problems people might face when they are actually using the document. But it is important to get more information from the test than just whether people get the answer right or wrong. You should also ask participants to make a note of how they reached their answer the sections of the document they consulted to find each answer – and the time each answer took. Remember, people might get the answer eventually, but take more time than they should because they are confused or sidetracked.

5. *Check the response time*

Another kind of test just asks one or more simple questions about a document, and then times how long it takes the participants to find the answer. This would be suitable for a simple kind of document, where the purposes and uses of the document are pretty clear, and you can phrase your questions accordingly.

6. *Ask them to fill in the gaps*

    In this test, called a "Cloze" test, you test whether the readers
    understand a section of a document (often a 100-word sample)
    by giving readers that section, but with a word removed at
    regular intervals (often every fifth or sixth word) throughout
    the section. Then you ask readers to fill in the gaps. This test is
    used to gauge a reader's overall understanding of what they've
    read. A poor result on a Cloze test tends to show that people do
    not grasp enough of the context to enable them to have an edu-
    cated guess at the missing words. It can show that you need to
    concentrate on giving *more* information – more context – in the
    document, or outside it. Cloze tests are often preferred to tra-
    ditional multiple-choice tests for testing reader comprehension.

    There is a more recently developed alternative to the Cloze
    test called the C-Test. Using four to six short texts, you delete
    the second half of every second word, beginning with the
    second word of the second sentence. The first and last sen-
    tences remain unchanged. The students have to restore the
    missing parts of the words. Typically there are 100 gaps. The
    restored words must be 100% correct.[28]

7. *Ask them to paraphrase something*

    This test is usually given to one person at a time. Participants
    have to read out the document, one sentence at a time, and
    then paraphrase that sentence in their own words. This not
    only allows you to hear what errors the participant has made,
    but also gives you an idea of why the participant made the
    errors – which words caused the problem.

8. *Ask them to think aloud as they read*

    This test is similar to the paraphrase test, in that individual
    participants read the document aloud one sentence at a time.
    But instead of paraphrasing the sentence, the participants just
    say what they think about whichever aspects of any word or
    sentence (or the whole document) they want to comment on.
    The idea is to understand the thought processes that the reader

---

28 For more detail, see <http://exchanges.state.gov/forum/vols/vol31/no1/
    p35.htm>.

goes through in trying to understand the document – what words cause them problems, where the information gaps are, what extra information they need when, and so on. Sometimes this can be an uncomfortable process for one person on their own, and some experts suggest that you do the test in pairs, with both people talking about the document as they work through it together.

9. *Do a formal usability test*

This type of test usually combines elements of the other tests I've just described, but on a one-to-one basis, closely observed by experts. They devise real-life problems and as the participants work through the questions and problems they are encouraged to speak their thoughts out loud. The experts often videotape the sessions so that they can continue to analyse the sessions in more detail later. This visual evidence is said to be very valuable, especially when you need to convince others that there is a problem with a document. Dr Janice Redish has described it this way:

> Seeing readers hunting for information, looking for an index, or going to the table of contents over and over as each section they look at turns out not to have the information they need and hearing them voice their frustration is more powerful than just counting their incorrect answers on a comprehension test.[29]

There are several good reference works that either deal specifically with testing legal documents or describe methods that can easily be adapted to testing legal writing.[30]

---

29 Krongold, S, "Writing Laws: Making them Easier to Understand" (1992) 24 *Ottawa L Rev* 495 at 548.

30 For more detailed information about testing, see Dumas, JS and Redish, JC, 1999, *A Practical Guide to Usability Testing* (cited at note 15). There is a section written by Dr Redish on testing a statute, in Krongold, S, "Writing Laws: Making them Easier to Understand" (1992) 24 *Ottawa L Rev* 495 at 544. See also Goldsmith, P, Reid, G and Sawyer, S, 1993, *Reaching your readers: A fieldtesting guide for community groups*, Legal Services Society of BC, Vancouver. There is also a chapter on testing in Eagleson, RD, 1990, *Writing in Plain English*, AGPS Press, Commonwealth of Australia, Canberra p 80. Martin Cutts describes his testing of the Clearer Timeshare Act in Cutts, M, 2000, *Lucid Law*, 2nd edition, Plain Language Commission, High Peak, England, pp 22-28. And there is some information about testing in Duckworth, M and Mills, G, 1996, *Organising a Plain Language Project*, Federation Press, Sydney, at pp 18-19 and 63.

What to do with the results

Once you have your test results, you have to decide what to do with them. You may agree or not agree with some of the test group's comments. You may agree, but not be able to come up with a good alternative. You may need to do more testing, perhaps with a different range of alternatives or a different group. There are no rules to tell you exactly how to take test results into account. Testing might show you where the problems are in your document, but it will not always give you solutions to those problems. Usability testers recommend that once you have gathered information about your "users", their goals and their tasks, you should set goals for your document. Once you have those goals, you can then work on specific ways to achieve those goals.[31] The idea here is to recognise that you may not be able to satisfy the needs of *all* readers, so it may be helpful to have set some general goals to return to when solutions seem elusive.

There are two further factors to keep in mind when considering what to do about test results. The first is this: the "victims" of a situation or the people with a problem are not always the right people to suggest the solution. They are experienced with the problem and they will help you identify it, but finding the *solution* is up to you.

The second thing to remember is that in testing we are looking for objectivity about our documents – not justification for our writing style or the decisions we made in our drafting. We must be careful not to taint our test results with enthusiasm for our own ideas.

Testing keeps us honest

I see the role of testing in plain language writing as a way of keeping ourselves honest. We must work hard to simplify our documents, and to eliminate legalese from legal writing. We all need to keep building up our plain language writing skills, and honing them by practice. The process never ends, even for a plain language expert. But we must also keep asking the question: are we considering our reader? Are we doing everything we can to make

---

31   Dumas, JS and Redish, JC, 1999, *A Practical Guide to Usability Testing*, pp 348-351 (cited at note 15).

our writing as clear and plain and readable as we can? Will our readers understand what we have written?

We have good evidence that using plain language writing techniques does make our writing easier to read and does improve reader comprehension. And we now have powerful incentives to make us write in plain language. But much of the time, when we write in plain language we do not actually know for sure whether our efforts are hitting the mark.

Testing allows us to tell, with some objectivity, if what we are doing is working.

Chapter 18

Any questions?

I said at the beginning of this book that the conclusion would be in Chapter 1 with the introduction. And it was. I said in Chapter 1 that this book was about drafting in a new way. Drafting to communicate, rather than just to record. I said that when we draft legal documents we should be able to use some of the same techniques that we use in everyday communication. I wanted to convince you that there is no need to cling to old formulas and archaic language, because new simple language can do the same job just as well.

I should have done that by now, and given you some of the tools you need to begin writing in a new way – unless of course you are already writing in plain language, as many lawyers do, sometimes without realising it.

If I have been successful, there is no need for any more encouragement from me now. But I suspect you might have a few questions still nagging away. Or you might have to answer questions about plain language from other people. So in this, the last chapter of this book, I have tried to anticipate those questions.

Is plain language a new language?

It is not a new language. It is just an attempt to write English (or French or German or whatever else) in a clear and simple style.

Is a plain language document always shorter than a document written in traditional legal style?

Not always. It depends on whether the traditional version contained much unnecessary material. Sometimes a plain language document is longer than the traditional equivalent: for example, if the plain language version needs to have a lot of explanatory material in it. Brevity is *one* of the aims of plain language, but not the only one. We never sacrifice clarity for brevity.

Is it possible to be too brief?

Yes. Sometimes in our eagerness to cut out unnecessary material we cut out necessary material as well. But we must give the reader everything they need to understand what we write.

There are some words and phrases that might not be *strictly necessary* to convey our meaning, but might assist the reader to understand our meaning more easily. They do serve a useful purpose and don't need to be cut. If we simply aim to reduce the number of words in our document it might be as unreadable as an overlong document. As Horace said:

> I strive to be brief, and I become obscure.[1]

Remember that some words don't necessarily add to meaning, but do add to readability. Again, brevity is *one* aim of plain language writers – but not at the expense of clarity.

Is it possible to oversimplify?

Of course it is. Remember Albert Einstein's warning:

> Everything should be made as simple as possible but not simpler.[2]

There is no need to choose every word to suit the lowest common denominator. That might be offensive to readers of average intelligence. All that is necessary is that you pitch your writing at the appropriate level for your likely audience. Only you can judge that.

Why should we break with the past?

We are not really breaking with the past. We are simply recognising that our readers are changing. We have a responsibility to serve the changing needs of our clients and the others who might read our documents. This might involve updating our writing style to suit the requirements of the present (and the future). It might mean that we must be more selective in what we keep from the past, recognising that tradition alone is not enough to justify using difficult or unfamiliar words.

---

1   Ars Poetica.
2   Attributed to Albert Einstein by *The Bloomsbury Treasury of Quotations*, 1994, Bloomsbury Publishing plc, London, p 629.

What about the "time-honoured" words?

Just because a word or phrase meant one thing in the past, even the recent past, that is no guarantee that it will mean the same thing at all times in the future, and in all other circumstances. And it does not mean it is the best word or phrase for the purpose. It is the legal principles that matter, not the forms of words. We have a responsibility not just to know and understand the law, but also to write so that we can be understood and so that the intention behind the document is clear. "Time-honoured" words may or may not do that. Only you can judge.

But why should we bother? We've got on well enough until now

Our clients are asking questions. They are demanding a change. Our governments, our legislators and our courts have taken a fresh look at lawyers' language. There are new dimensions of professional liability for the language that lawyers use. Plain language allows us to show our skills as lawyers more dramatically and efficiently. Today clients are prepared to pay for legal services in plain language. Soon they will not pay for legal services *unless* they are in plain language.[3]

But we don't have time to rewrite all our precedents

No one is suggesting that we must start by rewriting all our precedents – although it is a great place to practise, and you certainly learn a lot from the exercise.

The best place to start is with a clean sheet of paper. Next time you write a letter of advice. It is easier to write in plain language if you are starting from scratch. Writing in plain language is not as daunting if you don't have pages of legalese to "translate". The best advice is to start small, and gradually hone your skills.

As their writing skills improve, most people eventually get so enthused about plain language that they can't stand the look of traditional style documents and can't wait to rewrite any documents they are likely to use often.

---

3 To paraphrase Christopher Balmford (see p 75).

How do I deal with amending a document that is written in the traditional style? Plain language really stands out next to legalese.

That is true. You certainly shouldn't insist on rewriting the whole document to make the styles accord. Apart from the fact that it would take too long – and the client probably wouldn't want to pay for it – it might also seem discourteous to the writer of the document. But there is no need to imitate the traditional style either, if you are not in the habit of writing in plain language. Just try to state what you have to state as plainly and simply as possible, making sure that there are no ambiguities created in the process.

And don't be tempted to ridicule the writer's "traditional" style. Your own clear writing style is likely to be a more persuasive advocate for plain language.

I've got rid of the legalese. Is that all there is to plain language?

No. Plain language writing is about more than just the words on the page. It involves looking at the whole process of communication. It considers the needs and abilities of the reader, the purposes of the writing, the way the material is organised and the layout and design of the document. It looks at ways of finding out whether the document is going to do its job. And the definition of "plain language" continues to expand as we learn more about communication and writing. So plain language is not just a matter of "translation" of words on a page. It looks at writing and documents in a much wider context than that.

Should I write differently for email?

No. Email and the internet are simply different media for the writer. But the immediate, international and informal aspects of email and the internet do have implications for the way we write. We need to be aware that we are writing for a potentially limitless audience, and one that may not be familiar with our conventions of communication. And despite the informal nature of email, we still need to check our writing carefully for typing, spelling and other errors.

How closely should I follow all these plain language guidelines?

That is a difficult question to answer without a context. In fact, most things about plain language are difficult to discuss without a context: without using concrete examples. Most objections to plain language drafting that look sensible enough or plausible enough in theory, fall away when put to a practical test.

We need to be flexible in the way we apply plain language guidelines. There are no hard-and-fast rules, other than "consider your reader".[4] If you try to follow the guidelines set out in this book too rigidly, you will probably end up too inhibited to write anything at all. Start gradually, look critically at your writing, try practising one or two of the techniques I've described, and let your talent for plain language writing emerge. It will.

How will I know when I'm writing in plain language?

Just as there are no hard-and-fast rules in plain language writing, there are no standards to measure yourself against to tell you *when* you are writing in plain language. There is no one "orthodox" form of plain language. If you follow the guidelines in this book, or even some of them, your writing will be simplified. It will be easier to read than it was before. It is a gradual process. There is no line with "legalese" on one side and "plain language" on the other.

What is more, any document that is said to be written in "plain language" (including this book) can probably be improved, simplified further, redesigned, and made easier to read in many different ways. No one has all the answers and all the techniques. It is important to be flexible and listen to criticism carefully, without getting discouraged. It is also important to offer criticism sympathetically.

Remember that just putting in a lot of effort to write in plain language does not guarantee that what you produce will be in plain language. People often "confuse the effort with the outcome".[5] That's one reason why so many documents that are claimed to be in plain language are clearly not.

---

4   See Chapter 5.
5   This useful phrase was used by Dr Mark Hochhauser, in "Some pros and cons of readability formulas", *Clarity* No 44, Dec 1999, p 27.

One way to find out whether there is room for improvement is to consider testing your document, using one of the methods described in Chapter 17.

There is always room for improvement, and any improvement will be gradual. The most important thing is to be alive to the issues and aware of the potential problems with legal writing.

How do I start?

The best way to learn plain language drafting is by practice. Any document at all is suitable to practise on. Start now.

Thank you

There are many people who have helped me with this book. Some were plain language specialists, and some were not. All were very generous with their time, and very patient with my (often obscure) questions.

I want to thank in particular Mark Adler, Christopher Balmford, Peter Bartlett, Professor Peter Butt, Sir Edward Caldwell, Dr Nittaya Campbell, Richard Castle, Martin Cutts, David Elliott, Nicole Fernbach, Derrick Fine, Dr Jacqueline Harrison, Professor Joseph Kimble, Phil Knight, Robert Lowe, Professor Margaret McLaren, Mary Montague, Hilary Penfold QC, Wai-chung Suen, Anne Wagner, and Simon Williams and the UK Tax Law Rewrite Project Team. My account at your favour-banks is considerably overdrawn. Joe Kimble now *owns* the bank.

To all the others who have helped me by spending time on the phone with me, or sending me copies of a report, a judgment, or an article, thank you. *You know who you are.*

And finally, to my husband Lindsay Powers. In countless ways you have made this book, and so much else, possible. No plain words can express my gratitude.

Index